Battlegrou

The Battle for
Vimy Ridge 1917

Battleground series:

With the continued expansion of the Battleground Series a **Battleground Series Club** has been formed to benefit the reader. The purpose of the Club is to keep members informed of new titles and to offer many other reader-benefits. Membership is free and by registering an interest you can help us predict print runs and thus assist us in maintaining the quality and prices at their present levels.

Please call the office on 01226 734555, or send your name and address along with a request for more information to:

Battleground Series Club Pen & Sword Books Ltd,
47 Church Street, Barnsley, South Yorkshire S70 2AS

Battleground Europe

The Battle for Vimy Ridge 1917

Jack Sheldon and Nigel Cave

Series editor
Nigel Cave

Pen & Sword
MILITARY

The authors dedicate this work to the Directors of the Vimy Memorial, whom they have come to know well over the years: Clermont Chamberland, Jacques Morel (and his wife Diane) and, most particularly Al Puxley and his wife Susan who, ably abetted by Friday, always provided a most hospitable welcome to their house and were unfailing in their efforts to help in any way they could.

First published in Great Britain in 2007 by
PEN & SWORD MILITARY
an imprint of
Pen & Sword Books Limited
47 Church Street
Barnsley
South Yorkshire
S70 2AS

ISBN 9781844155521

The right of Jack Sheldon and Nigel Cave as Authors
of this Work has been asserted by them in accordance
with the Copyright, Designs and Patents Act 1988.

A CIP catalogue record for this book is
available from the British Library

Printed and bound in Great Britain by
CPI UK

Pen & Sword Books Ltd incorporates the imprints of
Pen & Sword Aviation, Pen & Sword Naval, Pen & Sword Military,
Pen & Sword Select, Pen & Sword Military Classics
Leo Cooper and Wharncliffe Books

For a complete list of Pen & Sword titles please contact:
PEN & SWORD BOOKS LIMITED
47 Church Street, Barnsley, South Yorkshire, S70 2AS, England.
E-mail: enquiries@pen-and-sword.co.uk
Website: www.pen-and-sword.co.uk

CONTENTS

LIST OF MAPS AND DIAGRAMS

1. German map showing how the opposing forces lined up for the battle from March 1917. Also shown are the Allied gains on 9 April **p41**
2. Subways constructed in support of the attack on Vimy Ridge [©GPGRobinson/DurandGroup] **p55**
3. Modern survey of the German tunnel T 19 in the La Folie area [©GPG Robinson/Durand Group] **p56**
4. German mining diagram of Sector *Döberitz* March 1917 **p58**
5. German mining diagram *Völker* Tunnel and Sector *Arnulf* (North) February 1917 **p62**
6. Canadian Corps Attack frontages, 9 April **p76**
7. 20th Battalion boundaries, 9 April **p91**
8. German *Zweitestellung* [Second Position] Thélus – Farbus sector, 9 April **p96**
9. Third Canadian Division Planning Map **p97**
10. A Canadian map of the La Folie Farm area. The 'Ecole Commune' was located alongside the *Route Pietonnière*, which runs through the modern Vimy Forest. In the colour section.
11. A German map of the same area, showing depth positions around the Ecole [*Schule*] and La Folie Chateau [*Schloss*] **p99**
12. A German sketch map of the 79th Reserve Division Sector **p124**
13. An extract from the Artillery Intelligence Map, Group Vimy showing battery positions which had definitely been located during the week 15 – 22 March **p129**
14. A German map of the 16th Bavarian Infantry Division area, including battery locations **p130**
15. A German map showing the main Allied thrusts and move of reinforcements between Vimy Ridge and the Scarpe, 9 April.**p134**
16. Situation map of Bavarian RIR 3-9 April, showing reverses in Thélus area **p138**
17. A detailed map of Sector *Arnulf,* defended by RIR 263 9 April **p140**
18. Situation map afternoon 9 April 1917 showing planned counter-stroke *Krummel* **p143**
19. Sector *Fischer* April. Note the numerous minor stop lines dug in the attempt to overcome the inherent weakness of such a shallow position. Determined defence from these locations caused the Canadian 4th Division major problems and high casualties on 9 April **p150**
20. Large scale map illustrating the German front line in Sector *Fischer.* The modern road between Broadmarsh Crater and Canadian

6

Diagrams

ACKNOWLEDGEMENTS

The writing of this guide has been greatly assisted by the help of a number of people. The authors are indebted to the historians of the Canadian, British and German armies, who wrote about the history of the area and the battles which occurred there almost a century ago. Without their careful recording of events, modern interpretation of the battles would be impossible. They also wish to express their grateful thanks, in particular, to Lieutenant Colonel Phillip Robinson RE, who placed at their disposal his superb collection of maps, diagrams and photographs and went to considerable trouble to prepare it for publication. Other members of the Durand Group were also extremely helpful, providing technical advice and assistance with a wealth of material relating to the underground workings beneath Vimy Ridge. Our thanks go, too, to Lieutnant Colonel Mike Jackson of the Canadian Army, for information relating to his uncle, Corporal AH Clubbe. We are also grateful to Laurie Sheldon who drew the maps for the car tour and Arlene King for her kind assistance and hospitality. As always, we wish to express our appreciation of the friendly and supportive team at Pen and Sword Books.

Lieutenant Colonel Phillip Robinson in action with the Durand Group below Vimy Ridge

CANADIAN INTRODUCTION

The Battle for Vimy Ridge, 9 – 14 April 1917, was a seminal moment in the history of the Canadian Corps and of Canada itself. For the first time all four Canadian infantry divisions that were to serve in France attacked together; in this set piece attack they took the great majority of the famous heights (neighbouring British divisions took the northernmost and southernmost parts of the ridge), which had become a major feature of the German defences north of Arras. Theirs was a vital contribution to the opening (largely very successful) of the Battle of Arras.

In the earlier volume in the *Battleground Europe* series, *Vimy Ridge*, events from the beginning of the fighting in the area through to its capture in 1917 were included. Consequently there was much emphasis on French and British activity there, as well as the period from October 1916 to April 1917, when the Canadian Corps held the line and then took the ridge. This book concentrates on the Canadian Corps and the final, successful assault on the ridge. It also includes a detailed account of the defence of the ridge by the Germans, thereby giving a much fuller picture of the battle.

Since *Vimy Ridge* was published in 1996 our knowledge of the ground has been enhanced considerably through work with Veterans Affairs Canada (VAC), which organisation is charged, amongst other things, with the maintenance of the Canadian National Memorial at Vimy. In recent years VAC has considerably developed the site: it has been declared a National Heritage Site (one of only two outside of Canada, the other being the Newfoundland Memorial at Beaumont Hamel); there has been a complete review of all aspects of the site; international conferences to ensure that best practice is followed have been arranged; and efforts have been made to improve the understanding of the battlefield – for example there is now an interpretive centre. Much of this work was organised by David Panton and Al Puxley of Veterans Affairs, whose endeavours in this regard have so contributed to public understanding of the importance of the sites here at Vimy and at Beaumont Hamel on the Somme.

Work has had to be carried out on Health and Safety grounds and there has also been a major effort to ensure that the most appropriate methods are used in ensuring the long-term viability of the site and safeguarding it from further degradation. This has meant limiting public access where once people could freely roam (such as walking, or running, up and down the Durand and Grange group of craters) and the

Casualties being pushed to the rear using a light field tramway.

initiation of a complex scheme of tree felling and removing of old and diseased trees. As part of this operation it became essential to know more about what actually took place on the site during the war, and so there has been considerable research in the British and Canadian archives as well as surviving German archives during recent years.

Another feature of this work has been the extensive investigation into the war effort underground, in particular that of the British. Most of this has been done by the Durand Group, working in close co-operation with VAC, which has resulted in the clearing of any remaining British mines under the site. This work has also resulted in opening up parts of the underground systems previously unseen since the war ended – for example much of the Goodman subway has been accessed, as well as a limited part of the O Sector, on the southern fringes of the site. Recently access has been gained to part of the German system as well, bringing new knowledge about an aspect of the war about which relatively little is known, certainly on the 'British' sector of the Front.

Although the primary aim of many of these endeavours has been to ensure visitor (and staff) safety, it has also led to a considerable inten-

Left: Contemporary press report from the *Toronto Globe* April 1917. Right: Press report published to mark the first anniversary of the battle in April 1918.

sification and deepening of the briefing for the guides in their initial training programme as well as providing much of the material for the Self Guided Tour that is now available on the site. The restoration of the Vimy Memorial has been a huge task: the actual work might have lasted a couple of years, but there was an enormous amount that had to be done before the contractors could move in. The full glory of the Memorial has been revealed once more and this time new technology and improved construction techniques should mean that it will better survive the elements.

The completion of the restoration seemed an appropriate time to publish a new Battleground Europe book on Vimy, this time incorpo-rating the German side of the story. The men who fought here in those tense days have now all 'faded away'; the names of the many Canadians who died here are safeguarded (and, in the nearby cemeter-ies, some of their fellow members of the then Empire and Dominions as well as their German enemy), but their deeds – or at least the deeds of some of them – still need to be recorded in words, so that memory can also include understanding.

Nigel Cave
Rosminian Postulancy, Gare, Tanzania

GERMAN INTRODUCTION

Vimy Ridge and the heights of Notre Dame de Lorette to the northwest of Souchez were bitterly contested during the autumn of 1914. The French army managed to retain the town of Arras, but the vital high ground just to the north remained in the hands of the German army. From the commanding positions on the ridges the invading German army was able to dominate the area in all directions. This situation was clearly intolerable to the French army, which took early steps to alter matters. As a result the favourable situation from the German point of view did not survive the major offensives of spring and autumn of 1915, because the French army, at great cost, succeeded in regaining Notre Dame de Lorette and reducing very considerably the depth of the defensive positions to the west of Vimy Ridge.

By the end of the 1915 fighting the German defensive lines, which protected what was now the key terrain in the area, were confined to the narrow crest of Vimy Ridge itself and the western slopes below it. The eastern slope of the northern section of this ridge fell away steeply, whilst that in its southern sector was altogether more easy-angled. Vimy Ridge is located to the west of the villages of Givenchy, Vimy and Farbus and, had it been in the possession of the Allies, its sixty metre elevation would have given them long views over the Douai plain. Throughout 1916 the ridge was the scene of constant minor actions and an intense period of mining and counter-mining once the British army took over the sector in March of that year. In May 1916 a German attack with strictly limited objectives succeeded in pushing the British back down the western slopes below where the Canadian memorial is situated today. This gained slightly more depth for the defence, but did not solve the fundamental problem that the ridge was far too narrow to permit meaningful defence in depth to be conducted.

In order to pre-empt the anticipated major offensive by the French and the British armies in early 1917, the German Supreme Army Command decided to withdraw from the great salient of Arras - Roye - Soissons, pulling back to the newly constructed Siegfried Stellung [Hindenburg Line], whilst simultaneously and extremely controversially, laying waste to the territory in between the new positions and the old. This considerably shortened the length of front and yielded strong reserves, by releasing the equivalent of approximately fourteen divisions from the ground holding role. As a result of this decision, during mid-March 1917 when the Allies were about to launch their attacks after several months' preparation, to their surprise the German front melted away and withdrew behind a broad swathe of destruction, which for the time being ruled out further major offensives.

In making its operational plans, the German Supreme Army Command had had to take into account that, following the strategic withdrawal, further offensives would undoubtedly be directed to the sectors north and south of the zone of devastation, aiming to unhinge the strong Siegfried Stellung by means of assaults on its flanks. It was quite obvious, therefore, that one of the objectives of any such push would be Vimy Ridge; a prospect which caused them some considerable concern. Although Vimy Ridge is generally portrayed in the anglophone literature as virtually impregnable, in fact it was nothing of the kind. The Germans knew it and it concerned them seriously – so much so that a fall-back Third Position was prepared up to five kilometres to the east of Vimy Ridge.

As has been mentioned, the position crucially lacked depth. In an attempt to overcome this problem and in accordance with prevailing doctrine during 1916, the method adopted was to pack the forward area with troops, a decision proved by the disproportionate number of dugouts associated with the front line itself. The priority which had had to be given to operations on the Somme the previous year, meant that neither manpower nor resources had been available to improve its run down defences, to rectify structural problems or mirror on the ground doctrinal developments applied elsewhere. Experience bought at a high price on the Somme, in particular the fact that stationing large numbers of infantry in the front line simply exposed them to destruction during bombardments, could not be applied here.

Short of abandoning the ridge, which was never seriously contemplated, nothing could be done about the geographical deficiencies of the position and, which was worse, constant Canadian pressure in the form of raids and patrols following their arrival in November 1916 made it almost impossible to improve the defences significantly, though emergency repair work, mining and counter-mining operations continued at a furious rate through the winter. Later, once heavy preparatory shelling began, all such work came to a virtual standstill. Throughout late February and March, the German defenders hoped and intended to launch a limited counter-attack, codenamed Operation Munich, towards Zouave Valley, to increase depth and so improve the defences, but this proved to be impossible: the means were lacking and the weather unfavourable.

Vimy Ridge lay in the German sector La Bassée – Arras, which in early 1917 was the responsibility of Sixth Army, commanded by

Generaloberst Freiherr (Baron) von Falkenhausen. The sector was further sub-divided into five 'Group Sectors', each the responsibility of a corps headquarters. Already by February 1917, in anticipation of the forthcoming offensive, no fewer than twelve and a half divisions were in the ground holding role and three others were held back in reserve behind the threatened area. This amounted to a doubling of the density of defensive forces along the most threatened Souchez - Arras sector, compared with the situation that had obtained in 1916.

As the intelligence indicators for the opening of a major offensive multiplied, concerns about the vulnerability of Vimy Ridge in the face of determined attack grew. Despite the known risks associated with 'front loading' the defence, in early February 1917 Army Group Crown Prince Rupprecht requested further reinforcements for I Bavarian Reserve Corps, commanded by General der Infanterie Ritter von Fasbender. The request was granted, the sectors were reduced in width and the defence of Vimy Ridge itself was entrusted to the Prussian 79th Reserve Division. Commanded by Generalleutnant von Bacmeister, the division (which only arrived from the Eastern Front at the beginning of December 1916) spent several weeks learning to master the characteristics and battle procedures of the Western Front. This began with training in the Lille area and continued with deployment to the La Bassée-Lens sector.

From the end of February it was then deployed in the cratered landscape of Vimy Ridge, between Givenchy and Thélus (Divisional Headquarters was well to the east in Beaumont), where it concentrated on reinforcing the shattered and ploughed-up position in anticipation of the expected assault. Division of responsibility for the three kilometre-wide position was as follows: right flank (Sector *Fischer*) Reserve Infantry Regiment 261 (Oberstleutnant von Goerne), centre (Sector *Zollern*) Reserve Infantry Regiment 262 (Major Freiherr [Baron] von Rotenhan), left flank (Sector *Arnulf*) Reserve Infantry Regiment 263 (Oberstleutnant von Behr). Two battalions from each regiment were made available to man the positions. The third was held back at the disposal of higher command.

As has been noted, the main problem for the defence was the lack of depth: only 700 – 1,000 metres. Should an attacker succeed in the first rush in pushing the defence back from the narrow crest, its recapture through counter-attack would be very unlikely to succeed. The First Position ran forward of and along the crest line and comprised three very poorly constructed trench lines, whose dugouts – which quite wrongly (in post-Somme thinking) had been sited mostly

Generalleutnant von
Bacmeister.

Generaloberst Freiherr (Baron)
von Falkenhausen.

Generalleutnant Dieterich.

General der Infanterie Ritter von
Fasbender.

in the front line trench – could not withstand the impacts of heavy calibre shells. Defence of the Second Position, which was most unfavourably located at the foot of the eastern slope, offered no prospect of long-term success.

The divisional batteries, under the command of Oberst Bleidorn, the artillery commander, were located in concealed positions to the east of the ridge. The direct support artillery (Reserve Field Artillery Regiment 63 and 2nd Bn Field Artillery Regiment 69 – Major Cropp) was deployed all along the Infantry Regiment Sectors, being split into three sub-groups, each of four batteries [4x4 = sixteen guns]. Sub Group Arnulf was further reinforced by one heavy field howitzer battery. To this must be added the close-quarter battle weapons in the first infantry position (mortars and grenade-launchers. The long range artillery under Major Kemmer, which comprised nine batteries (three equipped with field howitzers, four with heavy howitzers and two with heavy field guns) was split into two sub groups. Vimy Ridge, though short of space and often under heavy fire, provided the observation posts.

Generalmajor Freiherr [Baron] von Pechmann.

The amount of work needed to prepare the position for the expected attack, meant that every element of the division, including the troops theoretically at rest and the medical units, were pushed to their limits during the days and weeks which led up to the battle.

Despite constant heavy enemy harassing fire and terrible winter weather, work went ahead continuously in the attempt to strengthen the positions, renovate destroyed trenches, construct new dugouts and improve the barbed wire obstacles. Trackways to facilitate the nightly forward move of reserves had to be established. Regimental and battalion command posts had to be equipped with air recognition panels, which could be laid out as German infantry cooperation support aircraft approached, in order to show them where orders or reports had to be dropped. The shift of sector boundaries, which occurred when the division was deployed, meant that new command posts had to be constructed. For the staff of Reserve Infantry Regiment 261 this was in the foundry north of Vimy, for that of Reserve Infantry Regiment 262 in one of the trenches of the Second Position and for the staff of Reserve Infantry Regiment 263 on the eastern slope of Vimy Ridge. The infantry regimental staffs linked up with the artillery groups. A brigade command post, which was the headquarters of Generalleutnant Dieterich, was begun at the cross tracks known as La Gueule d'Ours to the east of Vimy, as was another nearby for the commander of the long-range artillery. By 9 April 1917 when the offensive was launched, lack of manpower and higher priority tasks meant that the brigade command post was not ready. The brigade commander and his staff set themselves up, therefore, near to the cross tracks, in the abandoned command post of an anti-aircraft troop.

To the left of 79th Reserve Division, between Thélus and the Scarpe, were 1st Bavarian Reserve Division (Generalmajor Freiherr [Baron] von Pechmann) and 14th Bavarian Infantry Division, (Generalleutnant Ritter von Rauchenberger) which, together with 79th Reserve Division made up 'Group Vimy' under command of I

Generalleutnant Ritter von Rauchenberger.

Generalmajor Ritter von Möhl.

Bavarian Corps (General der Infanterie von Fasbender). South of the Scarpe, along the high ground from Wancourt to Quéant, were the divisions of 'Group Arras' (IX Reserve Corps). To the right 16th Bavarian Infantry Division (Generalmajor Ritter von Möhl) of 'Group Souchez' (VIII Reserve Corps) defended against attacks directed towards The Pimple. Behind these groups, which formed the ground holding part of Sixth Army, were several reserve divisions, which were stationed in the area between Douai and Cambrai and which increased in number up until 9 April.

Increasingly accurate intelligence estimates, frequently based on the interrogation of the stream of Canadian prisoners produced by the active raiding policy, meant that by the time the Canadian Corps launched its attack, there was no question of surprise. The German chain of command knew almost every detail of what was planned. Despite this, the Battle for Vimy Ridge was a Canadian triumph. This guidebook is designed to explain why this was so.

Jack Sheldon
Vercors, France
October 2006
jandl50@hotmail.com

A captured German machine gun pillbox near Thélus.

Chapter One

VISITING VIMY RIDGE

General

If you are planning to visit the Vimy area, you are advised to base yourself in the town of Arras, with its magnificently restored Flemish Gothic architecture. Information concerning facilities and accommodation is best obtained via the website of the Tourist Office in Arras. Because there are several ways of accessing this site, it is recommended that you carry out an internet search for **Office de Tourisme Arras Pas de Calais**. With a little persistence you will find that the key information is available in English. Should you wish to contact the office in writing or by telephone (English is spoken), contact details are as follows: Office de Tourisme, Hotel de Ville, Place des Héros, BP 49, 62001 Arras CEDEX, France (Telephone: 0033 321.51.26.95; FAX: 0033 321.51.76.49. Accomodation in Arras, which ranges from four star hotels to Gîtes and a campsite, often gets fully booked, so you are strongly advised to reserve in advance. In addition, if you have particular questions concerning a visit to this area, or any other aspect of the Great War or its battlefields and you wish to obtain friendly advice from an extremely knowledgeable group of enthusiasts, you should visit the Great War Forum at http://1914-1918.invisionzone.com/forums   This very busy forum has well over 10,000 subscribers world wide; somebody is sure to be able to answer your queries, or to point you in the right direction.

Insurance and Medical

Travel and breakdown insurance is very cheap in comparison to the potential cost of an emergency, so although you are merely embarking on a simple visit to a nearby EU country, the peace of mind obtained is probably well worth the modest outlay involved. In any event do not venture out of the UK without a European Health Insurance Card, the successor to the old E111 form. You can apply online for the card at www.ehic.org.uk or by calling 0845 606 2030. Cards take about three weeks to be delivered, but it is possible to obtain a temporary number at short notice. For those living in France it is normal to have top-up medical insurance to complement state provision, so this is another argument for taking out some form of travel insurance, in order to ensure that you are entitled to the highest standards of treatment, should it be necessary. You will be visiting an agricultural area where there is a risk of tetanus. Make sure that your vaccination is up to date.

Independent Travellers
Most visitors from the United Kingdom tend to travel independently by car. This method probably provides the best combination of value for money and flexibility and, if you prepare carefully and bear a few straightforward rules in mind, you should have a trouble-free trip. The first point to remember is to drive on the right. This may seem obvious, but visitors from the UK are involved in accidents every year because they forget this simple fact. Danger times are first thing in the morning, or setting off after a stop for refreshments or to visit a point of interest, especially if you are on a minor, quiet country road. Put an arrow on your windscreen or have a drill to help you to remember. Carry your driving licence, log book and proof of insurance and passport at all times, *but do not leave them unattended in the car.* You also need a red warning triangle in case of breakdown and spare light bulbs. If you are stopped by a policeman and informed that a light is not working, production of a spare bulb from the glove compartment means that no offence has been committed.

A small first aid kit and fire extinguisher are also sensible items to carry. Make sure that you familiarise yourself with the speed limits in France (motorways 130 kph in dry weather, 110 kph in the rain; dual carriageways 110 kph; normal roads 90 kph; urban areas 50 kph, or less) and about the need to give way to traffic approaching from the right, unless you are on a priority road. Do not even think about drinking and driving. The legal limit is lower than in the United Kingdom and easily breached.

The best way to approach the battlefields of the Vimy area is to take the A26 autoroute from Calais and follow signs to Paris. The journey to Arras takes about one hour.

Useful Books
Over the years large numbers of books have been written about the battle for Vimy Ridge. They are almost all written from the Allied and, in particular, the Canadian perspective and therefore little is available concerning the defence of the ridge. Two recent books which provide a broader view are the *Battleground Europe* guide *Vimy Ridge* by Nigel Cave (Pen and Sword 1996 and subsequent reprints) and *Vimy Ridge 1917* by Alexander Turner (Osprey 2005).

Maps

The maps in this book should enable you to navigate around the area following the walks and drives without problem. It is a good idea to have an up to date road atlas in the car, the IGN Green Series 1:100,000 Map No 2 (Lille-Dunkerque) covers a large swathe of territory in this area and, if you wish to have access to the best readily available mapping, then the IGN 1:25,000 maps may be found in Arras. The sheet which covers almost the entire area to be visited or toured is 2406 E (Arras).

Clothing and Personal Equipment

Clearly this will depend on what time of year you intend to visit. Good boots are essential for all but the simplest walks and, regardless of the season, Wellingtons to wear when squelching up to distant cemeteries and points of interest are a good idea if space allows. This minimises the amount of mud transferred into the car each time you get in and out. As a general rule always carry a waterproof jacket and wrap up warmly against the wind and rain in the winter. In the summer the sun can be fierce. Wear a hat and use sun screen. None of the walks described is off the beaten track, nor are they particularly long, but you may wish to carry drinks and snacks so as to be self-sufficient. You will find a compass and a lightweight pair of binoculars useful as you orientate yourselves at the numerous recommended viewpoints during the car tours. Do not forget your camera and notebook and a day sack with which to carry everything.

Refreshments

It is easier to find refreshments in the Vimy area than it was up until a few years ago, but options in the rural areas are still fairly limited. Arras has a full range of facilities, but it wastes time to return there at lunchtime. Drinks are available in various places as you tour the area. Good modestly-priced food is available at lunchtime (opening hours restricted) at the Relais St Vaast on the D 937 at La Targette and the café located to the left of the D55 by a 90 degree turn to the right just before Givenchy en Gohelle as you descend from the Canadian Memorial. A range of sandwiches and other snacks is available from the café a few metres to the north of the Canadian artillery memorial where the Thélus-Neuville St Vaast road crosses the N17. Finally there are convenience stores and bakeries in several of the villages around the Vimy area.

Dogs

Now that the quarantine laws have been changed, it is a relatively straightforward matter to transport domestic animals to and from the United Kingdom. The latest rules which govern the import and export of pets may be found at www.defra.gov.uk. The critical point, which travellers often get wrong and which makes the vets in Calais wealthy, is the fact that dogs arrive at the terminals not having been treated for internal and external parasites in the correct manner. They should arrive at the port in France having been treated by a vet more than 24 hours and less than 48 hours previously. Make sure when you have this done that the vet signs and dates the paperwork, *adding in the time the treatment was administered.* If not, the dog does not travel and it is another job for a vet in Calais, not to mention a twenty four hour delay. Dogs are welcomed, or at least tolerated, in a wide range of hotels and gîtes in France, but it is as well to check in advance, unless you intend to use a chain such as Campanile/Première Classe www.envergure.fr or Formule 1 www.hotelformule1.com, where pets are automatically welcome. However, it must be said that the Vimy area is not a good place to bring a dog. They are not permitted anywhere on the grounds of the Canadian Memorial. Much of your visit will comprise touring in your vehicle from one viewpoint to another and, even when walks are described, none of them is suitable for a dog off a lead.

Battlefield Debris

Generally speaking there seem to be fewer dud shells lying around the edges of the cultivated fields in this area than is the case, for example, on the Somme, but you need to be aware that, in general, the woods in the Vimy area have, at best, only been partially cleared. Danger lurks in the undergrowth. It is for this reason that much of the Vimy Memorial is fenced off. If you stick to the main tracks through the woods, as described in this guide, you should have no problem, but elsewhere lie many hazards, ranging from dud shells and mortar bombs (both conventional and chemical) to rusty old caltrops (metal spikes designed to penetrate a boot sole). If you come across any sort of battlefield debris, leave it all strictly alone. Do not touch or kick it; above all do not tamper with it. Even after all these years dud shells can still be lethal. Possession of live or defused items is a criminal offence in France, as is the use of metal detectors on the battlefield; so be warned and do not indulge in souvenir hunting.

Chapter Two

THE CANADIAN CORPS:
AN OUTLINE OF EVENTS AT VIMY RIDGE

The Official History of the Canadian Corps was not printed until 1962; an earlier project had fallen foul of the outbreak of the Second World War, with only one volume of a planned multi-volume version printed (plus a volume of appendices). Although out of print for some years, it is available on the internet; because of the vagaries of web addresses, it is best to put the title on a search engine and take it from there. The author was Colonel GWL Nicholson of the Army Historical Section, who did a superb job within the constraints of a single volume. He also had the advantage over other Official Historians that Canada's version was so late in coming out: the Second World War had intervened and much had been written about the war by military historians and analysts. He was able to synthesise all this information and make good use of it, producing both an accurate and readable history. Much of what follows in this section is closely derived from what he wrote.

When Britain declared war on Germany in August 1914 Canada was automatically at war as well. Her constitutional position as a Dominion gave her no say in declaring war or in making peace, but she had the right to decide what form her contribution to the war effort should take. Loyalty to the Empire, ties with the Motherland and the sense of patriotism were very strong then, and there was never any doubt that Canada's response would be anything other than wholehearted. Sir Robert Borden, the Prime Minister, expressed the

General Sam Hughes taking a salute.

feeling of the nation at the opening of a special war session of Parliament on 18 August: 'As to our duty', he said, 'we are all agreed; we stand shoulder to shoulder with Britain and the other British Dominions in this quarrel. And that duty we shall not fail to fulfil as the honour of Canada demands.'

At the outbreak of war the Canadian regular army or, to give it its proper title, the Permanent Active Militia, numbered just over 3,000. It comprised two cavalry regiments: The Royal Canadian Dragoons and Lord Strathcona's Horse; one infantry battalion, The Royal Canadian Regiment (RCR) and some artillery, engineer and service support units. This small force was strengthened a few days after the declaration of war by the forming of a new infantry unit, Princess Patricia's Canadian Light Infantry (PPCLI). Named after the daughter of the then Governor General, it was rapidly brought to full strength with veterans volunteering from all over Canada. When it first paraded virtually every single regiment of the British Army was represented in its ranks. The PPCLI was the first Canadian unit in the front line when it went into the trenches with 80 Brigade, 27th Division on 6 January 1915 some two months before the 1st Canadian Division took over its first sector of the front. Ironically, the only pre-war regular infantry unit, the RCR, was sent to Bermuda to relieve 2/Lincolns and did not get to France until November 1915.

Behind the small regular force stood the Non-Permanent Active Militia, equivalent to the Territorials in the UK. Numbering some 60,000, it included 36 cavalry and 106 infantry regiments. Although improvements had been put in hand in the years immediately prior to 1914, Canada's armed forces were still ill-equipped and only partially trained when war broke out, but they provided a basis on which to build. A mobilization plan existed whereby a division and a mounted brigade would be made available for active service overseas. The activities of Sam Hughes, the controversial Minister of Militia, is not part of this brief outline, but he should take much of the credit for the enormous increase in manpower of the Canadian forces and the dispatch with which it was sent overseas. By New Year 1917 there were 7,240 officers and 128,980 other ranks of the Canadian Expeditionary Force (CEF) in the UK and 2,526 officers and 105,640 other ranks in France (in this case France also means Belgium). In March 1917 a form of regimental territorial system was introduced: reserve battalions in the UK were grouped with their affiliated battalions in France into Territorial Regiments bearing provincial designations. That summer the same system was extended to Canada itself.

In the Battle of the Somme, which started on 1 July 1916, the then three divisions that made up the Corps arrived on 3 September 1916 and the Corps took a prominent part in the major British assault on 15 September 1916 (including the first use of tanks). In the attack it successfully stormed Courcelette and in the ensuing weeks continued operations in the dreary fields nearby (and appalling conditions) that followed. On 17 October the Corps was relieved and sent to the Vimy front; but the 4th Division – which had arrived from England in August 1916, minus its artillery – moved to the Somme front on 10 October. It continued the fight in the same area as the Corps, struggling forward through to the muddy, waterlogged end of the battle and firmly establishing its reputation as being well up to the standard expected from a Canadian division. It left the Somme on 28 November 1916 to join the remainder of the Corps at Vimy; the Somme operations had cost the Corps some 24,000 casualties.

The new line of the Corps ran two miles north of Arras to two miles northwest of Lens, a front of about ten miles. By the beginning of December the missing elements of the Corps, the 4th Division and the Corps' artillery (which had been left behind at the Somme), had all come together. In the early months of 1917 the Corps engaged in a number of large scale raids, something the Canadians had made a specialty of since their striking success at La Petite Douve Farm (south of Messines) in November 1915. These were often quite successful, though success came at a price. A raid on 13 February by 10 Brigade – about 900 men strong – suffered 150 or so casualties: but it had occupied a good chunk of the German line and caused the Germans an estimated 160 casualties, including fifty prisoners. Sometimes these raids went terribly wrong, such as that on the night of 28 February/1 March. The raiding party was 1700 strong and suffered 687 casualties. See Chapters 3 and 5 for further details of this from both perspectives. In the lead up to the attack on 9 April, the Canadians launched raids every night from 20 March onwards – the cost was about 1,400 casualties in two weeks. The purpose, to gather intelligence about the state of the defences and the enemy opposite made the price, arguably, worth it, but it also resulted in a constant leakage of intelligence, derived from prisoner interrogation by the German defenders.

Arras: The Plan
The idea behind the Battle of Arras (9 April – 15 May 1917) was that it would act as a support for the assault of General Robert Nivelle to the south. All this was planned in the winter of 1916/17, but the key

point of the assault, the French attack, was seriously undermined by the German withdrawal to the Hindenburg Line. It was not so much the main offensive area that was affected, but rather a subsidiary one to the north, in an action designed to co-operate with the British assault around Arras. This withdrawal left the British with the responsibility in the north and also with the task of setting the whole action off with their assault. This was launched on 9 April; the attack on Vimy Ridge being an important part of the whole scheme. The French began their Chemin des Dames offensive on 16 April, but it was quite clear within a few days that it was not a success. The British had to continue their grinding attack at Arras, even after the French attack had been called off. Arras is another example of a battle the British High Command would rather not have fought.

Even before Nivelle had come up with his plan, an Allied conference in November 1916 had selected the Lens area as part of the offensive plans for 1917. The Canadian Corps (part of First Army, commanded by General Sir Henry Horne, a gunner) began planning for its part in possible operations in the Vimy area. In 1914 the Germans had ended up substantially to the west of the Vimy Ridge, occupying a sizeable segment of the western end of the Lorette spur. In a series of bloody French offensives in 1915 (including one glorious moment when the Moroccan Division actually took Hill 145, the highest point of the ridge), the line was advanced so that both sides disputed the highest ground along part of the ridge. The Germans gradually eased the French off the high points; but the prize of the high ground overlooking the Douai Plain to the east was tantalisingly close. The British took over the line in March 1916; they lost a slice of ground in May 1916, but otherwise were content to hold the line and engage in operations that effectively led to them winning the mining war, fought with considerable ferocity deep underground. It is a common misconception that the British attempted an assault on the ridge: far from it. When the ground was lost in May Haig specifically forbade any large scale operations to recover it, regarding them as a distraction from the main matter in hand, the forthcoming Battle of the Somme.

By mid January 1917, Lieutenant General Sir Julian Byng, Corps Commander since late May 1916, was quite clear in what was being demanded of his Corps by First Army: it was to capture the whole of the main crest of Vimy Ridge. There were various key features on the ridge that would seriously threaten the success of the assault further to the south – Hill 135 [modern Hill 139, known to the defenders as

Above: A scale model of Vimy Ridge laid out during the planing stages for the assault.
Right: Lieutenant General Sir Julian Byng, Canadian Corps Commander.

Telegraphen-Höhe = Telegraph Hill] and Thélus; La Folie Farm and Hill 145 – all of which had to be captured in the earliest stages of the battle. The Corps front, therefore, for the attack on 9 April extended over 7,000 yards. On the Canadian left there would be the 24th Division and on the right the 51st (Highland) Division.

By 5 March 1917 the Corps had come up with its operational plan, which survived more or less unscathed through to the attack. The stages of the attack were determined by the German defence system: the Black Line covered the German forward defence zone; the Red Line included the German *Zwischenstellung* [Intermediate Position], including La Folie Farm

27

and Hill 145 – this marked the limit for the northern divisions, the 3rd and the 4th. To the south there were two further bounds – the Blue Line, including Thélus, Hill 135 and the woods overlooking Vimy; and the Brown Line, which covered the German Second Line. Because of the nature of the task, 13 Brigade of the 5th ('Imperial' or British) Division was added to the attacking formation. Fortunately for us, the divisions were in the attacking line in numerical sequence from the left – ie the 1st was the southernmost and the 4th was the northernmost division; it is sheer serendipity that the British division happened to be numbered 5 (13 Brigade operating in the 2nd Division's area).

The assault would be launched at 5.30 am, each division having two brigades in the initial assault. After thirty-five minutes the Black Line would be taken; after forty minutes for re-organisation, then the Red Line would be taken after twenty minutes (ie by 7.05 am). The two reserve brigades in the 1st and 2nd Divisions, plus 13 Brigade on the left (5th Division) would take the remaining two lines. Two and a half hours were allowed for them to get into position; by 1.18 pm all lines should have been taken, some local tactical advances made and the line consolidated. In all there was to be an advance of some four thousand yards into the German defences.

Consolidating the line was essential: the Germans had an outstanding record for launching fast and co-ordinated counter-attacks to recover lost territory and inflict damage on an enemy which was still in a state of disorder after the attack. It was essential that a clear plan existed to ensure that the newly won positions could be held, and so Byng's Corps staff spent considerable time on managing this aspect of the phase. Artillery provision was vital for the success of the attack. The Canadian Corps had an enormous amount of artillery made available to it: apart from the 24th Division, it was the only formation from First Army committed to the Battle. The result was that instead of two Heavy Artillery Groups, for example, it had eleven. On the Corps front there was one heavy gun for every twenty yards of frontage (in the preparation for the Somme there was only one for every fifty seven yards) and a field gun (18 pounders and 4.5 inch howitzers) for every ten yards, compared to the Somme's one for every twenty yards. In addition, I Corps on the left had reinforced artillery capability; although not taking a direct part in the attack on 9 April, its artillery could certainly be used.

The artillery plan was the responsibility of Brigadier General E Morrison (a Canadian). The Germans were to be bombarded during the day from 20 March by observed fire on all features of their defensive

A supply of shells arrive at the gun position.

systems for almost a three week period. At night both artillery and machine gun fire were to continue to harass the approaches to the German front line, hindering resupply and ration parties. The artillery also had supplies of a graze fuze (No. 106), which had not been available on the Somme. This made high explosive fire far more effective against barbed wire. A rolling barrage, working on approximately hundred yard lifts, was to precede the assaulting infantry, whilst known defensive systems further back were to be kept under continuous fire from guns of all calibres. The Canadian Corps and I Corps between them had a daily allowance of 2,500 tons of shells, with an initial stock pile of 42,500 tons: again, a contrast to the Somme, where shells had been both in short supply and not of the right type for the task in hand (partly because there were not the right type of guns available, in the latter case).

Counter battery fire (i.e. the destruction of the enemy's guns, thereby providing protection for the advancing infantry) was the responsibility of specifically detailed heavy guns. Although the concept sounds refreshingly obvious, execution is entirely another matter, especially in the confusion of battle, with observation obscured by bad weather and the smoke of battle. Recent innovations, such as sound ranging and flash spotting, were added to intelligence sources such as aerial photography, wireless interceptions, interrogation of prisoners and evaluation of captured documents. The key here was the rapid use made of such information and then getting it to the batteries concerned as quickly as possible. This is complex now and was much more so then, given the considerable limitations of contemporary communications technology.

To the requirements of the artillery had to be added the logistical nightmare of feeding the huge number of troops concentrated in the Canadian Corps area: to the 97,184 Canadians in the Corps were added over 70,000 British troops – infantry, gunners, engineers, labour corps personnel, making a total of some 170,000 men under the Corps' command. On top of this there were 50,000 horses and mules to be watered and fed, roadways, light railways and tramways to be maintained, timber prepared for the creation of corduroy roads, miles of signalling cable to be buried deep in the ground and many miles more to be laid on the surface. It was – and still is - quite impossible to keep preparations for a major offensive away from the enemy; the only element of surprise that might remain would be when such an attack would take place.

Moving up for the assault on Vimy Ridge.

The initial part of the preparatory bombardment was carried out without the use of about half the batteries; British corps on the left and right shelled positions on the flanks of the Canadian assault area. On 2 April the bombardment became intensive: as Nicholson describes it a crushing bombardment fell on the German positions. Approximately one million rounds were fired, 50,000 tons in weight, utterly devastating the attack zone. The villages were shattered, the communication trenches severely damaged (with consequent interminable delays in getting rations up to the forward troops), the defenders had to put up with the seemingly endless and nerve wracking torment of being under heavy artillery attack. Many patrols were sent out to gauge the effect of the shelling, often at quite heavy cost. The Royal Flying Corps and Royal Naval Air Service flew numerous missions, some taking photographs and others protecting these vulnerable machines. During this period the Germans enjoyed the benefit of superior machines; 'Bloody April' was a horrendously bad month for the allied airmen. All the intelligence systems applied to learning the location of the German artillery paid off: about 83% of German gun positions were established.

The troops were well prepared. What Nicholson called 'a full scale replica' of the battlefield was laid out a few kilometres to the rear, and the attacking troops went over this again and again, rehearsing their attacks. At Lillers (First Army HQ), a detailed model was viewed by even the most junior of officers. To provide protection against enemy fire in the approach to the front line, a number of subways were constructed along the front by Royal Engineer Tunnelling Companies. The original intention had been for the assault to take place on Easter Sunday, 8 April. The French wanted a delay, and a compromise of twenty-four hours was reached. Perhaps it was as well: Easter Sunday was a sunny, clear day: Easter Monday saw the attack launched in snow and sleet, fortuitously blowing into the face of the enemy, enhancing the problems of the defence.

The Assault

The attack at Vimy was launched, promptly at 5.30 am, accompanied by the deafening sound of 983 guns and mortars: 'The main field artillery barrage was provided by one gun to every twenty five yards of front. These guns, opening at zero hour, fired for three minutes on the enemy's foremost trenches at three rounds a minute, and then lifted a hundred yards every three minutes, slowing their rate of fire to two rounds every minute. This was supplemented by 18 pounder standing barrages, 4.5 inch howitzer concentrations, barrages by heavy guns and howitzers and the continuous fire of 150 machine guns [ie Vickers guns], creating a bullet swept zone four hundred yards ahead. This employment of machine guns for barrage and supporting fire was unprecedented in military history. Other guns and mortars bombarded German battery positions and ammunition dumps with high explosives and gas shells [gas shells were not available to the British for most of the Somme], while some mortars laid smoke in front of Thélus and Hill 135.' (Nicholson). The German artillery's response was weak and ineffectual – German communications had been largely destroyed and SOS flares could not be seen clearly.

The 1st Division (Major General Arthur Currie) faced their biggest problem on the far side of the Arras-Lens road, but resistance was overcome, albeit at the expense of heavy casualties. The 2nd Division (Major General Burstall, the only regular Canadian soldier commanding a division at the time) had similar problems from the German defence as it came up to the Black Line: but both divisions were at the Black Line by 6.15 am. The 3rd Division (Major General

Lipsett, a British officer) had taken the Black Line, including the main points, La Folie Farm and the École Commune, by 6.25am. The 4th Division (Major General Watson) had a more difficult time. 11 Brigade, whose objectives included Hill 145, was initially successful on the right, adjacent to the 3rd Division; but the attack on the left failed. It was not until shortly before dark on the 9th that the Black Line was, more or less, secured.

Problems on the right naturally affected 12 Brigade's attack on the left; progress to the Black Line was made, but German machine gun fire from the Pimple and a German counter attack near Givenchy, along with considerable German resistance, combined to ensure that by 6.00 pm the main objectives were not taken. 10 Brigade (which had been ear marked to take the Pimple, to the north west of Hill 145, on 10 April) was brought in to replace the exhausted 11 Brigade, and on the afternoon of the 10th carried 11 Brigade line through to the Red Line. With Hill 145 secured, 12 Brigade was able to take its objectives on the Red Line with relative ease.

Whilst the 4th Division struggled with its problems against the tenacious German defence, the southern divisions continued their operations. The 1st Division, helped by the wind, which obscured the view of the defending Bavarians with a mixture of snow and smoke, soon were on to the Red Line (on the left this was part of the

Zwischenstellung = Intermediate Position). The 2nd Division encountered increasingly coherent opposition in its advance to the Red Line, which included the hamlet of Les Tilleuls. But by 8.00 am both divisions reported that they had taken the Red Line. The Third Division, meanwhile, had continued to make good progress and took the Red Line as well, fending off localised German attacks. However, it had to provide left flank protection by creating a defensive line to the original trenches to deal with the unsatisfactory situation on their left, in 4th Division's sector.

The 1st and 2nd Divisions took the Blue Line by about 11.00 am; the main problem had been encountered by the 1st Battalion at the Intermediate Line. The British 13 Brigade was brought into this part of the attack, on the left of the 2nd Division. There was now a halt of ninety minutes whilst machine guns were brought forward; by about 3.00 pm the Brown Line, too, had been secured. There had been problems – for example 1 Brigade faced a temporary problem on its right because the neighbouring 51st (Highland) Division had been held up in its attack; whilst the German resistance continued to be strong and determined.

A patrol of Canadian Light Horse sets out for Willerval on the first afternoon of battle.

The final notable event on 9 April was the attempt to use some cavalry to take advantage of the German confusion. In fact, Vimy Ridge was always regarded as a limited objective (it was the overlooking positions on it that were the essential features that had to be captured to provide British divisions to the south with security from enfilade fire), and First Army did not have a cavalry division under command. Nevertheless, a squadron of Canadian Light Horse was instructed to head for Willerval, which it entered, but then had to withdraw with considerable losses. However, its presence allegedly caused some concern to the German command.

With the exception of the difficulties of the 4th Division, the Corps had achieved its objectives more or less to schedule: a considerable achievement. When the 4th Division completed its part of the operation on the 10th, the Corps had advanced about four thousand yards on a seven thousand yard front: 7,707 men were casualties, 2,967 of which were fatal. 13 Brigade had lost about 380 men. 3,400 German prisoners had been taken by midnight on the 9th.

The Pimple
The Pimple is a height of about 140 metres at the northern end of Vimy Ridge. The Germans had being planning an assault of their own, based on a massive use of gas shells, from this feature (and further south, to Hill 145) a few days prior to 9 April: the aim was to complete the domination over Zouave Valley, immediately behind the Canadian

Front Line and across which the Canadians had to move men and supplies to reach the trenches on Vimy Ridge. Adverse weather conditions, the state of the ground – and probably the ferocity of the final week of the preliminary bombardment – meant that it never happened. The Pimple provided the ground from which the German defenders could make themselves very awkward against any advance to the south, over Hill 145; and also offered excellent views down much of Zouave Valley. Because of manpower constraints, the original plan was that it would be attacked by 10 Brigade only after the rest of the Ridge had been taken, therefore on 10 April. It would be fought in conjunction with the Imperial 24th Division, which would take Bois en Hache, the easternmost part of the Lorette Spur.

Because of the hold up on Hill 145, the operation had to be postponed for forty eight hours. The Germans used the time to stiffen their new line with two battalions from 4th Guards Infantry Division. Again, the Canadians were fortunate with the weather: 11 April was bad and 12 April brought a westerly gale, with snow and freezing rain, gusting into the eyes of the defenders. On the other hand the extremely muddy conditions made any movement difficult for the attackers and retaining cohesion in the assault all but impossible. The Royal Engineers launched forty thirty-pound drums of mustard gas into Givenchy, using Livens projectors, prior to the attack and around one

A view across the killing fields towards the captured German trenches.

hundred guns opened up in support of the assault, which commenced at 5.00 am. Although the highest point of the Pimple was taken relatively easily, (by the 44th Battalion: the last vestiges of their memorial which stood there were destroyed and removed in 2004), progress for the 46th, on the left, was very slow and came upon very determined defenders from Grenadier Guard Regiment 5. However, by about 8.00 am all but a very small section of the Ridge was firmly in Canadian hands and even this small section fell after the resolute defenders were withdrawn on 13 April.

Consolidation

The German position on Vimy Ridge was a powerful one, doubtless; but – especially at the northern end – it suffered the problem of providing very little room for defensive manoeuvre. Once the defenders were ejected from their positions it was difficult to envisage a successful counter attack to get them back up on the heights. This conclusion was doubtless assisted by the speed with which the

Canadians established a sound system of defence of the newly won ground. Accepting the loss of the Ridge, Crown Prince Rupprecht ordered a withdrawal to the German Third Position on 12 April (this was, of course, not unique to the Vimy sector: the German defenders had suffered reverses all along the line of attack, most notably north of the River Scarpe in the area defended by 14th Bavarian Infantry Division). The new position meant that the Canadians would have to advance into the plain and thus lose the advantage of an immediate dominance over the new German line. It also meant that all the Canadian artillery would have to be brought forward, a difficult task because supply lines were stretched and new roadways and light railway tracks had to be laid over the utterly devastated terrain. To disguise the move, the Germans left enough manpower and guns behind to create a sense of continued occupation and resistance in the old line; whilst on the night of the 12th the remainder were withdrawn to the new positions and fresh troops were brought up to them. Lacking powerful fire support, the Canadians and British advanced by the use

The view over the Douai Plain, 1917.

of powerful patrols. To the south they took a position on the Arras – Lens railway line; the 3rd Division occupied the line from Vimy to La Chaudière and the 4th Givenchy. The neighbouring British Corps – XVII and I – similarly advanced.

The Battles of Vimy Ridge and of the Scarpe had undoubtedly been very successful; but German resistance was nothing if not tenacious and the battle soon returned to a traditional format of attack and counter-attack and was reduced to an attritional struggle. Vimy Ridge was, however, a name to conjure with. During the Artois offensives of 1915 it had rarely been out of the papers. Censorship rules allowed that the name of Corps involved in an operation could be freely used – but not that of the divisions. Since British Corps were simply titled by Roman numerals and their composite divisions frequently changed, such a name did not mean much. The Canadian Corps was self evidently Canadian, consisting of its four divisions who never left it (except for a short period in 1918): Canada's position on the military map was clearly established. The capture of Vimy Ridge was described as an Easter gift to the people of France from Canada. George V sent a message of congratulations to Haig, including the comment: Canada will be proud that the taking of the coveted Vimy Ridge has fallen to the lot of her troops.

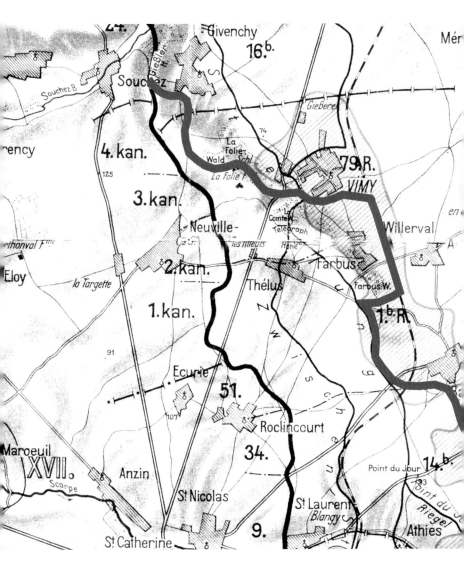

1. German map showing how the opposing forces lined up for the battle
from March 1917. Also shown are the Allied gains on 9 April.

Major General Arthur Currie
Commander 1st Canadian Division

Major General Harry Burstall
Commander 2nd Canadian Division

Major General Louis Lipsett
Commander 3rd Canadian Division

Major General David Watson
Commander 4th Canadian Division

Chapter Three

THE PRELIMINARIES: HOLDING THE LINE, RAIDING AND PATROLLING OCTOBER 1916 TO MARCH 1917

The months the Canadians spent in the line were chiefly ones of patrols and preparations for the great assault in April 1917. One of the finest regimental histories of the war is that of the PPCLI – Princess Patricia's Canadian Light Infantry (The PPCLI 1914 – 1919, H Williams, 1923). It was a regiment formed at the outbreak of war and was named after the Governor General's (the Duke of Connaught's) daughter, Princess Patricia. Its first recruits were all originally ex-soldiers of the British army; thus effectively fully trained, it was the first Canadian unit sent to serve on the Western Front. Concentration is given to the PPCLI, partly because of the quality of its history and partly because the actions described below all took place on the Memorial site, many of them accessible to he public.

The move to Vimy almost coincided with a change in the Battalion's commander: Lieutenant Colonel Pelly went on to greater things (in due course he commanded 91 Brigade in the 7th (Imperial) Division). He was replaced on 31 October 1916 by Agar Adamson, who remained in command until he was invalided home on 27 March 1918.

The Battalion undertook twelve tours in the line during the period October 1916 – March 1917. It 'was to hold a line of trenches about 900 yards long which clung to the western edge of the Givenchy – Neuville St Vaast road. Two craters – Broadmarsh at the north and Devon at the south – marked its extreme limits; and the whole dividing line between friend and foe, except for about 250 yards on the left, was the series of craters that had mostly been blown in the fighting of the spring. At no point were the outpost lines more than seventy five yards apart; these consisted of a large number of crater posts, connecting with intricate systems of fighting and communication trenches behind.'

Because of the proximity of the lines and the particular problems associated with the Vimy position, the line was more strongly held than usual. 'The "crater war" of the first months was very lively, and kept the Patricias far busier than during the previous winter. On the other hand, their movements during this period were regularised as never before or after, following the unchanging routine of front line, brigade reserve and divisional reserve, until they were withdrawn on 11

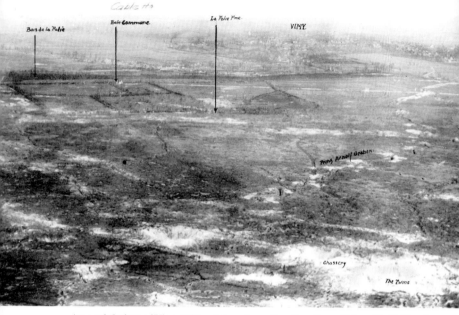

An aerial view of Vimy Ridge taken from the direction of Neuville St Vaast.

February to Bruay to train for the great assault. When in the line they shared the same sub-sector with the 42nd Battalion [The Black Watch of Canada] in every brigade tour, garrisoning the front trenches for five days at a stretch [although there was at least one occasion when it did six days at a stretch]. In brigade reserve they were always stationed in the cellars of Neuville St Vaast, and provided working parties to help the battalion in the line. In divisional reserve they were encamped in hutments beside Mont St Eloy [sic].' By and large, the early months in the line were relatively calm and casualty lists low.

Due to the length of the Canadian Corps' line when it arrived in October, some formations were placed considerably further north than the ridge area: thus many of the units of the 1st and 2nd Division were to spend a large amount of their time in the winter enjoying the line in Souchez and to the north of it; it was only much nearer the time of the attack that all the Canadian divisions took up the positions from which they would launch their attack. Large raids, involving many men, became more common on the Canadian side from December onwards. The PPCLI never took part in one of these large raids, but was constantly sending out patrols. For example on 5 December two officers, Reynolds and Burness, made a daylight reconnaissance in front of Durand and Duffield craters to explore the enemy post that linked the two. The enemy spotted them and they withdrew. They returned again twenty minutes later, accompanied by a sniper, Private

Svienbjorn Loptson. Having thrown some bombs into the enemy post and removed several barbed wire frames, they entered the post to find no one there. They did what damage they could and returned with a German trench pump as a trophy. The same evening Loptson went out again to the same place, accompanied by two NCOs; they shot the sentry who challenged them and took a German prisoner, who provided the desired identification – 23 RIR. (Loptson went on to be commissioned but was killed in September 1918; Reynolds was killed whilst serving in the RAF in June 1918.) On the following day another regimental officer, Lieutenant Donald MacLean, was wounded by a sniper whilst trying to bomb him out of his position (MacLean was later killed in July 1917 and is buried in Villers Station cemetery in Grave VIII E 2).

On 7 December a patrol went out to examine the enemy position in front of Commons crater (again in daylight). 'Next day a stronger patrol of ten men under the Bombing Officer, Lieutenant AA McDougall, left the line at 3.20am to raid the post. The officer and Private Mullin crawled to within six feet of the post; and after listening there for a minute or two Private Mullin crawled up and discovered two enemy sentries. Lieutenant McDougall decided to rush the post to secure prisoners and brought up the rest of his party. Then, covering the sentries with revolvers, he ordered them to surrender. The sentries, however, showed fight. One of them fired his rifle, and then both threw up their hands, but at the same time dislodged a bomb from the parapet by using a foot attachment, and wounded the officer badly. [This use of prepared bombs on the parapets to be released by sentries under attack seems to have been common in this sector.] The sentries were at once shot down but, as the alarm had been given, the first consideration was to get Lieutenant McDougall back to the line. This was not an easy matter, for the officer, a man of magnificent physique and weighing 230 pounds, had both legs terribly mauled by the explosion and was utterly helpless. Four of the party, however, managed to carry him back overland while the remainder, under Sergeant Dow, formed a covering party for the retreat. When all was clear, Sergeant Dow destroyed the post with a carefully timed Stokes shell, which had been carried up with the raiding party with no little difficulty. The whole party was back in the trench within fifteen minutes of the beginning and the enemy's only retaliation was to bomb his own communication trench leading to the invaded post.' Lieutenant McDougall wrote to Adamson a week or so later: "My left leg is off, my right leg is shattered below the knee, my left arm is broken, I have some shrapnel in my hip, but otherwise I am 'jake'!"

The next tour of the line between the 13th and 19th was very quiet until the last day. 172 Tunnelling Company blew three mines on both sides of the Tidsa crater, 'using 11,000 pounds of ammonal for the charge'. The explosions made good lips and increased the height and extent of the crater. On a rocket signal from the Tunnellers, two parties of the Patricias, each consisting of thirty men with a Lewis gun and all commanded by Lieutenant Pearson, advanced through lanes in the wire that had been cut earlier in the night and over shell holes which had been spanned by duckboard bridges. The near lips of the new craters were successfully consolidated, though with nine casualties… At Colonel Agar Adamson's request the First Army Command sanctioned the official name of Patricia for the main crater.' After the Ridge was captured a wooden obelisk ten feet high, with Patricia Crater inscribed on it, was put up by the Regimental Pioneers.

The regimental history notes that, on Christmas Day, a number of enemy troops, under a white flag, came out into No Man's Land, in a desire to fraternise, and wandered around there. The gesture was not reciprocated, though they were not fired upon. In January the arrival of two heavy German mortars, dubbed Josephine and Ananias, was soon made apparent. Front line tours were resulting in more casualties, but intensive patrolling went on as before, despite the consequent leakage of intelligence when raiders taken prisoner were interrogated. It is worth noting here that, amongst other means devised to protect their outpost positions, the Germans in this sector made extensive use of caltrops; essentially these were metal spikes, maybe a metre long, which could be stuck into the ground, leaving a sharpened point sticking up, catching the unwary in the foot as he walked forward or in the eye if he were crawling. They are very nasty things and a large number of them still exist in the areas barred to the public: notices to stay out are not there for the amusement of the site authorities.

On 26 January at 8.20 am a large raid was launched at a point between the Duffield and Durand craters. The fifteen or so men went forward under the cover of a Stokes mortar barrage 'to destroy dugouts and listening posts which had long been troubling the sentries on the Canadian side. The post was found unoccupied and the party moved down the saps towards the enemy line and bombed deep dugouts with Mills and Stokes [sic] grenades. A bombing counter attack was beaten off; a charge was exploded at the Durand post; and the party returned safely to their own trenches in seventeen minutes with two captured sentries, identified as belonging to the 3rd Battalion Bavarian RIR. 16'

Another raid was launched at 4am on 28 January on the observation line at Birkin Crater with 'the hope of discovering and destroying a nearby dugout. Moon and stars were shining and there was snow on the ground; so the raiders dressed in white canvas clothing made and fitted by the regimental tailor. As the sides and bottoms of the craters were not entirely covered in snow, black patches were sewn on to the garments to make the camouflage complete, while boots, steel helmets and rifles were also covered with white canvas... they came within ten yards of the post, which was then rushed. Three sentries threw up their hands but one of them first dislodged from the parapet a bomb that seriously wounded Lieutenant Mortimer and Corporal Stangroom. In spite of this, both the officer and the NCO jumped down and, after a struggle, overcame the three sentries. But the garrison was now alarmed and some twenty men appeared at the foot of the sap leading to the post. Lieutenant Mortimer and his corporal were unable to help themselves, the former being temporarily blinded by his wound, but were brought back safely by two of the party. The remaining two men, Lance Corporal C Sinclair and Private W Davies, performed their allotted task with great coolness, Davies placing the explosive [they

Canadians resting in 'funk holes' on Vimy Ridge.

had taken two ammonal charges with them] while Sinclair kept the enemy at bay by steady bombing.' Unfortunately the charges did not go off - the history suggests possibly this was because they were frozen. Sinclair was killed in March 1918 in England whilst serving with the RFC; he is buried in Stamford, Lincolnshire. Davies was killed on 23 March 1917 and is buried in the nearby Ecoivres Military Cemetery.

In early February the PPCLI moved back to Mont St Eloi for a week's training and relaxation and then moved with the Brigade to Bruay to begin a period of six weeks intensive training for the offensive, which 'in the later stages included operations planned to the minutest detail over practice trenches'.

This tale of trench life in these months was repeated along the Canadian line. Mine warfare continued to play a prominent part in operations after the Canadians arrived, though not with the intensity of the spring and summer of 1916. For example, the 14th Battalion CEF (the Royal Montreal Regiment) was involved in the heavy fighting that followed the firing of two mines, creating one crater, by 176 Tunnelling Company at 9.50pm on 27 November. The regimental history (The Royal Montreal Regiment, 14th Battalion CEF 1914 – 1925, ed. RC Featherstonehaugh, 1927) gives a very full account of the whole operation. The orders included the creation of three separate storming parties (each of about twenty men, including stretcher bearers, sappers, bombers and, for the left and right parties, Lewis gunners), each with a reserve storming party of the same strength. There were to be wiring parties whose job it was to wire the flanks of the crater. A force of 51 men from the 13th Battalion was positioned to act as an emergency support force; each of the storming parties was to have two runners: 'all runners to wear distinguishing marks and to have absolute right of way over all traffic'. Eleven light to heavy mortars were made available; twelve 18 pounders and four 4.5 inch howitzers were to be used to engage enemy batteries and mortars, with an FOO (Forward Observation Officer) positioned in Ersatz crater, equipped with telephone and runners. The Brigade machine guns (ie Vickers) were to put down a heavy barrage behind the enemy lines – '... to open fire when the mine is blown and NOT BEFORE [sic].' Digging parties (to match the storming parties) of a dozen men were detailed off to dig communications trenches in a 'zig zag fashion' to the crater from the present location. Before the crater was fired 'all ranks must clear the area bounded by Uhlan-King-Gobron-Chalk Trenches to half way between Tranchot and Uhlan. Company commanders must personally see that this is done and advise Battalion Headquarters in writing.

After debris from the explosion has fallen, positions will at once be reoccupied. All ranks must be warned to clear dugouts for explosion and to take shelter from falling debris immediately after.'

The attack required detailed rehearsal: the attacking and consolidating parties therefore went to special billets near Villers au Bois and went over a taped replica of the ground (including the likely size, shape and location of the new crater).

The mines were fired on schedule. 'Contrary to expectations, little debris fell and no delay ensued from this cause, the consolidating parties moving forward without having suffered losses. For a full minute after the explosion the enemy appeared dazed, then a Minenwerfer came into action and white flares rose from behind the crater, red distress flares following from the same locality and obviously calling for SOS [artillery] fire. Eight minutes elapsed; then a barrage fell on the crater area, preceded [by] several seconds by a number of fish tailed mortar torpedoes that burst in the Canadian front line.

Meanwhile the consolidation parties of the Battalion had advanced to their respective objectives. Ten minutes after zero the parties on the left reached their assigned locations and found that the explosion had affected the positions hardly at all. Accordingly, they set about improving the existing trenches and clearing them at the few points where parapets had fallen in.

The right also worked on their trenches, both parties taking some casualties from German shelling, which subsided after twenty minutes and died away altogether half an hour later.

To cover the working parties, a bombing post was pushed forward to the right in the old German front line. Between 11 and 11.30pm a party of one hundred Germans advanced across the open from their support line and dislodged the 14th Battalion bombers, who withdrew on the main body. Bombs and machine guns soon dispersed the enemy, who retreated in disorder, leaving a number of dead behind and yielding two wounded prisoners. On the retreat of the enemy, the 14th bombing posts, doubled in strength, were pushed forward, these dealing successfully with a group of about nine Germans who attempted to interrupt the consolidation parties on the right.

Failing to achieve success with a small party, the enemy sent forward a stronger force at about 2am. Retiring before this attack, the 14th's bombers and a patrol took cover in the mine crater while two machine guns opened fire and drove the enemy back. Shortly afterwards two lines of French wire were staked,

49

*pinned and strung from the south lip of the crater outside the
right T-head to Harting Street, and simultaneously the enemy
began to consolidate his lip of the great hole in the ground.'*
The job was completed by 6am.

The operation had cost the 14th Battalion thirty nine casualties, of
whom eleven were killed; it was estimated that the Germans had lost
seventy five men, over and above those killed in the explosion. The
crater was named Montreal Crater in the Battalion's honour. This
account gives a good idea of how operations involving the blowing of
a mine were conducted: by this stage in the war both sides had
developed considerable expertise in this type of attack, and Vimy
Ridge (and the area around it), because of the geological conditions,
was an ideal location for this particular type of warfare.

It is interesting to note the Battalion's strength in mid December. In
theory, and at full establishment, a battalion would number just over a
thousand men and officers. At this time the front line strength of the
14th Battalion consisted of: twenty six officers and 430 bayonets,
seventy machine gunners, five bombers, twenty four signallers,
seventeen stretcher bearers and eighteen Intelligence men, or 590
altogether. This total was in turn divided among the companies as
follows: No 1 Coy, five officers and 109 other ranks; No 2 Coy, five
officers and 110 other ranks; No 3 Coy, four officers and 114 other
ranks; No 4 Coy, four officers and 151 other ranks; HQ, eight officers
and 80 other ranks. On top of this there would be men involved in
support functions, clerks, cooks and the like. In all, the Battalion was
probably about three hundred men short of establishment.

Raiding was not a one way activity. On 25 February, when the
Battalion was in the line well to the north of Vimy Ridge, near the
Double Crassier, an enemy raid got into 2 Company's position. Under
cover of darkness a party penetrated the Canadian wire by way of a gap
in it made by trench mortars. With skill the raiders evaded the 14th's
listening posts and surprised the front line, killing two men, wounding
six, and vanishing with two wounded prisoners when attacked by a
party organised and led by Lieutenant D Woodward. The enterprise
and the daring of the Germans on this occasion confirmed reports that
the enemy had trained raid specialists. Certainly the operation reflected
credit on those who planned it and the party who carried it out.

The 14th was not going to let this particular raid go unanswered. On
the night of 1/2 March it launched a raid consisting of eighty six men
with the object of damaging 'enemy trenches, inflict loss and capture
prisoners'. Some of the general instructions are of interest and, as

Keeping a watch on Vimy.

mentioned above, would have been standard practice amongst the combatants by this stage of the war. For example, time allowed in the enemy trenches was limited to fifteen minutes – raiders could not afford to get caught in a trap by an alerted enemy who had time to consider the situation. 'Company commanders will take all necessary precautions to avoid casualties in the event of enemy retaliation. All killed and wounded **must** [original emphasis] be brought in. Officers and other ranks are to be stripped entirely of identifications, particularly cap badges, numerals, sleeve patches, identity discs, pay books, buttons, letters, etc.' All of this was now standard practice. German interrogation reports show how often prisoners talked – often quite willingly. There is no reason to doubt that German prisoners spoke equally freely. Therefore it was essential to ensure that no wounded fell into enemy hands during such raids. There is an interesting detail explaining how the boundaries of the raid were to be marked. A reliable NCO will 'take up position inside our trench at the northernmost tape. This NCO will be provided with a watch that will be synchronised at Advanced HQ at 1.45am. At 2.15am [zero was at 2am] this NCO will fire a succession of Very lights towards our support line in a north westerly direction. Major D Worrall will personally show this NCO in which direction he is to fire. The object of this is plainly to mark the boundary.' The signal for the return was to be given by a mixture of a bugle, Strombos horns and the burning of ground flares on the enemy's parapet. Special flare arrangements were laid down for signalling to the Brigade machine gunners. Artillery co-operation was laid down. The raid went more or less to plan, there was one Canadian killed (Corporal Henry Price – actually from Manchester, who is buried in Maroc British Cemetery) and ten or so wounded. Six prisoners were brought in, several dugouts (and their occupants) were bombed and a number of Germans killed.

Not all raids went to plan, no matter how much work, preparation and planning had gone into it. The most disastrous raid launched by the Corps, and possibly by the BEF, and, as Nicholson describes it, 'the most elaborately planned Canadian raid of the winter' was that by the 4th Division, carried out on the night of 28 February/1 March.

It involved some

> *1,700 all ranks, representing from left to right the 73rd, 72nd, 75th and 54th Battalions,* [who were] *to reconnoitre and inflict damage on German defences on Hill 145. To achieve surprise the planners ruled out any preliminary bombardment or wire cutting. To aid the attackers cylinders of tear gas and chlorine had been installed along the whole divisional front, but the preliminary discharge of the former served only to alert the enemy, and a changing wind prevented use of the lethal chlorine – indeed the attackers themselves suffered casualties when German shells breached some of the cylinders. The venture was almost a complete failure. While 12 Brigade on the left* [72nd and 73rd Battalions] *reached most of their objectives, the enemy discovered those of the 11th Brigade before they were well clear of their own wire and brought them under withering fire. The Canadians took thirty seven prisoners; their own casualties numbered 687, including two battalion commanders killed* [Kemball of the 54th and Beckett of the 75th, buried with many of their men at Villers Station Cemetery]. *During the next two days the Germans permitted and even helped our troops to recover the dead.*

The failure of this raid became common knowledge amongst the men and it can have done nothing for the morale of the 4th Division.

The events of that terrible night took place, at least for some of the ground involved, in part of the Vimy Memorial site, and it is possible for the visitor to get a good view over both the Canadian and German line there. Besides Villers Station Cemetery, about forty of the casualties were buried in Zouave Valley Cemetery, on the other side of the autoroute. Big raids had a far greater tendency to go wrong than the smaller ones, and their efficacy and value was at least questionable. On the other hand, it left the enemy in a perpetual state of alert and nerves; combined with the ever present risk of a mine exploding under their feet, the situation for the man in the trenches must have made for, at the very least, enormous anxiety and tension.

The assistance of the enemy with the removal of casualties was not confined to this occasion. Lieutenant Clifford Wells (8th Battalion CEF) wrote to his mother in January 1917 about an event on the Somme:

> In one of my letters a long time ago I spoke of a remarkable experience which I had. Briefly, it was this. I met a German in No Man's Land one morning. He was a stretcher bearer and carried a Red Cross flag. He was out on the same errand as I – looking for wounded. He offered to guide me to a number of "verwundete Engländer", lying in various shell holes. He did so and I got a stretcher party (six men) and brought them all in – nearly twenty in all – with the assistance of five other German stretcher bearers. The Germans brought the wounded to a point about midway between the lines, and my men carried them the rest of the way. Sometimes I had a German and a Canadian carrying a stretcher between them. When all the wounded in sight had been brought in, the Germans returned to their trench and we to ours. All the while the German artillery and ours were pounding away, and we were really safer between the lines than in either. The Germans lent me one of their stretchers, on which we brought in a wounded man, and then returned it to them. The German in charge told me he was an Alsatian [ie from the 'lost' French territory of Alsace], which spoke volumes. He belonged to the Medical Corps and hence was a non-combatant, I presume. When no other Germans were around he would speak to me in French. He did not speak English at all. The skill of the Germans in binding up their wounded, their strength and endurance in the exhausting work of carrying stretchers over ground which was one mass of shell holes and their quiet disregard of stray shells and the possibility of being sniped from our lines, command my highest ad-miration... They treated me with great respect, calling me 'Herr Leutnant'. We saluted before

parting. ... For various reasons I do not want you to say much about this incident – at least outside of the immediate family. It all happened months ago. The courage and humanity of the Germans under the circumstances was very remarkable. They risked their lives to rescue our wounded, when they could not even make prisoners of them and at a time when our bombardment of their positions passed description. I have very special reasons for not wanting you to say much about the occurrence...

In the days immediately before the attack the raids increased in intensity.

The War Underground

A considerable amount of space was given to this subject in *Vimy Ridge*, in particular Chapter 7. For what follows below we are indebted to the work of the members of the Durand Group, an organisation of volunteers with a wide range of appropriate

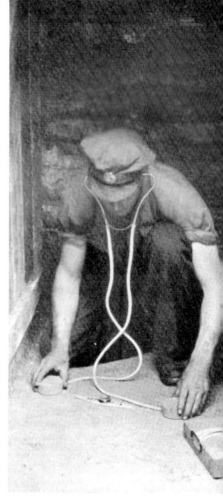

Engineer officer listening with a geophone for the sound of enemy tunnelling.

skills, which studies and explores underground warfare and whose work has been largely centred on Vimy and at Beaumont Hamel. Above all, we must express our thanks to Lieutenant Colonel Phillip Robinson, a retired Royal Engineer officer, who is responsible for much of the hard work synthesised below and who is also responsible for much of the correlation of mapping and surveying. One of the driving forces for the creation of the Durand Group was Colonel Mike Watkins, one of Britain's foremost ordnance disposal experts, who was tragically killed whilst working at Vimy in the summer of 1998. His

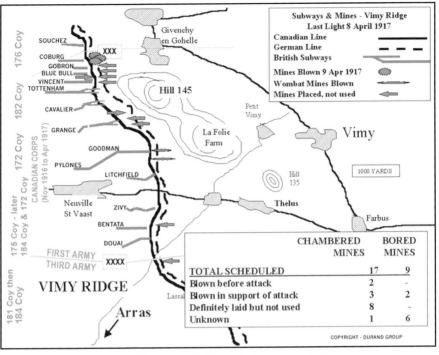

2. Subways constructed in support of the attack on Vimy Ridge
[©GPG Robinson/DurandGroup]

The sixty metre Crater VIII occupied by German troops May 1916.

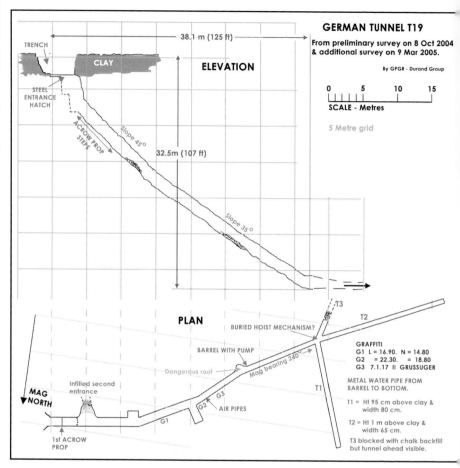

3. Modern survey of the German tunnel T 19 in the La Folie area
[©GPG Robinson/Durand Group]

memorial stands near the publicly accessible parts of the Grange Subway.

The Grange Subway is a unique feature of the Vimy Memorial site. Its opening up after the war was the by-product of a hiatus in the construction of the memorial proper, due to delays in the delivery of stone from the quarry in what is now Croatia. Not only was a section of the subway made safe (by contemporary standards) for the public, but also the outpost line on both sides was restored and put into a permanent state of preservation by using concrete filled sandbags. But what the visitor experiences here is only a small glimpse into the war underground, which got under way on the ridge as soon as the French armies advanced their line several thousand metres from the west to a point where they were able to struggle with the Germans for the summit of this tactically important high ground.

The area under the Ridge (as it was elsewhere on the front) was divided into sectors. Within the area of the memorial site access has been gained to the La Folie sector (named after the nearby eponymous farm, behind the German line), which runs more or less parallel to the line from the area of Broadmarsh Crater to a few metres beyond Goodman Subway, and therefore falling almost entirely in the area of the 3rd Division at the time of the attack on 9 April. It was the responsibility of 172 Tunnelling Company.

Tunnelling Companies were formed by the British in February 1915, under the dynamic inspiration of Major Norton Griffiths. The French and the Germans had already been engaged in tunnelling activities and at the beginning of 1915 the British had suffered from a series of mine attacks, the first being near Festubert, in December 1914. Although the British did use mines before the formation of the Tunnelling companies, it was clear that specialists units were needed and Griffiths had the full and enthusiastic support of the army commanders in France. When the Tunnellers were first recruited it took only four days from them being enlisted in Manchester on 17 February, processed at the RE depot in Chatham and shipped to France, arriving at Hill 60 in Belgium on the 21st. Those recruited initially were specialists in a technique known as 'clay kicking' and were enlisted on a rate of pay much higher than that of a private soldier or their sapper colleagues.

By June 1916 the BEF had thirty three Tunnelling Companies: twenty five British; three Canadian; three Australian; one New Zealand [which did much of the work under Arras itself]; and a specialist Australian company, the Electrical and Mechanical, Mining and Boring Company (known as the 'Alphabetical' Company). A Portuguese mining company was incorporated into the BEF in 1917. The strength was fixed at 585, including nineteen officers; however, when engaged in major mining operations (such as the creation of the subways at Vimy), considerable numbers of infantry would be 'attached', acting as unskilled labourers, so that a company might double in effective numbers. The attached infantry did not benefit from the pay rates, however! Higher command was exercised at Army level, where there was a Controller of Mines; whilst each Army also had a mine school and a mine rescue organisation. The Tunnellers came directly under Army command; and although organised as a company, this could be – and usually was - split into three semi-independent

German troops occupying a crater on Vimy Ridge. Note the prominent tunnel entrance.

4. German mining diagram of Sector Döberitz March 1917.

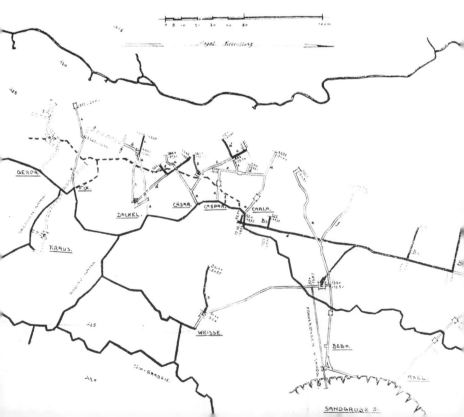

sections or groups, working on different projects or different aspects of a project.

In June 1916 the British fired 101 mines and the Germans (in the British sector) 126 – on average, one every three hours. At Vimy, between October 1915 and April 1917 there were an estimated 150 mines fired by both sides, the bulk of them, as mentioned above, before the end of the summer of 1916. The ground at Vimy was especially suitable for mine warfare, as not far below the soil there is chalk, ideal for tunnelling.

Mine warfare was complex. One might think that a mine blast is a mine blast, but in fact mines were fired for a variety of purposes. An offensive mine could either be a common mine, designed to blow up the enemy, or a fougasse mine, designed to throw debris over the enemy and bury him. Tactical mines, which could be fired anywhere in the front line area, were designed to create high ground from which the enemy could be observed or to screen part of the front from enemy observation or approaches.

A good example of this type of mine is the Longfellow series, fired in March 1917 by the Germans – see Chapter 5. The craters created a significant new obstacle in the path of any attackers as well as disrupting British mining operations that the Germans knew were taking place in this area. There were also defensive mines, designed to hinder the enemy's mining effort. These were most commonly camouflet mines (although the Longfellow could be described as a defensive mine), small charges, placed close to an enemy tunnel, designed to destroy his workings and which would not break the surface. The Durand Group has made safe a number of this type of mine in the British tunnelling systems on the site over the last ten years or so. Finally there were bored mines, usually known as wombat mines because of the (extraordinary to say) hand drilling rig that was required to create them. A large drill was driven deep into No Man's Land from a gallery and the resulting bore then filled with explosive. When fired, these provided an instant deep trench into No Man's Land, with the added bonus that the resultant debris would also fall, at least to some extent, on the enemy. The Memorial site at Vimy has two of these wombat craters, unique vestiges, certainly in the British sector, on the Western Front – though they are not available to public access.

The British initially deployed five Tunnelling Companies on the ridge area – from north to south, 176, 182, 172, 175 (until October 1916) and 185. Part of 252 was attached to 172 in early 1917. The Canadian Tunnelling Companies were attached to Second Army in

Flanders; Later in the war some of the tunnelling companies were turned into other type of engineers (a process which began towards the end of 1917); the remaining Canadian Tunnelling Company, the 3rd, did not actually join the Canadian Corps until February 1919, to take its place in the queue for repatriation to Canada.

The British came up with a system to deal with German mining at Vimy. Essentially this involved the digging of a deep lateral system, running more or less parallel to the British front line positions, at a depth of between sixty and a hundred feet. This effectively blocked the Germans from mining under the British, and later Canadian, positions. From this tunnel further tunnels were driven forward to lay a mine and to create underground listening posts (to monitor German mining activity). The subway systems dug before the Vimy attack all connected in some form to these deeper systems.

The British became adept to the mine warfare on Vimy Ridge – and very quickly. The German limited offensive of May 1916 (only a couple of months after the British took over the line from the French)

German troops rush to occupy a crater they have just blown Vimy Ridge. Early 1917.

was in large measure the consequence of the success of this work: for more details about this attack see *Vimy Ridge*. Although this was a splendid example of a well executed limited attack, it actually caused only a negligible delay to the British tunnelling programme. By the time the offensive opened on 9 April the British had dug about twelve kilometres of tunnels, on average about five feet high and two and a half feet wide. This excludes the subways and other workings close to the surface.

All of this is fully explained and illustrated in an excellent DVD, *One of Our Mines is Missing*, by Durand Group founder member Andy Prada. The film provides a moving tribute to the work and courage of the tunnellers from all the armies involved in the underground war at Vimy Ridge. We must admit an interest here; Nigel Cave was an historical consultant. The film had its origins in the examination of a mine laid by the British to be fired in conjunction with the attack on 9 April. This mine, which would have gone off under what is now a road junction near the Grange Subway car park, was not fired (as were hardly any of the pre-laid mines) and doubts arose as to whether it had ever been disarmed. Because of concerns about visitor safety, it was

decided that an attempt should be made to access it and determine its status. Because the approach through the La Folie deep lateral was both blocked and would have involved a long carry of material through unstable tunnels, access was made from the ground above. In the course of an investigation that lasted about a week it was found that the mine was still charged, but with a lot less than the 20,000 pounds of explosives that had been originally laid.

The Germans knew that the British were laying mines in this area. They brought up 16,500 pounds of explosives and laid them at the ends of four mine galleries: and these mines were fired at 4.10am (German time) on 23 March 1917 (though the Canadian battalion opposite stated that they were fired promptly at 3.00 am British time). The troops in the line occupied the

61

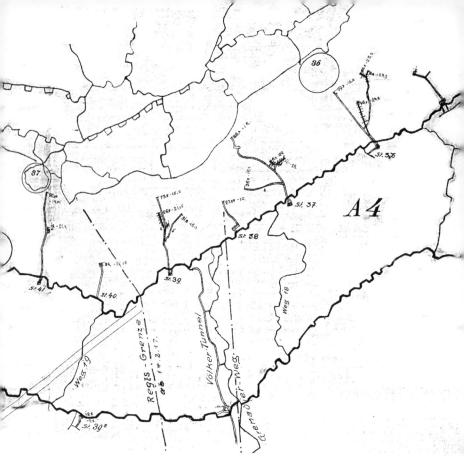

5. German mining diagram: Völker Tunnel and Sector Arnulf (North), February 1917.

easternmost of the four craters thus created. The nearest British operations in the area involved two mines, Broadmarsh and Durand. In fact neither was destroyed by the blast, but the Broadmarsh (just next to the old Broadmarsh mine [German name: Schleswig Holstein], in the corner of the present road junction, which had been turned into a significant strong point in the German line) was damaged. After the battle, it would seem – or possibly before - the detonators and a substantial part of the ammonal, packed in tin boxes weighing fifty pounds, were removed.

It was decided, presumably by Corps Headquarters, that this mine and the neighbouring Durand and Duffield mines, would not be fired as part of the attack. The reasoning may well have been that the combination of the newly created craters of the Longfellow mines and the pulverising of the ground in the preparatory bombardment meant

62

that the infantry faced enough obstacles in their way without adding the complications of further huge craters. The German mining attack did, however, destroy a wombat mine, which had been drilled out of the end of the Black Watch tunnel (part of this tunnel may be viewed during the Grange Subway tour). The Durand mine was also defused by the Durand Group, in 1998. It was found that this relatively small mine (of about 6,500 pounds) still had the potential to cause significant damage not only to the Grange Subway but also had the power to break the surface. It had been anticipated that the ammonal, packed in twenty five pound canvas bags, would have leached and lost most of its potency, but such was the quality of the waterproofing that this was not the case.

The Subways
Both sides built subways and they were not unique to Vimy. However, the chalk sub-strata, so close to the surface, meant that the construction of this type of protection was a relatively straightforward process. The Germans, for example, had two major subways, the Prince Arnulf and the Völker, several smaller ones as well as large underground 'lagers', effectively barracks, some of which could accommodate hundreds of men. They also made use of dugouts built as offshoots to interlinking tunnels. Along the Canadian front there were thirteen subways, the longest of which was the extended Goodman/Pylones subway, 1,722 metres in length. The Grange was the third longest, measuring 1,228 metres, of which the public get access to rather less than a third (the rest is blocked). Both of these subways, along with Cavalier, are at least partially under the memorial site.

Operations began to construct the subways towards the end of October, about the time that the Canadian Corps moved to the front here; the decision to extend them and make them more complex came in January 1917, when the details of the Arras Offensive became clearer. One reason for digging them was the difficulty of access from the rear to the front line positions along communications trenches that were either under observation or all too well known to the German artillery; the subways provided a secure route. One of Byng's main concerns was to provide as much security for his men as he could. Most, but not all, of the subways were not designed to be lived in – to act as barracks, as it were. They were usually simply a secure (they had a minimum of twenty feet, approximately six metres of overhead cover) means of moving up to the line, with a number of exits (inclines) to various points in the trench system.

They were much bigger than the usual tunnels used in mine warfare, being about two metres high, enough for a soldier to pass through with a slung rifle, and about a metre wide. They could contain dugouts (for example the Grange incorporated existing headquarters dugout systems), living accommodation, latrines, water reservoirs, telephone exchanges, power houses, forward dressing stations, tramways and mortar positions. Most of them were lit by electric lighting – but this should not be confused with what is found in the Grange now. There was a bulb for about every twenty metres in that subway, for example. A few subways were lit by storm lanterns.

The subways were constructed, usually, by four tunnellers working at each of several faces (one of whom was resting), with two others handling the trolley, air pumps and timber. Infantrymen were used to remove the spoil to the surface and dispose of it, making use of shell holes and any other place that was handy, or sending it back on the light railways which were such a feature of the line here. The Canadian Corps, with its great number of experienced railway construction workers, built and maintained a notably efficient light railway network. The subways were also begun at different points, with the digging parties working towards each other – it needs to be recalled that there were a variety of exits along any one given subway. The digging rate, including any chambers added to the sides, was about twenty feet a day. Additionally, the Royal Canadian Engineers dug further dugouts and constructed, from underground, mortar positions to be broken out immediately preceding the attack.

The Germans were aware of what was going on, but because of the deep laterals could not interfere underground and the tunnels were too deep to be affected by anything but the heaviest shells; though they could (and did) shell the entrances. The work was, therefore, done quite speedily, though some of the subways were only finished a matter of days before the assault. A number of myths have grown up about the subways. None of those at Vimy connected with any medieval tunnel systems. These so-called tunnels, in any case, related to the excavation of stone that was used for building. An example of such a medieval system may be found at La Targette, and there is another under Maison Blanche; whilst Arras itself is built on top of a maze of underground quarries which, in this case, were connected up by the New Zealand Tunnelling Company. Another myth has the miners working away on the subways silently and using vinegar to loosen the chalk. Whilst the former was certainly true for the fighting tunnels, there was no such need in the construction of the subways, as they were secure from underground intervention by the Germans. We have found no authoritative reference to the use of vinegar, In order to be effective a tremendous amount of it would have been required, and the smell and chemical reaction would both have been off-putting, to put it mildly. In chalk, in any case, the face could be as easily softened by the use of water. Because dugouts are incorporated into many of the subways, some of which were battalion headquarters, people think that the officers all lived down there, nice and secure. In reality these dugouts were, in principle, no different to dugouts elsewhere along the line – they just happened to be connected to a subway system.

The use to which the subways were put for the attack on 9 April was left to the individual divisional commander to decide; invariably, however, they were used to bring the troops up to the line and to shelter some troops for the hours between moving up and going over the top – but, excepting Cavalier and Tottenham, usually never for anything more than a few hours. They were also used to hold battle stores necessary for consolidation, aid posts for the wounded, a holding point for rations, a place to stockpile munitions to replenish the fighting line and so forth.

The Canadian line at the northern end of the ridge had to be approached through Zouave Valley. Use was made of this feature by trench railways, as the 16th Battalion history relates:

> *One convenience of the new sector gave much satisfaction to the Battalion; its rations and supplies were delivered by trench railway at the door of the Battalion HQ in Zouave Valley.*
>
> *Vimy was the ideal front for that form of transportation.*

Iron Duke **moving through Arras prior to the battle, April 1917.**

Vimy, March 1917.

Vimy from the air, April 1917.

Before Mont St Eloy, close to the town [!] *of Ecoivres, in the valley of the Scarpe, stood the Bois de Bray. Under the shelter of its trees lay the forward headquarters of the light railways with all the paraphernalia in miniature – sidings, lines of trucks and engines, blowing off steam and puffing around – of a real railway terminus. To this spot the transport sections of the various battalions repaired on the afternoon of each day and, on to trucks previously allocated to them, loaded up the rations, ammunition and the sundry other requirements of the men in the line. When darkness fell, off went the train, pulled by the tiny engine, across the devastated area. It circled round Berthonval Farm and Berthonval Wood* [Bois l'Abbaye], *rattled through junctions, stopped at various battery and reserve positions* en route *and in due course arrived at Zouave Valley, where the freight was delivered. From there it was merely a carry of a few hundred yards to the front line.*

On quiet nights the train, as it turned into the valley, engine panting, wheels squeaking, made noises loud enough to reach well into the German lines. The disturbance did not seem to worry the ration guards, who sat stolidly on top of their sacks; nor did the enemy seem to be interested in the target. Yet there, and throughout the valley, the track was within easy trench mortar distance of the enemy and a "minnie", nicely placed, would have made a sad mess of rations and men.

An example of a forward 'station' was near Aux Rietz corner. The railway running from Ecoivres had three branches in the area, Claudot, Bessan and Vistula, with a spur into the Elbe. Two depots, containing engineer and trench stores, known respectively as Glasgow Dump and Liverpool Dump, had been formed close to the road and the main communication trenches. It was not only a substantial light railway network that had to be maintained; there was a substantial traffic in freight trains bringing in all the materiél necessary to keep this great body of men and horses supplied with food and water as well as all the equipment of war. Roads, which were originally designed for the sleepy traffic of rural France, needed to be maintained and required hundreds of men using trainloads of hard core to keep them operational. Corduroy roads were laid down – essentially railway sleepers (or equivalents) bound tightly together by cable - which could sit on the surface, requiring relatively little ground preparation. Hutments had to be erected and a great sweep of camps erected several kilometres behind the line; hard standing had to be laid for as many of

The remains of Vimy after the battle.

the guns as possible, especially the heavies. Practise areas occupied substantial parts of the countryside behind the lines as the various formations practiced and practiced again their actions on the day.

The 2nd Battalion history describes one of these areas:

On the rolling ground west of the Chaussée Brunehaut, between Estrée Cauchie [sic; inevitably known to many of the troops as 'Extra Cushy'] *and Les Quatre Vents, an almost complete reproduction of the Vimy Ridge area had been taped*

out. The Zwischen Stellung, Nine Elms, Island Traverse Trench, Bois Carré, Commandant's House and Farbus Wood were indicated with great precision. For weeks this country was practised over until the exercise became almost monotonous. From the beginning the Battalion adopted the dispositions to be employed on the day of the attack. Platoons and sections were given special tasks and every individual was made to familiarise himself with them.

Byng was an avid observer of these practices, 'patiently accompanying battalions over the tapes and explaining details to all and sundry. … In the YMCA hut at Camblain l'Abbé he assembled all the officers within the area and diligently expounded his principles of leadership. "Make sure that every man knows his task. Explain it to him again and again; encourage him to ask you questions. Remember, also, that no matter what sort of fix you get into, you mustn't sit down and hope that things will work out. You must do something. In a crisis the man who does something may occasionally be wrong; but the man who does nothing is always wrong."

All of this preparation of positions and stores required a lot of labour; troops who were not in the front line, in Brigade Support, Brigade Reserve, Battalion Reserve or even just not manning the line, were likely to find themselves called upon to provide large working parties. Thus the 13th Battalion reported, after a thaw in January: 'Under the rays of a warm sun, followed by slashing rain, parapets softened and trench bottoms, formerly hard as rock, melted into thigh deep morasses of clinging mud. Only the labour of every available man for hours at a time preserved the trench system from disintegration.' The same battalion, when in Brigade Reserve at Maison Blanche ('three companies in billets and one being billeted in a large cave') provided five hundred men and five officers for five days in the second half of March for work, carrying material, cleaning trenches and constructing dugouts. The 16th Battalion was similarly engaged, 'it furnished some of the large working parties necessary for the carrying up of the ammunition and trench supplies required in the coming offensive and for the digging of the deep dugouts nearby, indeed under, the front line, where the advancing troops were to assemble. The 13th Battalion was asked, at short notice, in late March to provide fifty men to lay half round logs over a stretch of road that had become well nigh impassable: the job was urgent. The CO, Lieutenant Colonel McCuaig, ordered out a party of two hundred men and instructed them to 'clean up the job without delay'. 'Acting on these orders, the party worked like the proverbial beavers and had the road open for through traffic in a surprisingly short period of time.'

The 20th Battalion also took its part in proceedings. 'Safe accommodation had to be made in the forward area for the forming up of the assaulting troops before the attack. ... Our tasks included the construction of machine gun and trench mortar emplacements, shell-proof bomb stores and the assembly of the material for building them – the heavy beams, the large semi-circular "elephant" shelters, the corrugated iron and the revetting wire. The Engineers planned the works, but we supplied the labour, becoming in the meantime expert builders and miners. Mining the deep dugouts was a slow business: the chalky earth, which was soft and slimy, had to be put in sandbags and carried outside.' When in divisional reserve at Bois des Alleux, in addition to infantry training, it had more fatigues – for the artillery, trench mortars and engineers.

Work under Engineer supervision was also done on some of the caves close to the line. Thus Zivy Cave, which was in the forward support line, was turned into living quarters and electric light installed. At zero hour 'it was to be occupied by the advanced HQ of 4 Brigade, a battalion of infantry, a company of infantry and a dressing station, complete with temporary operating tables and beds made with chicken wire. An ample supply of water was available from pipes connected to water tanks in the rear. A tunnel to the front line [ie a subway] provided safe communications. There were three entrances to the cave, two in Ashton trench and one in Territorial

Left: Lieutenant General Hon Sir Julian Byng Right: Major General AW Currie.

Avenue.' Zivy Cave was a few metres down the metalled track, off the Neuville St Vaast – Thélus road, now signed to Nine Elms and Arras Road cemeteries. In fact the track goes right over it. Then there was the small matter of getting the material far enough forward for the infantry (and further back) the gunners to get it to the right place. The principal road was the Chaussée Brunehaut, an ancient Roman road which ran north west from Arras to Houdain (and beyond). The 2nd Battalion history (WD Murray, 1947) described a typical afternoon on it at this period:

> *During the weeks preceding the attack the orderly confusion of the Chaussée Brunehaut was a strange and inspiring spectacle. At Mont St Eloy the road ascended and descended until about half a mile south of the village it came under the*

71

observation of the distant ridge to the east. From that point northwards, extending for several miles back to Camblain l'Abbé, the afternoon hours witnessed a unique procession. Day after day a long and unbroken column of transport limbers, motor lorries, engineer wagons, ambulances, guns, tractors and troops, its head halted just short of a point where enemy observation began, stretched along the chaussée. The assembling of this mass occupied hours. The earliest vehicles to arrive were forbidden to cross the crest in daylight, but they secured as a reward for their long wait the privilege of leading the procession forward when twilight hid the vulnerable portion of the road from view.

Men might be exhausted, but they were not the only ones engaged in the struggle to bring up all that was required for an offensive on this scale. The weather was very changeable, but the thaw period soon returned to one where snow storms, hail storms and rain storms alternated. 'The horses were in a sad plight. They suffered heavy casualties from exposure. The burial squads could not overtake their tasks. Carcases lay for days on the roads or in the fields where the animals had dropped in their tracks' (16th Battalion history).

An important development, which commenced in the dying days of 1916, was the reorganisation of the platoon. There is a tendency to think of the First World War armies as being unimaginative, not learning lessons, adverse to new technology, besotted with visions of wars previously won, commanded by hard hearted and inflexible generals. Whilst obviously there is much room for criticism of the

All that was left of the Lens-Arras Highway.

Canadian engineers building a corduroy road in the rear area.

conduct of the war and no general (or politician, for that matter) was perfect, simplistic judgements are invariably over generalised, sweeping, often quite inaccurate and usually flawed. The 16th Battalion history, for example, details the changes and their impact on one battalion:

'*The new tactical policy vitally affected battalion tactical organisations. The platoon was entirely remodelled. In the light of the lessons gained in the Verdun and Somme operations* [it is important to note that British and French officers visited each others' major battle zones after the battle to learn new techniques] *the importance of that unit began to be realised. The High Command came to believe that "the efficiency of its platoon commanders will often be the measure of an army's success", and thereupon all hastened to give these officers and their men the range of weapons and organisation best suited to their important work. One, then two Lewis guns (the automatic rifles which had come into use), rifle, bayonet. Rifle grenade and bomb were all placed at the disposal of the platoon; the Lewis gun – a weapon of opportunity – and the rifle to deal with the enemy in the open, the rifle grenade and the bomb to get at those behind cover and the bayonet for hand to hand fighting. With the combination of these weapons, each supporting the advance as the need arose, it was possible for the commander and his men to initiate tactics suitable for a variety of conditions and ground. In other words, the purpose behind this grouping was to create a*

73

balanced, self-sufficient fighting body which could act as the spear head of the attack, ready at a moment's notice to exploit the advantage of battle. Towards the attainment of this end all existing battalion organisation was adjusted.

The specialists, so much to the fore in 1915, instead of interfering with and acting independently of company officers, now worked through them, assisting and advising when required. In this way the old quarrel between the two parties was settled once and for all to their mutual satisfaction. The rights of the company officer were respected, and the specialists, except our friend the bomber, who fell from his post of honour to the level of his comrades in the platoon, retained or increased prestige as the value of their work was manifested.

This was all part of what some military historians have termed the 'learning curve'; as the war progressed the reorganisation continued, with platoons designating particular roles to sections. For this sort of system to work effectively it required effective command; the infantry soldier became, perforce, a much more adaptable soldier from his experience in battle, which in turn made for a much more effective fighting soldier, section, platoon and battalion. Initiative and adaptability at a junior level of command was as vital to success in the Great War as in subsequent conflicts: and the fighting at Vimy showed this just as clearly as elsewhere.

Germans clearing away their dead.

Chapter Four

THE CANADIAN CORPS IN THE BATTLE FOR VIMY RIDGE 1 – 14 APRIL 1917

As mentioned above, raiding was intensified in the days leading up to the assault: the 1,700 casualties suffered as a consequence were about fifteen percent of those incurred during the main battle. It is difficult to be able to assess the value of such raids: in an ideal world they would provide prisoners and valuable information on the state of preparation and morale of the enemy opposite; they would give a good indication of what effect the artillery bombardment was having on the enemy wire (bearing in mind that aerial observation was made difficult by frequent adverse flying weather); and it would provide information on the ground conditions, inevitably made worse by the bombardment. The negative side involved casualties suffered and the consequences on morale if a raid failed. 'Accidental' Fire could also produce casualties – probably in excess of twenty percent of casualties were the consequence of 'friendly fire' and accidents, if recent studies on the matter are to be believed. One such casualty was an officer of the 2nd Battalion, Captain Eric Dennis MC. A raiding party (on 5 April) returned to No 2 Company HQ soon after he arrived there himself. A German officer's body had been brought back for identification.

A non-commissioned officer of the party, extracting the Lüger pistol from the dead man's holster, was handing it to the company commander when the weapon discharged. The bullet penetrated the head of young Dennis, who was seated on a chicken wire bunk, killing him instantly.

He is buried in Ecoivres Military Cemetery, grave V B 6. This Battalion alone carried out eight patrols or raids in the three days 3 – 5 April.

One battalion was equipped as follows: rifle; complete equipment less pack; 120 rounds of small arm ammunition (SAA); two Mills bombs (grenades); five sandbags; forty eight hours' rations; unexpended portion of current ration; waterproof sheet; box respirator, worn at the alert; smoke helmet; goggles; one ground flare; and filled water bottle. Specialist – bombers, rifle grenadiers, Lewis gunners and runners – only had to carry fifty rounds of SAA. Officers were to carry revolvers and a Very pistol. It was a considerable weight to be taking into battle, especially given the ground conditions, but each item was

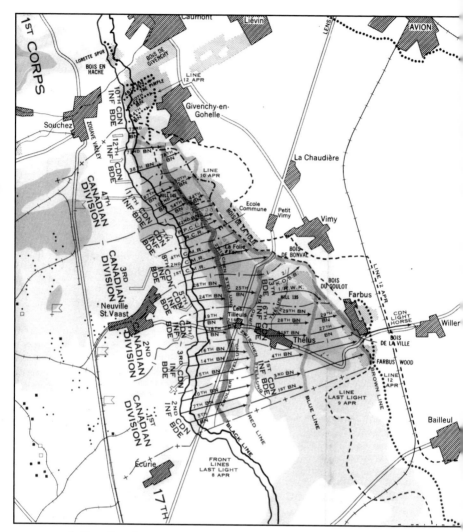

6. Canadian Corps attack frontages, 9 April.

essential for the maintenance of the individual in the fighting line. Each half of the attacking battalions (they usually attacked two companies up, or the equivalent, as a sizeable proportion of each battalion left at least a hundred men behind to act as a reserve to be called up when required and upon which the battalion could be rebuilt if heavy losses were suffered) also had to carry forward thirty three picks and sixty seven shovels, which would be in addition to the small entrenching tool that every man had with him. Those who were so lumbered with this extra burden were able to carry rather less SAA to compensate them for the extra weight. This load seems to have been widespread amongst the attacking troops, with some variations according to their assigned role. The outline of the attack has already been given above. It is impossible to cover all the battalions that took part in a book such as this, but an idea is given, using mainly regimental histories but also some extracts from relevant war diaries and battle narratives.

Lieutenant Clifford Wells served with the 8th Battalion (the 90th [Winnipeg] Rifles), nicknamed 'The (Little) Black Devils', at Vimy, part of 2 Brigade, 1st Division; its role was as support battalion to the Brigade, which was attacking on the extreme right flank of the Canadian Corps. He described the day in a letter to his mother (with all the limitations that that imposes as regards to what he felt able to write), dated 20 April 1917; before it reached her she had received notification that her son had been killed in action on 28 April. What follows is an edited extract.

Yes, I was in it! And I am glad and proud that I was. You probably know more of the success of the great offensive than I do, for newspapers are very scarce articles out here now. But, on our part of the line, everything went smoothly.

The Huns were completely surprised, strange as it may seem, and made very little resistance. Our artillery barrage was wonderful beyond description, lifting forward from objective to objective with clockwork precision, and practically obliterating the German trenches as it passed them. The men followed the barrage steadily and fearlessly, and prisoners were streaming back five minutes after we went "over the top".

Most of the prisoners were entirely cowed, and thankful to be prisoners. They worked hard carrying in the wounded. One slightly wounded officer, however, was very cocky. He appeared at the entrance of a dugout as I passed. He was very indignant when I had him searched for papers, and was furious when I sent him back with three of his own men under a single escort. He actually refused to go without with his greatcoat, which he had left in the dugout thirty feet underground [Wells spoke German fluently]. *As we had no time just then to act as valet to German officers, and as the exploration of a German dugout requires great care, he had perforce to go without his coat. We had been warned to be on our guard against infernal machines in dugouts but, so sudden was the attack, that the Huns had no time to*

The advance across Vimy Ridge 9 April.

prepare traps for us.

Some of the German dugouts, especially those of the artillery, were wonderfully comfortable. Some had electric lights, arm chairs, cupboards, beds with white [sic] sheets, etc. These were not the front line dugouts of course. An hour after the attack, all our men were smoking Hun cigars and were laden with souvenirs of various sorts. I was fortunate enough to secure a pair of field glasses, one of the things I have long wanted.

After we had taken and consolidated our objective [the Red Line], fresh troops went through us to capture a distant wood [Farbus]. As they pressed on behind the barrage, which moved forward like a flock of dragons, the sky suddenly became overcast and a blizzard raged for a few minutes. That picture is one I shall never forget – the dark scarred wood in the distance, the line of bursting shells creeping toward it, the long lines of khaki figures following the barrage and minding the shells and bullets which thinned their ranks no more than the driven snowflakes which overcast the whole scene. It is a wonderful picture, and I wish I could paint it more accurately.

I came through it all without a scratch...

The **14th (Royal Montreal Regiment) Battalion** (3 Brigade, 1st Division [Major General A Currie]) was the centre battalion of a three battalion assault by the Brigade, with the 16th on the left and the 15th on the right; the 13th was in immediate support and came up behind the 14th Battalion. The 14th had completed its move into jumping off positions by 3.50am on 9 April, with Battalion HQ in the Bentata Subway. It advanced, two companies up, promptly at zero towards the German front line 'which at the moment was suffering the destroying wrath of a marvellously placed barrage.' The first obstacle to be overcome was the Eisener Kreuz Weg, the main line of the German first position on the reverse slope to the west of the Lens road (and now west of where Nine Elms and Arras Road cemeteries are located). As the regimental history notes, 'here the defending Bavarian troops fought gallantly, holding back the Canadian advance until killed or wounded by bomb or bayonet.' By the time that the position was taken, both the leading company commanders had been killed or mortally wounded.

Brigadier General FOW Loomis Commander 2 Brigade.

Unusually, particular mention is made of a German machine gun crew that was operating on the left of the Battalion's attack and that also affected the 15th (48th Highlanders of Canada) Battalion. 'German machine gun No 10294 shot down many men of both units. Realising how serious an obstacle this gun presented, Lieutenant BF Davidson organised and led an assault on it. Game to the last, the gun crew met the Canadian assault with a shower of bombs, which dropped several of the Royal Montrealers in their tracks. Davidson, however, penetrated the grenade barrage, shot the crews and put the gun out of action.' The action of this gun crew was typical of many others, and it required deeds of considerable heroism to overcome them. Most of the Battalion's casualties would appear to have been suffered whilst storming the Eisener Kreuz Weg. What was significant, however, was that although the casualties caused by the defenders of this line were significant – indeed heavy – it did not break up either the co-ordination or impetus of the attack. The Battalion halted on the Black Line (in this case just to the east of the

Lens road) and reformed, under the shelter of the standing barrage, for the onward move to the Red Line, which commenced at 6.55am.

His second phase of the attack went smoothly and at low cost:

> *The effect of the barrage in the area beyond the Black Line was marked, the ground being ripped and torn and the German trenches utterly demolished. Garrisons in many cases had been wiped out; elsewhere individuals remained alive, but too dazed to offer resistance. Attack schedules were accordingly maintained and the Red objective was captured at 7.10am.*

In the day's fighting the Battalion lost six officers killed and three wounded; there were 265 other rank casualties, of whom ninety two were killed. A number of the dead may be found in Row IA in Nine Elms cemetery.

An interesting observation is made in the history about the scenes immediately behind the old front line when it was moved back on the evening of 10 April: 'Thousands of troops were employed on the construction of roads and light railways; huts to shelter reserve units were springing up in all directions; guns were being manipulated and tractor-hauled forward…'

The **16th (The Canadian Scottish) Battalion** (3 Brigade) was on the left of Major General Currie's 1st Division. Its main body moved up to the assembly trenches by moving through Bentata Subway. However, a small Battalion HQ group, including the CO, Lieutenant Colonel Peck, decided to go overland to the battle HQ, partly because the subway was so crowded and partly because its exits were some distance from the site of the new HQ. 'Going forward the mud was terrible. In one place I had to get out of my boots, climb on the bank of the sunken road and then pull my boots after me', one participant of this move wrote afterwards. Not long after it set off, a shell landed in the middle of the small party, killing the artillery liaison officer and two orderlies and severely wounding the adjutant. Peck wanted to appoint the CO of No 3 Company, Captain Tupper, as his second in command, but he pleaded to stay with his men and the fortuitous return to duty of Major Hope, who had been lightly wounded the previous day, resolved the problem.

Once the barrage opened up the Battalion moved forward, led by No 3 and No 4 Companies, moving in files of sections. The first major problem was navigating the narrow paths between the old craters of the Claudot and Vissec Group, blown during the French occupancy of the line. 'Some of these were as deep as twenty feet with sides of greasy chalk sloping down to six or seven feet of water.' The enemy defensive barrage, such as it was, caused little trouble, but machine gun fire from the farther rim of some of the craters took a heavy toll. These were dealt with by flank attacks and the advance then proceeded towards the Black Line.

The fire from hostile machine guns now beat in on the advancing men from front and flank alternatively. It was evident that these weapons were scattered everywhere in an irregular pattern on the shell-pitted ground over which the Battalion had to go forward. Men began to drop singly, others in huddled groups. The action could perhaps best be described as a running fight, men rushing from shell hole to shell hole, the bodies of the fallen indicating by their position the locations of the enemy's guns towards which this fighting was directed. Organised infantry resistance was encountered at Visener Graben, thirty to forty yards short of the Arras Lens road; this trench had somehow escaped destruction by the supporting artillery. In it the Germans fought hard and the trench had to be captured at the point of the bayonet.

Over the road went the Battalion, towards the Zwölfer Weg; the right company passed through fairly easily, but No 4, on the left, was held up almost as soon as it moved on from Visener Graben.

From half left a German machine gun opened fire on the Company, inflicting many casualties. It could not be silenced. Groups crept up towards it from three sides, but with no effect; fan shaped around the position lay dead 16th men. It seemed as if a serious delay were to ensure when, as a further assaulting party was being rallied, a series of bomb explosions were heard in the direction of the enemy gun and a 16th man, Private William Milne, sprang up from the shell hole close to it, signalling to his comrades to advance. He had crawled around on his hands and knees to within bombing distance of the enemy machine gun crew and with hand grenades had put every one of them out of action.

Private WJ Milne VC.

He repeated this feat with another gun, between the Black and Red lines; for these two deeds he was awarded a posthumous VC. His body was never recovered and identified, and so his name is on the Vimy Memorial.

The Black Line was taken on time and the prescribed pause gave the necessary opportunity to reorganise. After some forty minutes the advance proceeded to the Red Line. Problems were greatest on the left flank, where a rifle grenade knocked out one machine gun crew and Private Milne the other. As the 16th came close to the Red Line 'the enemy's morale seemed to give way. The trench had a strong garrison, but the Germans, directly they realised that the Canadians had overcome the resistance in their front line system, retired. Many of them were shot as they retired eastwards.' The worst of the job was over and for the remainder of this part of the operation the men of the 16th were mainly spectators. Shortly afterwards the pipers played Colonel Peck and the RSM to the captured position. The RSM's batman (servant) was the last to arrive, 'with a jar of rum under each arm ... as the procession got nearer and got into the final objective, a volume of cheering broke out on all sides, apparently directed in greater part to the last figure with the jars.' In this short action twenty out of the twenty one officers who entered the battle were put out of action, the heaviest officer casualty list for the Battalion in any single action in the war. Three hundred and forty one other ranks were casualties – and the list was to increase considerably by the time the Battalion finally moved to the rear on 4 May. Two company commanders, both on the left of the attack, were killed: Lieutenant Charles Bevan MM, promoted from the ranks, a Welshman, who is buried in Quatre Vents Military Cemetery, grave III B 11; and Captain Victor Tupper MC, the man so eager to return to his men. He was killed in the early stages of the battle, trying to deal with the German guns in the Vissec Craters and is buried in Ecoivres Military Cemetery, grave V D 10. Colonel Peck went on to win the Victoria Cross in September 1918. He had been elected a (Federal) Canadian MP in the so-called khaki election of December 1917, and thus had the unique distinction, as far as is known, of being the only serving parliamentarian in a Commonwealth country to gain the VC during the war.

Lieutenant Colonel CW Peck VC commanding officer 16th Canadian Battalion.

Supporting the 14th and 16th Battalions was the **13th (Royal Highlanders of Canada)**. Even a cursory examination of the Battalion orders for the attack, selected extracts of which appear below, shows the range of activities that such supporting battalions were expected to perform:

The Battalion will go forward at zero hour, as close to the last wave of the 14th Battalion as possible until No Man's Land has been crossed. It will then move at a slow rate until there is an interval of 150 yards between the leading wave of the 13th and the rear wave of the 14th. The role of the Battalion is to give additional power to any one of the attacking battalions should the strength of any of the latter be insufficient to attain its objectives. The Battalion will not be merged into the attack, unless requested by one of the attacking battalions. The Battalion will not go through to the Black Line until the attacking battalions resume their advance to the Red Line at zero plus seventy five, and in the meantime will occupy the Eisener Kreuz Weg. When the advance to the Red Line is resumed, the Battalion will move up to the Black Line, B and D Companies extending to the right and left to cover the Brigade frontage. This line will be consolidated and the Battalion will be prepared to send reinforcing platoons if necessary.

After the Red Line has been consolidated, the 14th Battalion will be withdrawn from this Line, and the 13th and 14th will then become the Divisional Reserve.

A part of the orders deals with movement in the communication trenches and the use of the subways, again typical of what was required along the line. Thus, the 'In' communication trenches in this instance were Claudot and Bentata and the 'Out' ones were Paris, Douai and Sapper.

Bentata Subway runs from Claudot Avenue to the front line, between Roger and Claudot Trenches. This will be used as a covered route during bombardments previous to zero hour and after zero hour for runners. At the top and bottom of each entrance are notice boards showing to whom the entrance is allotted and where each entrance or exit leads to.'

Another interesting instruction relates to the question of inter unit communications and intelligence.

The [Battalion] OP [situated off Bentata] will watch the progress of the advance and will keep the Brigade Report Centre in touch with the situation by telephone or runner. Forward of this station communication will be maintained by visual signalling, carrier pigeons, runners and Aeroplane Contact Patrols. The Intelligence Officer, with his Section, six signallers and four runners, carrying signal fans, ground sheet, carrier pigeons and two signalling lamps will follow in the rear of the last wave and make for a dugout in Eisener Kreuz Weg. It will be the duty of the Intelligence Officer to collect and communicate all messages received from his observers and the company officers to Battalion HQ. This forward report centre will plant a red and blue flag... All messages must be numbered, bear the time, date and place, and be written on the back of maps which have been struck off and which show the German trenches. At the time of writing each message the officer will chalk in his position on the sketch. These will be issued as follows: To Company Commanders, 12; to Platoon Commanders, 8. Each Company Commander will detail two men with sandbags into which all papers found will be placed and forwarded by runner to Brigade HQ.

The Battalion also had to provide carrying parties, two platoons for each of the attacking battalions. 'As soon as the situation permits, these parties will commence to carry from the A Line dumps (previously created by battalions and located in the forward area) to the B Line dumps [on the Lens road]. They will then return to the Brigade Dump and carry forward the material to the B Line dumps. As soon as the Red Line is captured, C Company will detail one half of a platoon for each of the attacking battalions and will carry the material forward from the B Line dumps to the C Line dumps, situated in the Red Line objective.' It looks fine on paper, but one just has to consider how difficult this operation would be for men stumbling over pulverised ground and negotiating wrecked trenches and barbed wire defences whilst at the same time carrying heavy loads of ammunition and grenades.

Escorts for prisoners were to be provided on the proportion of fifteen percent, being provided as far as possible by lightly wounded men. 'Prisoners and escorts will march overland and not by communication trench.' Arrangements were laid down to begin salvaging equipment as soon as possible. Rather more unpleasant was the necessary task of burying the dead:

The 13th Battalion is responsible for the burial of all dead between Eisener Kreuz Weg and the Old British Front Line. Lieutenant JL Atkinson is detailed to supervise the clearing of the battlefield in the above area. He will report at Battalion HQ before dawn and will work in conjunction with, and under the orders of, the Divisional Burial Officer.'

To this Battalion belongs the origins of the Arras Road and Nine Elms CWGC cemeteries.

One thing that caused some murmurings in the rank was the order, on 6 April, to paint stripes of different colours on the men's haversacks,

> *so that the waves of the attack could be recognised at a glance and proper distances maintained [though one has one's doubts about the efficacy in the, at best, feeble light at the beginning of the attack]. Everyone was pleased with this arrangement, except the men of the third wave, whose distinguishing stripe was yellow. Only repeated assurance that the colour was fortuitously chosen and was in no way a reflection on their personal courage, satisfied the men of the yellow wave and enabled them to stand the jibes of the 1st and 2nd waves, whose respective stripes were red and green.*

The Battalion moved up to the front from its billets near Mont St Eloi at about 6pm on 8 April. All were impressed by the minute details of the preparations – for example, where the route lay overland beyond the Arras-Béthune road, a series of luminous stakes had been planted, leading them to the point in the communication trenches where guides awaited them. A quick look now at the ground between the two roads shows how vital this sort of action was; it is almost featureless today, and one can only guess at what it must have been like in April 1917, especially given the extremely heavy fighting over (and under) it in 1915, when the French had wrested it from the Germans. The Battalion was in position shortly after midnight, the only serious casualties being suffered by the company cooks, who had gone ahead to the assembly trenches to provide hot soup for the men on their arrival; several of them fell victim to shelling.

In the initial advance the Battalion suffered casualties, B Company in particular suffering: it lost seventeen NCOs, nine of whom were killed. On the other hand, the carrying parties suffered few casualties, when many had been feared. Battalion HQ was established in,

> *'a large German dugout, which rejoiced in the name of Neuberger Haus* [sic: Neuburger Haus, command post of the KTK (Commander of the forward troops) in Sector Wittelsbach, in the Black Line, the Zwölfer Weg]. *Here the Herr Commandant had just celebrated his birthday, the walls being festooned with wreaths of evergreen, while enshrined amongst*

these was an ornate sign, Zum Geburtstag = Happy Birthday.
Soda water bottles were much in evidence, but the only food that
the curious Highlanders could discover consisted of some very
filthy looking sausages and a large quantity of Kriegsbrot [a hard
loaf, frequently containing a high proportion of potato meal],
which resembled saw-dust and which the Canadians found
utterly unpalatable.

The Battalion remained in the forward area over the next days. A
tragedy was caused when someone kicked a Mills bomb which was
concealed in the mud, wounding several men, including several
officers (and amongst them the Medical Officer) and fatally wounding
one. The move up to the area of Farbus Wood on 13 April was difficult
for other reasons:

All landmarks had been obliterated and in the pitch darkness
of the night direction was hard to maintain. One company took
the whole night to advance a distance of approximately two
miles, arriving at its destination just at dawn. In the Blue Line
the Battalion spent two uncomfortable days. Shelling on both
sides was brisk and, although casualties were not heavy, there
was scarcely a moment when the German shell fire was not
distinctly threatening. Movement during the day was almost
impossible, owing to the enemy observation balloons, and for the
same reason cooking was considered inadvisable.

On 26 April the Battalion moved back to Pendu Huts, its time since 9
April resulting in a total of 186 casualties. These had been more than
made up when the 73rd (Royal Highlanders) Battalion was disbanded
and its manpower split between the 13th and the 42nd Battalions, also
Royal Highlanders. This was a consequence of the re-arrangement of
battalions mentioned earlier: Montreal was over-represented by
battalions at the front in proportion to the total of her enlistments and
ability to maintain reinforcements. One might well imagine the
reaction of the men of the 73rd (part of the 4th Division, 12 Brigade),
who had fought in the battle and who had gained a distinguished
reputation. The 13th gained the entire Pipe Band as part of its
distribution, which brought the size of the band up to almost fifty – 'a
formidable number when the authorized establishment was six. To
celebrate the union of the two battalions, the combined bands
attempted an entertainment on 23 April, but this was not an entire
success, as the enemy rudely disturbed the performers with some well
placed shells.' A consequence of this bounty of new manpower was
that, when the actions at Vimy ended for the Battalion in early May, it

was able to occupy comfortable billets at Chateau de la Haie boasting a strength of 1077, effectively a full establishment.

The **2nd (East Ontario) Battalion** (1 Brigade, 1st Division) joined the other battalions in the Brigade as being part of the onward move onto the Brown Line, moving the front to Farbus. The 2nd was the support battalion for the three others, the 1st, 3rd and 4th, who were primarily responsible for this third and fourth phase of the attack. The regimental history also spends some time discussing the changes in organisation within the CEF.

It is refreshing to note that when the preparations for storming Vimy Ridge were at the most tempestuous heights, there should be injected into the Battalion's hectic life such airy matters as regimental nomenclature. For some months someone on the staff, high above the Battalion level, had been trying to determine just what the style and title of the Battalion should be. For reinforcement purposes the Princess Patricias, the 2nd, the 21st and the 38th Battalions had been grouped into the 'Eastern Ontario Regiment'. For some reason, or for no reason at all, the 2nd Battalion had gravely asked that the 'Eastern' be abbreviated to 'East'. This apparently posed a problem for the staff. However, their judicial decision was rendered at about this time; and they insisted that the word 'Eastern' be spelled out. Characteristic of that perverseness that seizes battalions when they fail to get their own way, the 2nd accepted the decision but for ever after they wrote the word 'East' just the same, and no one ever questioned their right to do so.

Whilst such matters of moment were being finalised (and, needless to say, behind this triviality lay a serious issue), the preliminary bombardment had begun, and the Battalion, at the southern end of the Corps front, endured the German reaction: 'Standing waist deep in liquid mud, the Second suffered the savage retaliation that fell steadily on the front line, obliterating the trenches, crashing in dugouts, and sowing destruction with a liberal hand.'

On Easter Sunday the Battalion moved up to Maroeuil; and whilst they rested, around noon, it became quite evident that they were sharing the area with the 51st (Highland) Division: 'From all around was borne the brave music of bagpipe and drum as the Scots swung jauntily over the roads to their own assembly areas.' The Assembly area for the Battalion was around Maison Blanche (the farm of that name is opposite the massive German cemetery on the Béthune road). Interestingly, the regimental historian felt that the weather favoured the

Germans on 9 April: 'Meanwhile the elements aligned themselves against the Canadians. A drizzling rain had turned with the dawn into snow flurries, blowing directly in the face of the assaulting troops. The ground turned to slop and mud.' Other accounts have the wind blowing into the Germans' faces. On top of this, the Canadian assault was carefully planned and crafted: the defenders, especially if their front line positions were taken, would be left in confusion as to what was going on and their artillery would find it very difficult to maintain communications and even see the various SOS light signals that would go up. On balance, bad weather for a fully orchestrated major assault, especially in its earliest stages, probably was an advantage for the attacker – a similar situation, for example (on this occasion thick fog) helped the 51st (Highland) Division in its assault on Beaumont Hamel in November 1916.

The 2nd left its trenches at 7.30 am – ie some twenty minutes after the Red Line had been taken – and followed on behind the 4th Battalion. The German artillery was still operational, and casualties were caused before the Battalion reached the Old British Front Line, though the Battalion HQ party had a narrow escape when a shell burst in the middle of them but its force was completely absorbed by the thick mud in which it landed. By 11.00 am the two forward companies were well in advance of the Zwischenstellung and were able to fill a dangerous gap between the inner flanks of two of the forward battalions. This resolved what could have been a dangerous situation, but Major Malcolm Neilson, only twenty three years old, who had seen the danger and rectified it, was soon after killed by a shell from the Canadian barrage. He is buried in Ecoivres Cemetery (V D 5). By 1pm the Battalion had reached its final position, with the units in front on their objective.

A concern at this stage was the right flank. The Highlanders had a difficult task, involving a wheel in the course of their advance (because of the lie of the line) and because of the fact that there were substantial amounts of uncut German wire. At 5pm the Battalion made a reconnaissance forward to the Commandant's House, more or less south of Farbus, which marked, give or take a couple of hundred metres, the boundary between the Canadian Corps and XVII Corps. This was being held by part of 7/Black Watch, which had strayed slightly from their designated area. Late at night the 2nd was ordered into Farbus Wood to relieve the 3rd Battalion:

A long and hazardous undertaking. From time to time groups of the enemy would blunder into the Second's outposts and be

Farbus village captured by the Canadians.

greeted with rifle fire. In the darkness the rumble of vehicles and the champing of horses from the darkness of Willerval were mingled with the explosive crackle of machine guns. Battalion patrols searched the area between Farbus and Willerval and became engaged in occasional brawls; but in the pitch darkness the results could not be ascertained.

The situation on the right flank was not clear. At one point a young officer of 4/Gordon Highlanders, Second Lieutenant Alexander Stewart, appeared at Battalion HQ and asked for a message to be transmitted to his Brigade that he intended to bomb up Toast Trench and get on to his final objective. He succeeded in that venture, but was killed a fortnight later, at the age of 21, on 23 April: he is commemorated on the Arras Memorial to the Missing. Several histories comment on how captured German guns were turned onto their former owners. In fact a number of Canadian gunners had been specifically trained to make use of them – their additional firepower would be far from insignificant, given the great difficulties of moving British and Canadian artillery over the all but impassable ground that had been captured.

Moved, no doubt, by a laudable desire to assist the Canadian artillery in its work of making a quick job of destroying the enemy, several resourceful members of the Battalion turned some

89

of the guns around and had fun firing them at the Germans. They forgot for the time being that the one organisation on the Western Front that would have the position of these gun pits located to a fraction of an inch was the German artillery itself. They were unpleasantly reminded of this when a heavy bombardment descended upon them in indignant retaliation for this amusing diversion. Little physical damage resulted, but the troops' ardour for shelling the Boches with their own guns suffered a swift relapse.

By the 13th the Battalion was back at Maison Blanche; twenty eight men had been killed, and there were eighty four other casualties, eight of whom were missing. By the 15th the Battalion was established in Winnipeg Camp, in the woods to the north west of Mont St Eloi. **The 20th (Central Ontario) Battalion** (4 Brigade, **2nd Division** [Major General H Burstall]), was a support battalion for the Brigade, which was on the right flank of the Division's attack. For some weeks before the attack it took its place in the line in what was called the Thélus Sector. When in support, Battalion HQ and specialists were based in dugouts and in the 'Cave' at Maison Blanche, one of several such large underground refuges.

'The inhabitants, instead of quarrying, had mined the stone to build their homes. From the entrance, sloping passages running for from twenty to forty feet led into large caves, which inevitably had off-shooting galleries to other smaller caves. The engineers were converting them into 'glorified' and safe living quarters. The soil was clay loam, the sub-soil chalk.' Further along, a thousand metres or so away to the north, was a cave at Aux Rietz Corner which was, 'being prepared as the battle post for the 2nd Canadian Division Headquarters.' Until recently, this was open to the public, managed by a resolute and perhaps slightly eccentric Frenchman. The 1st Division Battle HQ was to be sited at Maison Blanche for the battle.

As the date for the battle approached, so the German shelling became more searching. On 24 March the Battalion was shelled out of its huts at Bois des Alleux and it had to be moved back to Yukon Camp, which existed effectively in name only. On the evening of 4 April the Battalion moved into the line in a relief that took some ten hours. 'We found that the trenches were muddy, with a layer of from one to two feet of liquid slime at the bottom.'

As soon as the light of morning appeared, organised shooting began at suspected strong points and, to test the artillery arrangements, the guns fired practice barrages. The visible effect

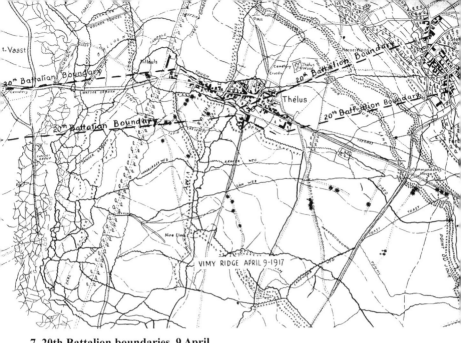

7. 20th Battalion boundaries, 9 April.

was devastating. A storm of steel burst in the enemy trenches, shooting sprays of earth, bags, beams and wire into the air. Trench mortar and machine gun emplacements were destroyed, trenches smashed in and wire torn and shattered. As a successful ruse to keep the enemy from guessing the day of attack, these practice barrages were continued daily at 5.30am for nearly a week beforehand.

For the attack, the two forward battalions, the 18th and 19th Battalions, were to move out beyond the British wire and occupy previously prepared Assembly Trenches. Two companies would act as 'moppers up' for them; the 21st would pass through the 20th's line and another company would then follow them, carrying out the same role as the two others. Because of the height of the trenches, the Battalion placed 150 scaling ladders in position during the night of 8/9 April.

There was naturally much congestion and confusion due to the assembling of about 3,000 troops in an area about 700 yards long and 200 wide. The arrangements for controlling the traffic were managed exceedingly well under the circumstances. Zivy Cave was like a beehive since, in addition to medical personnel, the 21st Battalion and 4 Brigade HQ occupied portions of it.'

The Battalion HQ was in a dugout in Zivy subway.

In the assault in this area the Black Line was taken rapidly – in about ten minutes. The German front line trenches, in fact, were only

91

about a hundred yards away. And given the number of men that had been assembled in No Man's Land, perhaps the rapid move forward should not come as a great surprise. Two companies of the 20th cleared part of the Black Line 'and sent back scores of prisoners of the 79th Reserve Division, who had offered no resistance and who appeared to be dazed.'

The 21st Battalion moved on to the Red Line, which was captured by 8.23am. A gap developed with the left (5) brigade, but C Company of the 20th filled that and also captured a German field gun at the entrance to Thélus in the process (probably in the area of the present Canadian Artillery Memorial at the Les Tilleuls crossroads). Whilst engaged in their mopping up tasks, C Company also found the Wasser Graben tunnel,

> leading from the German front line back to Les Tilleuls, a distance of nearly a thousand yards. It was deep and dry, with wooden plank sides, ceiling and floor, and lighted by electricity. The large rooms had been used as HQs, dressing stations and stores containing many articles of clothing and equipment. In one of them was found a large supply of black bread [ie rye bread].'

The German occupied the equivalent of the Maison Blanche cave at Thélus and there was also a German subway, called Thélus Tunnel.

The Battalion suffered few casualties – less than a hundred in total, of whom only six were killed, including Lieutenant James Little, who is buried in Ecoivres, grave V C 21 and Corporal Alfred Henry Clubbe, whose grave you will be visiting in Nine Elms cemetery during the car tour. Most of the casualties were caused by machine gun fire from the direction of Nine Elms – doubtless those same well handled machine guns that had caused units of the 1st Division so much trouble.

On the night of the 10th, 4 Brigade took over the line from the British 13 Brigade (5th Division), the 20th taking over from 15/Warwicks in a sector 'lying north and east of Thélus'. A couple of days later it moved away from the immediate front line zone. The 29th **(Vancouver) Battalion** (6 Brigade, 2nd Division) was to follow up the two assaulting brigades, and was posted on the centre of the divisional attack. 13 Brigade was on its left, with 1/Royal West Kents (RWK) on the left of the 29th and 2/King's Own Scottish Borderers (KOSB) on the right of 1st Canadian Mounted Rifles (CMR) of 8 Brigade, 3rd Division. The job of 6 Brigade was to follow through the attack of the other two brigades and take and hold the ridge in this sector.

The assembly area for the Battalion was on the northern edge of the

21st Infantry Battalion Memorial Cross erected at Nine Elms in May 1917. There were originally two such memorials in this cemetery. The crosses were transferred after the war to the grounds of the Royal Military College in Kingston, Ontario where they were displayed for the next sixty years. Despite being repaired a number of times, age finally took its toll. During the 1990s, the memorial to the 13th was sent to the Canadian War Museum in Ottawa, but because the 21st Battalion was a Kingston based unit, its cross was moved into the city of Kingston to the Armoury of the Princess of Wales' Own Regiment, the one surviving unit of the war time grouping. Essentially a replica of the original, it is still preserved there.

Neuville St Vaast cemetery (which is still in its original location). At 8.05am the Battalion moved forward to Turco Graben, on the Red Line. Amongst the few casualties at this stage was Lieutenant Ted Brown MM, who earlier in the war had built up a formidable reputation as a scout. He is buried in Barlin Communal Cemetery Extension (I H74), though his death is recorded as having occurred on 10 April. At 0935 the 29th Battalion began its attack. The regimental history notes that in training the British had decided to adopt the German method of advance, whereby officers were to 'steer' their men from the rear rather than leading them in the attack. This was to ensure that better direction and alignment were kept in the advance and had been followed on the training grounds. However, in practice the old method was adopted – old habits were too hard to be killed off that easily. This history has another take on the weather, noting that the snow flurries got into the enemy's eyes – 'Fickle Dame Nature seemed to be on our side' - Thélus Trench, although heavily defended, was taken quite easily as was the sunken road beyond it. Thélus Wood was considered to be likely a hard nut to crack, but in the event it proved to have been evacuated, though a couple of extremely well camouflaged German field guns in the Farbus Line were found to have barrels that were still hot and nearby there was an unconsumed hot breakfast prepared for the gunners.

The men of the Battalion could now enjoy the view over the Douai plain and see the German artillery moving off across it, though there were few signs of any infantry.

On 10 April the Battalion took part in an assault on the railway embankment at Farbus, which had been partially reoccupied by the Germans; due to the promised barrage not opening up – the problems of getting the artillery forward were hindering the Canadians at this stage – this was not a success. Lieutenant Benjamin Gray, the relevant platoon commander, was killed in the attack, and is now commemorated on the Vimy Memorial. On the night of the 11th the Battalion withdrew to Mont St Eloi but was spared the need to launch an attack on the railway embankment and beyond when the Germans voluntarily withdrew from what was a quite untenable position.

1/RWK (13 Brigade, 5th ('Imperial') Division) was transferred to the Canadian Corps, along with the rest of the 5th Division, on 16 March. The training that then followed included accustomising itself to the platoon reorganisation recently introduced (and discussed above), 'each platoon being constituted as a a complete unit with its proper proportion of riflemen, bombers, rifle grenadiers and Lewis gunners'.

On the morning of 8 April the men moved to Villers au Bois, where they were equipped with battle stores and then rested; at 9.30pm they commenced the long, five mile, approach move, heavily laden and over difficult ground, to the assembly positions at Neuville St Vaast. At 3am, with a battle strength of twenty officers and 655 other ranks, the Battalion was in position. Two companies were to assault Thélus trench and then A and B Companies were to take Goulot Wood and establish a position on its western edge.

At 7.30am the Battalion moved off; at 8.15am it advanced in three waves in artillery formation. 'The ground was fearfully cut up and very slippery, but the men kept well closed up and reached the Lille [Lens] Road, punctually to timetable, at 9am. When passing the German front line trenches, the tanks, which were to have supported the attack, were found sticking in the mud and being shelled by the Germans.' At the road the Battalion was deployed for its attack. 'At 9.29am the first wave advanced to close under our artillery barrage. So intense was the barrage that watches could be compared and all the men notified as to when it would clear the objective with the greatest impunity.'

As soon as the barrage cleared Thélus Trench it was rushed and captured; patrols then followed the artillery fire and cleared all trenches up to Telegraph Weg. B Company then moved forward on the north side of Count's Wood and entered Goulot Wood, which was found to be lightly occupied by the Germans. Finally, the eastern edge of Goulot Wood was seized; at this point the men came under German artillery fire and, as it was possible to hold the position from the less exposed western side, the main position was made in good dugouts that had been found there. At night time patrols were pushed forward to the Brown Line proper.

Nine guns were captured in the wood, namely four howitzers, four field and one 90mm gun. A few rounds were fired from them at close range as our men approached. The rifle grenade section of one of the platoons at once came into action, while the rest of the platoon charged. The German gunners then bolted, but most of them were accounted for by our Lewis gunners.

All of this was taking place in the wood roughly 1,200 yards due east from the turning off the Lens road to the Vimy Memorial.

Great difficulty was experienced in getting rations up at night. Pack animals, including officers' chargers, had to be used. The going was necessarily very bad indeed, and improvised bridges had to be made over old trenches. It took nine hours to reach Battalion HQ and casualties occurred on the way.'

1/RWK also pushed patrols forward onto the sunken road (now – and probably then – a track which links Farbus to the western edge of Vimy). The total casualties suffered were 138, of who twenty six were killed or missing. The only officer fatality, Lieutenant Francis Hyde, is buried in Nine Elms Cemetery, III E16.

The Battalion was relieved on 10 April, starting at 8.30pm but which was not completed until 4.20am on the 11th. It remained on the Vimy battlefield area for a week, based at Villers au Bois; during this time it furnished large parties for railway work and then moved back to rejoin the 5th Division. **2/KOSB** was the other forward battalion from 13 Brigade engaged in the fighting on 9 April at Vimy, though the regimental history is quite clear about the limitations of its role. 'The story of Vimy Ridge belongs to the Canadians. Theirs is the glory and 13 Infantry Brigade may mildly add *pars parva fuimus*.'

The Battalion moved closer to the battlefield, taking up billets in the woods near the Chateau of Olhain on 2 April. Living 'in bell tents without boards, a chilly refuge in the chill April of 1917, at an altitude higher than any part of Vimy Ridge. Mud, lost kits, colds, aches, sore feet and unchangingly vile weather were unpropitious preludes to an

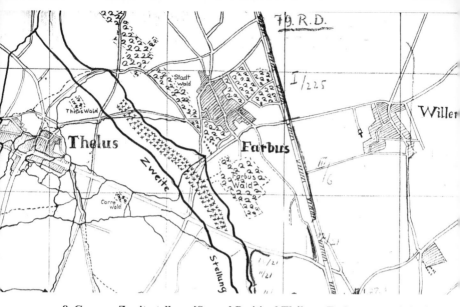

8. German Zweitestellung [Second Position] Thélus – Farbus sector, 9 April.

ordeal of life and death.' Like 1/RWK, the men set off from Villers au Bois at 9.30pm, having earlier loaded themselves up with battle kit; they were in position near Neuville St Vaast by 2.30am. The regimental history notes that the 5th Division artillery was too close to the line to be used for the first phase of operations, but was brought into action for the second phase, the advance to the Blue and Brown Lines.

The Battalion moved off initially at 7.20am, moving up by companies to a forward assembly area, from which point they continued their advance at 8.30am. The men moved in artillery formation, 'little columns or sections in fours, not too close to one another to risk being 'browned', and not too far apart to lead to loss of formation and control. It suggests troops engaged but not yet deployed for attack... Direction was hard to keep. It was daylight, yet the aid of the compass had to be invoked.'

At 9.30am the Battalion moved off from the Red Line to attack Thélus Trench, which ran more or less parallel to, and a half mile or so to the east of, the Lens Road. It lay in front (ie west) of Thélus village, running towards Vimy. The Battalion crossed the road more or less where the access road to the Memorial comes off it; and it faced the immediate problem created by Bonval Wood, whose southern point is on the east side of the road, a couple of hundred metres north of the turning. 'To skirt the south, or top edge, of the wood, ie to leave it on the left, it was necessary to move by file of sections before reforming for the final assault. It was here that enemy snipers, shooting across from the other side of the road from dugouts yet untaken, caused considerable casualties. The Canadians on the left had suffered a temporary check; in fact they continued to be held up long after the KOSB had stormed Thélus trench without much opposition and had done some mopping up.'

Once Thélus Trench had been taken, this area of German resistance was quelled by members of D Company and produced three officers and thirty three prisoners. Elsewhere the break in at Thélus Trench was exploited by bombing along it, pushing the length captured forward to the Quarry Dugouts. The right company, meanwhile, had had an easier passage to its objective, taking Thélus Trench as far south as the northern edge of Count's Wood.

It 'pushed on through empty gun pits to a network of trenches, the

9. Third Canadian Division Planning Map.

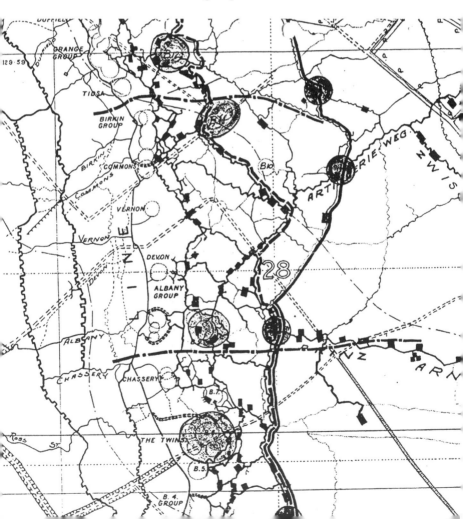

Gridiron. A certain adjustment of frontiers had to be made with 1/RWK. Both battalions had had to squeeze through the space, about three hundred yards wide, between Count's Wood and Bonval Wood. They were then to fan out, the KOSB going more or less straight ahead and 1/RWK more to the right to face their several objectives. The reason for this manoeuvre was that a thick belt of wire ran south east along the line of the ridge from Count's Wood, forming the second or inner defence of the Farbus line. It had not been continued north of Count's Wood and, thanks to our airmen and the Canadian Corps staff, it was turned [ie it was by-passed] intentionally – probably with economy to wire cutting artillery. 1/RWK did not deflect enough at first, but the slight overcrowding in the gun pits beyond the Gridiron was soon remedied.' The KOSB's objectives were taken by 11am; patrols were pushed into Vimy, which was found to be empty of Germans.

However, because the Pimple had not been taken, any further advance into Vimy was impractical; especially because the snow was settling and moving figures would stand out clearly against the white, making them easy targets for snipers. 2/KOSB came out of the line during the night of 10 April. Its men had captured some 250 prisoners, two 8-inch howitzers, four machine guns and a wireless installation. Its casualties were twenty one killed (including one officer), two missing and 138 wounded. The history notes a few points about the conduct of the battle: 'The value of practice was strikingly vindicated. But the infantry were loud in praise of the most important liaison of all – with the gunners. Only a perfect barrage can be "hugged", and that is what the KOSB and RWK were treated to.'

Optional Tour
The area of this fighting, which is outside the tour offered in this book, is easy enough to follow. Very shortly after the turn off to the Vimy Memorial to the west of the Lens road, there is a minor turning to the right (east) side: this road leads, eventually, into Thélus. Immediately on your left is the southern tip of what was then called Bonval Wood. After about six hundred metres you will find a track going off to the north. In approaching this intersection, within the last fifty yards or so, you will have passed through the wire defences of Thélus Trench. This trench followed, more or less, the track up past Count's Wood and beyond to the north and the road going off to the south, into Thélus. The track to Count's Wood should be tackled only on foot and the car must not cause an obstruction when parked, but it is an interesting area

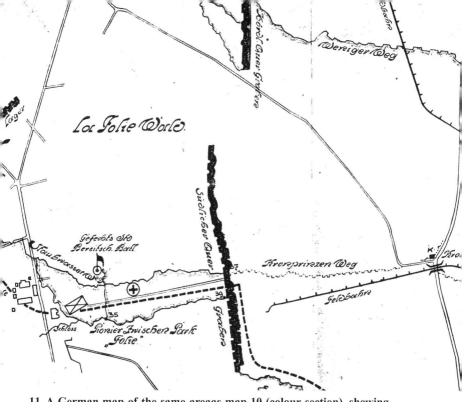

11. A German map of the same areaas map 10 (colour section), showing depth positions around the Ecole [Schule] and La Folie Chateau [Schloss].

La Folie Chateau March 1917.

99

to visit. Bonval Wood to the north of Count's Wood has grown much closer to it – originally there was a gap of three hundred yards or so between them. The motorist should carry on into Thélus and continue with his touring.

One other item of interest as regards Vimy comes out of this history; on 24 April the Battalion came out of the line in the vicinity of Givenchy and was due to move back to the area of Maison Blanche – which thus involved a traverse of the ridge. They used Tottenham subway for part of the trip, an indicator that at least some of the subways continued to be used for some time after the front had been pushed forward.

8 Brigade of the **3rd Division** (Major General Lipsett), which consisted of four battalions of the **Canadian Mounted Rifles**, the 1st, 2nd, 4th and 5th, had the responsibility of taking La Folie Farm and forward from there into La Folie Wood. In fact, the 3rd Division area (or, at least, a good chunk of it) is largely preserved in the sense that most of it lies within the Memorial site or in the Vimy National Forest. On the other hand, because much of these sites are forested (and particularly that of 8 Brigade), it is very difficult to get any real sense of what the view was for the men at the time. What woods there were were badly damaged or destroyed, and therefore the sight lines would have been significantly different. On the other hand, many of the craters have survived, a significant number of trench features and earthworks can be identified and it provides an atmospheric quality which is, perhaps, lacking on other parts of the battlefield. It is also a fact that much of the 'preserved' area is off limits to the public. Even where it is possible (such as in the Vimy National Forest) great care has to be taken because of munitions, 'man traps' and that scourge of battlefield visitors, trigger happy hunters during the season.

Hidden away in the closed part of the Memorial site, for example, are two wombat craters, probably unique on the Western Front. Drilled (by hand!) these provided immediate communication trenches across No Man's Land: thus the War Diary of 4/CMR notes at 5.32am: 'Tunnelling Officer reported that the TUNNEL SAP from GOODMAN TUNNEL to German Front Line had been successfully blown at 5.301/2.' The effect of such a type of mine had been demonstrated, amongst others, to the officers and NCOs of 5/CMR on 4 April, as related by the War Diary.

At 12 noon, officers and NCOs attended a demonstration by the 172nd Tunnelling Coy in blowing a tunnel trench, a number of which will be blown from our present front line into No Man's

Reinforcements and supplies entering Arras, 1917.

Land first prior to our attack on Vimy – preparations for which are being pushed with all possible dispatch. The weather conditions are abominable. Demonstration (at 2pm) quite successful, 170 feet of trench 'blown', average depth 8 feet – 10 pounds of ammonal per foot was used – width about 15 to 20 feet.

The CMR attacked in the order, from the right, 1st (plus one company of the 5th), 2nd, 4th, with the 5th in reserve/support. 1/CMR had some problems in its attack, not least the nest of machine gunners mentioned in the account of 2/KOSB above. They had a difficult task in that their final objective area fell just short of a part of the ridge where there is a re-entrant into it, as the Lens road begins its drop down its eastern side, bending noticeably to the right and passing by the west of Vimy itself. The original road carried straight on at this point (as is evident now) and it was between the two, approximately, that there were entrances to a number of tunnel systems, such as Schwaben Tunnel and 20th Tunnel.

2/CMR had four phases to its operation, and consequently the attack was launched with a front of a company, in four company waves, led by B, followed by C, then D and finally A, the latter of which would proceed to the right of the captured La Folie Farm to the final objective and then set up strong points. The different phases involved: firstly the capture of the enemy's front line system; secondly the capture of the main resistance line, known as the Zwischenstellung; thirdly the capture of the new subsidiary resistance trench (Fickle) together with La Folie Farm; and finally the Red Line, along with the immediate establishment of a protective outpost line.

Some of 2/CMR used the Goodman Subway to reach their assembly positions; right on time, the other Wombat mine, laid to the south of Chassery Crater, was blown and (the WD continues) 'the enemy barrage settled upon our lines and the glacis in front. Following our own curtain of fire, B Company crossed into the enemy lines, occupied the front line system and started collecting prisoners, whilst C Company passed through.' By 5.55am the Zwischenstellung was reported captured; Fickle Trench had been so pulverised by artillery that it had been all but completely obliterated and therefore the defensive line was established in Zwischen. At 6.50am La Folie Farm was reported as taken and an hour later so was the final objective.

Owing to the rapid advance behind our curtain fire, enemy machine guns had no time to get into action, and of the two that made an attempt to do so, both were wiped out immediately by our infantry... The Zwischenstellungwas converted into a main resistance trench, upon the Red Line objective a front line trench was dug, and an outpost of one platoon out forward in a SP [strong point] *as far ahead as tactical conditions permitted. From deep dugouts at the west end of the Prinz Arnulf Graben tunnel a large number of prisoners were taken. ... During the morning enemy aeroplanes were very active, at 10 o'clock several flying low over the Zwischenstellung and La Folie, and an hour later hostile artillery became very active upon these, and continued throughout the day, causing many casualties.*

The following day strong patrols were sent out from the front line battalions by Brigade at about 4pm, with the objective of establishing the location of enemy positions. 2/CMR's patrol was instructed to reconnoitre Petit Vimy and the Bloater trench system; they found this system to be heavily manned and considerable casualties were caused. Amongst those killed was the scout and sniping officer, Lieutenant R Spinks (Richard Spinks, who was 41 when he died, is buried in Ecoivres Military Cemetery, grave VI D 6), whilst the other officer in the patrol, Lieutenant Henekey, was severely wounded. All casualties were brought in. 2/CMR remained in the line until late on the night of the 11th, having endured heavy shelling for most of the daylight hours on that day. The Battalion had started the attack with twenty three officers and 654 other ranks (the balance were held back); upon relief the numbers stood at fourteen officers and 353 other ranks, 'During the advance the casualties were chiefly sustained from the enemy barrage on the Crater Line and his immediate front line system and later on during the process of consolidation.'

4/CMR was to the left of 2/CMR and to the right of the Royal Canadian Regiment in the line of battle. The WD in the days preceding the attack details the hard labour involved in getting the forward dumps filled with the appropriate stores and munitions, bailing out waterlogged trenches and sending small patrols forward to clear as much of the British wire as possible. The Battalion went into the attack with seventeen officers and 627 other ranks, with ten officers and 172 other ranks detailed as Carrying or Stretcher Bearers or being on duty at Battalion HQ. Of the 172 other ranks, about seventy were available to act as stretcher bearers, though initially only twenty five were specifically detailed for that task; eighty were detailed as a Battalion Carry Party and twenty one to do a similar task for Brigade.

The Battalion used the Goodman Subway to get the men up to the line, some members of which stayed in it whilst they awaited the move

Lieutenant Colonel Agar Adamson DSO.

to the assembly trenches. At the time of the attack, Battalion HQ was in the subway (seven officers and fifty five other ranks), whilst a number of others were in dugouts and saps nearby. The WD details the messages received as the action progressed, coming from a variety of sources, including one intrepid officer who had taken up an OP (Observation Post) on Edmonton Crater, out in No Man's Land. Reports initially came from OPs, but later these were replaced by reports from further forward in writing, making use of the message forms with the relevant part of the large scale trench map printed on one side. By 7.05 the signallers' were able to report that they had established a signal station in the enemy front line. By 7.50am Lieutenant Smith reported personally that 'we have reached all our Objectives and we are consolidating a position 100 yards in rear [ie to the west] of La Folie Road [ie more or less the pedestrian track that runs through the Vimy National Forest up to the Memorial area] and that two platoons of D Company had pushed forward to establish SPs in the wood.' In 1917 the wood, or what remained of it, was not as extensive or as dense as it is today; thus these strong points were about one hundred and fifty yards east of the present track and only just into the wooded area, whereas now the whole sector is wooded.

Thus far all seemed well; however, there were problems on the left. Lieutenant Pierce (A Company) reported in writing at 9am that 'some of the troops on the left overran their objective, and were now being driven back, and asked for reinforcements, and that A Company's left flank rests on a point 100 yards to the right of Ecole Commune.' Reinforcements were also called for from C Company, and eventually Brigade gave permission for the Carrying Party to be sent forward as reinforcements. Once signals were established with the Zwischenstellung, the CO (Lieutenant Colonel Gordon) got permission to move forward to that line at 9.30am; whilst at the same time 5/CMR were instructed to send forward two of their three companies to reinforce the line.

The next problem came in the area of the SPs; by 11am the men in them were suffering considerable casualties. Although the situation was 'well in hand' by 11.45am, with a considerable number of Lewis and Vickers machine guns deployed, the SP was coming under heavy fire and Brigade eventually agreed to Gordon's request to remove his men from there – but this could not happen until after dark.

What both these accounts underlines is that the initial assault was carried out very much according to plan; but that casualties mounted in the hours after the objectives had been taken as the Germans recovered from the initial shock and tried to restore the situation.

5/CMR, in support, occupied Goodman Subway at the beginning of the attack. A and D Companies moved into the Goodman at 2.30am, fitting in behind the elements of 4/CMR which were at the head of it; the others moved in after 4.30am, as the 4th moved into its jumping off positions. The Battalion's WD is almost poetic in its description of what happened at 5.30am. 'Zero Hour: Intense artillery bombardment – one continuous roar. The ground trembles and there is mingled with the roar of the guns the swishing and screeching of the shell-filled air. 60 guns are covering our own advance, forming a 'rolling barrage'. Smoke and debris, thrown up by the bursting shells, give the appearance of a solid wall.' At 5.50am 'A and D Companies filing out of tunnel via Albany Ave entrance (as the PS Line [ie front line] entrance had just been crumped in) and took up a position in our old front and support trenches, A Coy in area of 1/CMR and D Coy in area of 4/CMR.'

'As A Coy moved forward toward Zwischenstellung they came under the fire of a party of about 40 Huns who had been evidently hiding in dugouts in the Crater Line whilst our barrage was on and had been overlooked by 1/CMR as they moved forward. These were immediately engaged and after a number had been killed the remainder – about 23 – surrendered and were taken prisoners.' For the rest of the day the Battalion was involved in assisting with digging new lines (and holding them) and bringing up the battle stores.

8 Brigade's Battle Narrative reported at noon on 10 April that, 'The ground is particularly wet and muddy and the men are suffering severely from exhaustion.' On April 11th, at 10.00 am, the narrative states, 'Enemy commenced shelling our forward line and the crest of the hill – retaliation by CB [Counter Battery] work asked for. 2/CMR

suffered some casualties from our own howitzers. This bombardment lasted for four or five hours, after which it gradually eased off, and the relief of our front line by the 60th Battalion (9 Brigade) – a Battalion shortly to be disbanded in the general organisational reshuffle - was commenced.

The casualties suffered by the Brigade in the battle, as of noon on 12 April, were listed as follows: 1/CMR, thirteen officers and 323 other ranks; 2/CMR, eight officers and 319 other ranks; 4/CMR, nine officers and 172 other ranks; 5/CMR two officers and ninety other ranks; MG Company, two officers and eighty nine ranks. This gives a total of thirty four officers and 993 other ranks – that is about thirty percent of those involved in the attack. It should be noted, from the evidence of many CMR headstones in the cemeteries, where dates are often given as 7/10 April, that these figures probably relate to the period 7 – 12 April.

To the left of 4/CMR was the **RCR (7 Brigade, 3rd Division)**. 7 Brigade's task was 'to consolidate a defence line on the east of the Ridge with strong points in the final objective line and to push patrols through La Folie Wood.' The first objective was the enemy's first main defensive position behind the Crater Line, to be taken by 6.05 am; the final objective was a line through La Folie Wood on the forward slope of the ridge, to be captured by 7.05am, the assault commencing at 6.45 am. Battalions had to advance distances ranging from about a thousand yards on the left to 1,300 yards on the right.

The Battalion moved up to the line from Villers au Bois and made some use of a part of Grange Subway for protection and accommodation in the time prior to the assault; its HQ, however, was not situated in the subway, but nearby. 648 men went into the battle; in the early hours of 9 April they moved out to their jumping off position along the Observation Line (sometimes known as the Outpost Line) running north from Birkin crater to the northern edge of Vernon. A group of fifty men (with the assistance of Field Engineers) were to create a Strong Point a short distance behind the final objective, which was to be further strengthened by two Vickers machine guns manned by men of the Brigade Machine Gun Company. This use of the Vickers was common along the Corps front, designed to give the new line substantial fire power, especially applicable given the considerable views that would be available to the rear of the German positions. A number of smaller posts, each with about twenty men and equipped with Lewis guns, were to be established on or forward of the final objective

The first (or intermediate) objective was taken with comparatively little cost, but the second was more expensively won, with the defending machine gunners and snipers putting up a determined defence. The fighting thus far had reduced the two forward companies to about 110 men; casualties were being sustained as a consequence of the initial failure of the assault on the left in the 4th Division's area. It was far from plain sailing in the area to the front and right as well, but by midnight and, with the aid of reinforcements from the 58th Battalion (from the reserve 9 Brigade), it became possible to establish a continuous line. Nightfall had brought relief from the German fire coming from the area of Hill 145. Again, it is difficult to envisage this situation today as one walks through the National Forest towards Hill 145, the site of the Vimy Memorial; the thick woodland makes appreciation of the tactical situation difficult.

Three of the officer fatalities were buried together in Ecoivres Military Cemetery in Block V Row E – Lieutenants AS Churchill (8), Guy Beck (7) and William Blott (6). Lieutenant Lester Rooks is in VI G26, whilst Lieutenant Bole, the Brigade Bombing Officer, was wounded and captured by the Germans. He died on 13 May 1917 and is buried in Niederzwehren Cemetery, Kassel, Hesse, one of four cemeteries selected after the war to which the Commonwealth dead in Germany were concentrated. The centre battalion in 7 Brigade's attack was the **Princess Patricia's Canadian Light Infantry**. In the Corps' report of the battle, a comment is made on the problem of the difficult going:

> The difficulties of the first ground to be traversed were particularly great. The protracted mining activity of both sides in this locality had resulted in a chain of great mine craters, many of them impassable, and the others presenting a difficult obstacle for infantry. In addition the unfavourable weather of the preceding days and the continuous shelling had reduced much of the earth to vast puddles of sticky mud. The deep shell craters, the maze of shattered trenches and the remnants of torn and scattered entanglements added further obstructions to the heavy-laden infantry.

Two companies were already in the line some time before zero; the other two were in the Grange Subway, 'waiting near Colonel Agar Adamson's HQ in Grange Tunnel to debouch behind their respective odd numbers…' This HQ is the one visitors see on the guided tour of the Subway today. The Battalion was to attack on a front of approximately 250 yards, passing through the crater line before them, which included the Duffield, Grange and Patricia-Tidsa groups, all of which are clearly visible to the visitor today. They would end up in a position north west of the École Commune and establish SP 6 a short distance behind the final objective.

> *By 4.30 am all ranks of the Patricias were in position, and thanks to Grange Tunnel every man had a hot meal and his tot of rum two hours before action. It was still of course quite dark, and the men filed unobserved into the jumping-off trenches without hitch or interference from the enemy. Zero hour had been chosen so that there would be sufficient light for local movement and not enough for the enemy's snipers and machine gunners.'*

Over the men went at 5.30 am, the Regimental Pipers first playing the men over the top and then following as stretcher bearers.

Some casualties were suffered in the move to the first objective, but they were few and already a number of prisoners from RIR 262 were on their way back to the Canadian line. Heavier casualties were suffered in the next phase, particularly amongst the officers and, frequently, certain crucial command posts had to be filled by senior NCOs. SP 6 was to be build on the Staubwasser-Weg (portions of which are visible today on the Memorial Site), a little beyond the École Commune; again, there is evidence of this significant German trench in the National Forest, but none of the École Commune. Patrols were to be pushed forward as far as Bois du Champ Pourri, into which ran the Staubwasser-Weg; this little wood is still there, though access may be complicated by the construction of the Thélus by-pass.

The triumph of the attack and the successful consolidation of the objective were marred by the persistent problem of German sniping from the area of Hill 145. Because of the precarious situation on the left, the 42nd Battalion on the PPCLI's left had to refuse its flank and dig a new trench; consequently the PPCLI had to take over some of the 42nd's anticipated responsibilities. To the problem of German fire from the left was added heavy shelling, starting at about 3pm and not easing off until 2am on the 10th. The German artillery had the advantage of superiority in the air (at least in terms of quality of machines) at this time, and thus low flying aircraft fed information to their guns with expensive consequences for the Canadians. Number 2 Company, on the right, for example, had every NCO but one a casualty by the morning of the 10th. The Germans also identified SP 6, completed just before dusk, and flattened it, causing considerable casualties amongst its garrison. Eventually it was abandoned and the surviving guns placed elsewhere.

Liévin, near Lens, on the Canadian front.

Losses mounted – from about 50 at 10.30 am on the 9th to 215 twenty four hours later. There was some disorganisation in the consolidating positions of Numbers 2 and 3 Companies; the intentions of the Germans were far from evident. Eventually it seemed clear that, whilst the Germans were unlikely to launch counter attacks, they had every intention of remaining put as long as they could in their positions towards the foot of the ridge, a decision doubtless strengthened by the fact that the northern part of the ridge, through to the Pimple, was not in Canadian hands.

On 11 April the PPCLI were withdrawn from the line, moving back to Villers au Bois, relieved by the 43rd Battalion. The Battalion, in the period from noon on the 8th to noon on the 14th, had suffered 222 casualties, including eleven officers. Eighty three were killed or died of wounds, of whom three were officers: Lieutenants Reginald Sladen and Archie Wagner (the latter attached to 7 Trench Mortar Battery) are buried in Bois Carré British Cemetery (Graves V A 12 and IV A 5 respectively) and Lieutenant Robert Simonds in La Chaudière Military Cemetery (Grave VIII E 10).

The **42nd Battalion (The Royal Highlanders of Canada**, often known as The Canadian Black Watch) were the left battalion in 7 Brigade's attack.

They had an eventful time early on 23 March – only a few hours after they took over the trenches just before midnight on the 22nd, which was itself after a period of over a month out of the line preparing for the forthcoming offensive and enjoying some recreation.

The garrison had just settled down in their places when on the stroke of 3am the enemy exploded a tremendous mine on the Battalion front. There was a rending blast and the whole area rocked for a moment. Lights in every dugout were extinguished, extra trench stores, dishes and other movable objects crashed to the floor, while smoke, dust and debris were everywhere. The OC of B Company had just returned to Company HQ dugout in LaSalle [sic] *Trench after a tour of inspection of the crater posts when the explosion occurred and, on reaching the entrance, observed a tremendous wall of earth extending across the left of the front line for a distance which was afterwards found to be 250 yards. Proceeding forward immediately, he joined Lieutenant Small, who was on duty in the front line and, accompanied by Small and two Lewis gunners, at once rushed out and occupied the highest point on the near lip of the crater. From here parties of the enemy were observed digging in on the far side of the crater and the Lewis gun was promptly brought into action with good effect whilst the officers used their revolvers. Several of the enemy were seen to be hit and the consolidation work in the immediate vicinity terminated abruptly. Shortly afterwards severe enfilade fire was brought to bear on the B Company party, which was then withdrawn to a less exposed position after one of the Lewis gunners had been severely wounded; there being insufficient time to establish a post on the crater lip before daylight.*

At daylight it was found that the enemy had exploded a series of four large mines simultaneously. The new craters extended from Durand Crater in a northerly direction to a distance of 250 yards and consisted of a series of four separate craters merging into one. It was promptly christened "Longfellow"... The explosion of the mine itself caused no casualties, but there were several shortly afterwards while the crater was observed and the lip reconnoitred.

The blowing of the mine completely changed the configuration of a large section of the front over which the Battalion was to attack on the Ridge and formed a most dangerous obstacle which would have to be overcome just as the attacking troops jumped off. Its immediate and effective consolidation was imperative and during the day careful plans were prepared for this work. At dusk consolidation was energetically pushed forward. Every available man from the front line and support companies, in addition to 120 men who were brought up from the reserve companies, were put to work. On the first night Topp Sap [named after the OC of B Company] *was dug, extending from the observation line to the lip of the new crater, where a defended post was established. A post was also established at the southern end of the crater.*

The following night... Longfellow Trench was commenced, extending across the front line just under the lip of the crater. Four additional new posts were also commenced, together with a new communication trench. By this time the enemy had detected the new work and throughout the night heavy rifle fire was maintained from Broadmarsh Crater to the left, from which point the site of the new work could be enfiladed in some degree. Covering parties with Lewis guns were able to keep down enemy machine gun fire, but could not stop the constant sniping by individuals from numerous points of vantage in the enemy line, with the result that the work was carried out under most trying conditions. During the night three other ranks were killed; Lieutenant Robert Stewart was mortally wounded while carrying a wounded man to a place of safety [he died on the 25th and is buried in Aubigny CCE, V A 39] *and a number of other ranks were wounded. The men, however, did not pause in the work at any time and consolidation was well under way before dawn. On the night of the 25th the same procedure was followed and by this time the positions were deep enough to provide a fair measure of protection for the working party and fewer casualties were sustained. Daylight on the 26th found a number of new posts on the Longfellow sufficiently near completion to enable them to be occupied and the Battalion was able to retaliate for its uncomfortable experience of the previous days by maintaining most active sniping. It was found that the near lip of the crater was considerably higher than that on the enemy's side, with the result that much German territory previously not under observation could be completely dominated. From one post the snipers were able to enfilade an enemy communication trench and in this one place alone seven hits were obtained the first morning.'*

By 31 March, after successive nights of further consolidation, a complete new defensive system, complete with proper communications, had been constructed. The enemy suffered particularly on the morning of 30 March, as a relief had taken place and the incomers seemed unaware that previously screened places in the line were now under Canadian observation. This work was followed up by a successful raid, during the early morning of 1 April, on the German trenches opposite the new crater, which destroyed a number of German dugouts and brought back a prisoner of RIR 262. That night the Battalion was relieved and its history noted: 'Thus ended one of the most successful tours in the history of the Battalion.' From the platform outside the Interpretive Centre at Vimy one can see clearly most of the Canadian side of where this action took place, though trees tend to get in the way of the view off to the left; whilst the Germans' perspective is equally clear from their side of the line.

Until the 5th the Battalion was in bivouacs in Dumpbell Camp, situated in the northern end of Bois des Alleux behind Mont St Eloi; four uncomfortable days in miserable conditions. On the night of 5 April A and C Companies were in the front line, clearing and rebuilding assembly trenches. On the night of the 7th B and D Companies moved up to occupy space in Grange Subway (the Black Watch branch of the subway is named after the Battalion). 'The great Grange Tunnel, electrically lighted and supplied with water, was, with its numerous branches, tramways, recesses for supplies and room for Headquarters, of enormous value in facilitating the concentration of the troops and with ten [sic] other similar tunnels on the Canadian front saved hundreds of lives.'

Within just over half an hour of the launch of the assault the Battalion had taken its first objective; casualties were light, but seemed to be concentrated particularly heavily amongst the officers. Lieutenants Charles Tinling (Barlin CCE, I H 62) and G Sheffield (Boulogne East Cemetery, VII B 15) were mortally wounded and two others severely enough to put them out of action. There was, therefore, with this lack of officers, some confusion in the reorganisation on the objective, but this was resolved in particular by the good work of Lieutenant Dick Wattam. This officer was killed afterwards by a sniper (Villers Station Cemetery, VIII A 6). By 8am the final objective had been reached and consolidation was well under way.

However, very stubborn German resistance had held up the advance of 11 Brigade on the left, so that although some elements of the 54th Battalion had made reasonable progress, it was unlikely that they could hold their ground. With the Germans resolutely holding on to the high ground, sniping became a severe problem. By 0930am Captain Harry Hilton, attached to 7 Trench Mortar Battery, had also been killed

(Villers Station Cemetery, VIII A 8). Reinforcements were sent up from the 49th Battalion (the Brigade Support Battalion); and because the situation on the left remained confused, but certainly with clear indications that the Germans retained considerable control over the high ground, the Battalion hastily constructed a defensible line from Broadmarsh to the new line, a company of the 58th Battalion being lent to strengthen the line. In mid afternoon the Battalion estimated that it had suffered about two hundred casualties.

A further attempt on Hill 145 was made in the afternoon of 9 April; whilst not completely successful, it certainly eased the situation for the 42nd. It was now possible, in the darkness, to get all the less urgent casualties moved to the rear, something which had been impossible during the day due to a combination of a shortage of stretcher bearers and the intensity (and accuracy) of the German fire. But still, at places on the left, the enemy were only some forty metres away; fortunately the German artillery had not been able to place shells accurately on the new defensive positions on this flank. The weather was cold and there was a heavy fall of snow overnight on 10 April, adding to the discomfort of troops who were already very tired.

A small patrol exploring the situation further down the slope of the ridge had a torrid time of it, suffering many casualties; but the final and complete capture of Hill 145 during that day added much to morale. However, by now the German artillery, thanks to the work of their spotter aircraft work, knew full well where the Canadian positions were; thus the entire garrison of SP 7 for a time 'with the exception of an occasional sentry, was obliged to take cover flat on the bottom of the newly dug trench, and even then several casualties occurred.' On that evening, at 7.45pm, the 49th (Edmonton) Battalion took over the front line and the weary men moved back to Villers au Bois. The Battalion entered the line 722 strong; it suffered 302 casualties (eleven officers and 291 other ranks); five officers and forty nine other ranks were killed (Lieutenant Douglas Small is buried in Villers Station in VIII A 9, alongside two of his mess colleagues). Whilst at Villers the Battalion was reinforced with the arrival of an officer and 240 other ranks of the disbanded 73rd (Royal Highlanders) Battalion, practically cancelling out most of the losses suffered on the Ridge.

11 Brigade, 4th Division (Major General D Watson) had the task of taking the highest point of the ridge; on its left 12 Brigade would capture its allotted section of the German line and cover the northern flank, protecting the assault from interference from the Pimple, which would be taken on 10 April. It was substantially reinforced for the attack; an extra battalion was attached to it from 10 Brigade (47th Battalion), as was the 85th (Nova Scotia Highlanders) Battalion. This latter had arrived in France two months earlier to replace the 73rd Battalion, which was due to be disbanded as soon as its part in the battle was over (one wonders what that did for its morale?). The attack on the day on the Brigade's right started off well enough; the 102nd (at the time known as North British Columbians; redesignated Central Ontario in August 1917) got to its objective and the 54th came through to consolidate on Hill 145. However, on the left the 87th (Canadian Grenadier Guards) Battalion made very little progress. The Commanding Officer had requested that a section of the German trenches on his objective should be left largely unscathed by the bombardment by the heavy artillery. This might seem an odd thing to ask, but he was doubtless aware of the vulnerability of his new line from the German positions on the nearby Pimple and possibly wanted to be able to consolidate with the benefit of a largely intact trench. Whatever the reasons, it was to prove a serious tactical error. The German defenders were extremely resolute and this trench became the centre of stout resistance.

The leading wave of the 87th suffered enormous casualties, whilst the 75th (Mississauaga) Battalion, due to pass through it and move on to the final objective, was pinned down in its assembly trenches by well directed machine gun fire. Some men battled on, but then came under fire from flank and rear by machine guns from the uncaptured sector and from Germans who came out of their dugouts and mine shafts after the attacking waves had passed. The moppers-up had become completely enveloped in the push forward and thus this essential task was never effectively carried out. If this were not bad enough, the Germans in the second line position had plenty of time to man their positions, freed from the barrage, which by this stage had passed on over them. The end result was that 11 Brigade's attack on the left completely failed and the success on the right had to be largely abandoned; the 54th (Kootenay, redesignated Central Ontario in August 1917) Battalion had a completely open left flank to deal with and had to fall back to the line taken by the 102nd Battalion. As has been seen above, this had a serious knock-on effect on the neighbouring 3rd Division.

With the 102nd so close to the section of line that had been the cause of most of the problems, it was not possible to bring down artillery fire on to it. At 1pm the 87th Battalion managed to storm this trench, supported by Stokes mortars (one of the few times when this mortar was required in the initial phase of the attack) and machine guns. The 85th were then able to take the two remaining German defensive trenches on the west side of the summit, thereby removing the threat that the fire from these posed to the newly won positions of the neighbouring 7 Brigade. The Germans attempted a counter attack during the night of 9/10 April, using fresh troops who would be launched from positions on the Pimple. But this had all the hallmarks of a rushed decision based on what looked practicable on paper. The men did not get into position until after midnight (a reserve battalion of the 16th Bavarian Division) and even then a number had lost their way and some had even lost their boots because of the mud. The attack came to nothing, seen off by the fire of a single machine gun.

12 Brigade also had an encouraging start, aided by the firing of a couple of mines opposite the front of the 73rd (Royal Highlanders of Canada). Quite understandably, the remaining defenders here were not inclined to stay when the Canadians began to advance. The first German line was soon taken, and the 73rd set about creating a substantial flank defensive position. The **72nd (Seaforth Highlanders of Canada)** Battalion and the 38th (Ottawa) Battalion on the right, continued the move forward against increasingly strong opposition. The second trench was successfully bombed from the flank by the 72nd when a frontal assault failed. Whilst the Germans were kept occupied to their front, three men worked their way round to the right flank of Clutch Trench.

Armed chiefly with bombs, which they manipulated with unerring efficiency, the three proceeded to take, unaided, about 400 yards of the strongly held German support line. Slipping from traverse to traverse along the trench, the dauntless trio advanced, clearing or partially clearing each bay by throwing bombs into it before entering and finishing the job with revolver and cold steel. Time after time Boches, braver and more cunning than the rest, attempted to waylay them by lying in wait in the doorways of their dugouts, only to be met by a courage more deadly than their own. Pushing the now thoroughly demoralised Boches before them, the three of them continued their advance (northwards) until practically the whole trench on the Battalion front was cleared. Aided by the arrival of the frontal attacking troops, they drove the completely routed Bavarians to their destruction in the heavy standing barrage, which was protecting the left flank of the attack.

It was perhaps as well that they succeeded when they did; the Battalion started the attack with only 400 effectives; by the end of it only sixty two who went over the top were not casualties. The 38th Battalion, meanwhile, was losing the barrage as a consequence of the appalling nature of the ground, which was badly cut up. Nicholson notes that some of the wounded fell into the water-filled shell holes and were drowned. Germans emerged from previously undiscovered dugouts, relatively safe now that the barrage had moved on. It was during this phase of the action that Captain TW MacDowell won a VC to add to the DSO he had won on the Somme. 'Some 75 occupants of a dugout just over the crest were confronted by Captain MacDowell, who called on them to surrender, tricking them into supposing that he had a large force behind him. They were marched out in groups of twelve, only to find that the 'large force' consisted of two men' (Nicholson).

Despite the loss of the barrage, the advance of 12 Brigade had been shielded from effective observation and intervention from the Pimple by a smoke barrage and, fortuitously, by the frequent heavy snow flurries. As this cleared, however, heavy machine gun fire was brought to bear, which made the task of the 72nd Battalion ever more difficult. Having suffered very heavy casualties, the best it could do was to get a foothold into the third German trench, on the far side of the crest. The 78th (Winnipeg Grenadiers), meanwhile, passed through the remnants of the 38th Battalion, to become victims of the failure of 11 Brigade's attack. Besides losing the supporting barrage, the Battalion came under fire from the uncaptured positions on Hill 145; whilst it was also under observation from the Pimple. Thus, although very weak elements of the Battalion did approach the final objective to the west of Givenchy, they were driven back by a resolute German attack by men of Bavarian Infantry Regiment 11 which, however, failed to get the German line back to their second trench. The 46th (South Saskatchewan) Battalion provided troops in the afternoon who managed to capture some disputed craters just beyond this second trench.

It is probably worth noting here that much of the ground over which this attack was being conducted was behind the old British front line before it was lost in May 1916; the German second trench was largely a reversal of that British trench. Thus the ground had already been heavily fought over, and there were a number of craters in the area left over from the early days of the underground war on the ridge, some of them dating back to the French occupation of the line. At the end of the day the situation was far from satisfactory on the 4th Division's front. The attack by 11 Brigade had, to an extent, been salvaged from its initial setback; but the failure to take the final objectives by 12 Brigade (indeed, to get over the crest) meant that the projected attack by 10 Brigade on the following day could not take place. The original planning had allowed for this contingency, however. At 6.00 pm Watson ordered the unused two battalions of 10 Brigade to complete 11 Brigade's advance to the Red Line the following afternoon.

This time the attack proceeded much more successfully; which is perhaps understandable. For this time the artillery would be working closely with the attack, providing the covering barrage that had been lost in the attack the day previously. The German Hangstellung [Slope Position] (located to the immediate east of the road to the east of the Memorial) was brought under sustained fire and the 50th (Calgary) [left] and the 44th (Manitoba, redesignated New Brunswick in August 1918) [right] Battalions charged down the slopes and swept into the final objective. Though it was a highly successful operation, resulting in a large number of prisoners, the 50th Battalion suffered 238 casualties. In the process one of its members won the Victoria Cross. His citation reads:

> *For most conspicuous bravery in attack. When the advance of our troops was held up by an enemy machine gun, which was inflicting severe casualties, Private Pattison, with utter disregard*

Canadian troops delighted to have been relieved.

of his own safety, sprang forward and, jumping from shell hole to
shell hole, reached cover within thirty yards of the enemy gun.
From this point, in the face of heavy fire, he hurled bombs,
killing and wounding some of the crew, then rushed forward,
overcoming and bayoneting the surviving five gunners. His
valour and initiative undoubtedly saved the situation and made
possible the further advance to the objective.

The VC was gazetted in August; John Pattison was killed on 3 June 1917 and he is buried in La Chaudière Military Cemetery (VI C14). He was 41 when he won the VC; he had a son who also served in the war. He is the only one of the three VC winners that won their decoration in the battle and were subsequently killed in the war who has his own headstone (Sifton is in a mass grave in Lichfield Crater and Milne is on the Vimy Memorial. MacDowell died in 1960). The 44th Battalion worked its way into the northern end of La Folie wood, removing the last vestiges of German opposition there, and finally successfully connected the left flank of the 3rd Division with that of the left flank of the 4th. A thought should be spared for the quality of the German defence. Tiny surviving remnants of units put up an extraordinarily strong defence, having endured days of harsh punishment from the massed allied artillery, as well as undergoing the traumas of the attack of the 9 April. Those Bavarians were formidable and worthy opponents of the men of the 4th Division. On the morning of the 10th, 12 Brigade's forward battalions worked their way forward, completed the capture of Hill 145 and made their way to the final objective, the Givenchy Line.

The Postscript: The Capture of the Pimple, 12 April

The Germans retained their hold on the Pimple (and, indeed, put fresh troops on to it) after all the rest of the Ridge had fallen. From this height at the end of the ridge the Germans had reasonable observation along the Zouave Valley, which had to be crossed by allied troops approaching the front line. It was from here that the Germans had considered launching their own offensive in early April, discussed elsewhere in this book. It was quite evident that the defenders were in a very difficult position after the events of 9 – 11 April. A huge and overpowering number of guns were available to the Canadians; the British to the north had not so far been involved in frontal assaults and would doubtless be used in any attack on the position; whilst the Germans approaches to the Pimple sector were now generally dominated by the allies. However, it could be argued that by keeping this tactically very important piece of ground for as long as possible the Germans could hinder the forward movement of the Canadian Corps and certainly make the task much more difficult. It will be recalled that the original intention was to take the position on 10 April but that events to the immediate south, around Hill 145, meant that troops earmarked for this attack had to be deployed to complete the capture of the highest point on the ridge.

The Canadian attack was to be launched along a front of approximately a thousand yards by three battalions; from the right these were the 44th, the 50th and the 46th. To the north, their left, the 24th Division would complete the capture of the Lorette spur by taking the Bois en Hache, on its eastern slopes. To soften the defences up even further, a heavy bombardment was opened on the enemy's communication trenches and the approaches to Givenchy from the rear; whilst Givenchy itself was given harsh treatment as well as being gassed by the RE's Special Company (a euphemism for the specialist gas troops). At 5am the Canadian attack commenced, signalled by a massive barrage

Lieutenant Clifford Wells BA. A graduation photograph from John Hopkins University, June 1914.

provided by over a hundred field guns on the German front line trenches. The weather once more favoured the attackers, who had the benefit of a strong following wind, which was accompanied by blinding snow. Perforce, the Germans had brought fresh troops into the line – in one respect stiffening the defences, in another weakening them because of their limited knowledge of the terrain. On the other hand, the attackers had to make their advance over very difficult ground, waterlogged conditions making movement exceptionally difficult, with mud often thigh deep.

The 44th and 50th Battalions, setting off at 5.05am, had a reasonably easy approach and took the first two lines of German trenches on the Pimple itself and in Givenchy Wood. The bombardment had done its job, all but obliterating the trenches and making them practically indistinguishable from the shell ravaged landscape, further tortured by the consequences of the particularly heavy mine warfare that had been going on in the sector for well over a year. By 6am both of these battalions were on their objective, encountering more stubborn resistance as they continued their push forward. For the hapless defenders there was little prospect of a safe retreat into Givenchy, especially on the right where there were no shattered stumps of trees, the remnants of Givenchy Wood, to provide some sort of cover. For a time there were problems with maintaining contact with the Canadian brigade on the right of the attack: the ground was simply so churned up that it was practically impossible to identify the objective. One officer, Lieutenant Henry Lewis, was killed whilst trying to rectify this situation (he is buried in Cabaret Rouge British Cemetery, XV M 25).

However, the further to the north the battle raged, the more difficult the going was. German machine gunners were able to cause severe difficulties to the advancing men of 73 Brigade, 24th Division, especially on the right of its attack. They were able to fire in enfilade from positions inside Givenchy Wood, which was eventually cleared by the 50th Battalion. Equally threatened were the men of the 46th Battalion, which enjoyed the unofficial title of the 'Suicide' Battalion. Although they took their objectives, it was at a cost of some fifty percent casualties from amongst the men of the two forward companies. One survivor described the first moments of the advance: 'We hadn't gone three or four steps when the little fellow who loaded the rifle grenades for me had his head blown off. I was looking right at him and all of a sudden his face just vanished. I had bits of his brain scattered all over my tunic.'

Consolidation rooted out remaining Germans from Grenadier Guard Regiment 5 who had been able to take shelter in the confusion that was Givenchy wood (even now it clearly bears the marks of the war). Thus the ridge was taken and consolidated, not to pass into German hands again. The 44th Battalion commemorated their action here with a memorial; partially dismantled soon after the war, when work began on the Vimy Memorial, the concrete surrounds remained, with the number 44 clearly visible at the top, until the farmer decided to remove the last traces a few years ago.

Let the final words come from the farewell letter sent to Frances Wells, the mother of Lieutenant Clifford Wells, whose account of the battle opened this chapter. Clifford's father, an academic and Baptist minister, died when he was six and his mother married a widower, also an academic and Baptist minister. Clifford had a brother George, with whom he was very close; and his very close relationship with his mother ('Molly') shines out from his letters. The letter, of course, is sentimental – what else could it be: but it expressed sentiments that were repeated in thousands of similar letters sent home by soldiers of both sides during this horrific conflict:

My darling Mother,

I am sending this note to George for him to give you if I am killed. It is just a last message of love to you, Molly, for I do love you more than anyone else in the world. You have been the best mother I ever knew or heard of, and my greatest grief is the sorrow which my death will cause you. Please do not grief too

A beaming Vimykämpfer of RIR 262 extremely pleased to have survived.

much, mother dear. Remember that I died doing my duty – the very best I could do for the cause which we all believe is right – and that we shall be together in heaven, where God will wipe every tear from our eyes. God and heaven seem more real here in the presence of suffering and death than they ever did before.

Give my love to dear father. He has been all that a father could be to me for many years, and I am deeply grateful to him. If I had lived I would have striven to be a credit and comfort to him always. Emma and George and Ned and Rae and Croy [his brother and half brother and sisters] – *I think very tenderly of all of them, and feel that I have not deserved all the love that they have manifested towards me. I pray every night for their welfare and happiness.*

Molly dear, there is nothing more I can say. This is just a message of love and gratitude and, I trust, of love. Do not grieve mother dear. All is well with me, and we shall meet again never to part.

Goodbye, my own darling mother,

News of his death reached the family on 12 May; on 20 May his mother died after being fatally burned in a tragic accident a couple of days earlier. Lieutenant Clifford Wells is buried at Orchard Dump Cemetery, Grave IX J 1

Mass trench burial east of Vimy.

Chapter Five

THE GERMAN DEFENCE OF VIMY RIDGE
1 MARCH – MID-APRIL 1917

Note that German time, which was one hour ahead of Allied time, is used in this chapter.

In late February the Germans conducted a major reorganisation and strengthening of their positions on Vimy Ridge. 79th Reserve Division, a battle-hardened division, with a great deal of previous experience on the Eastern Front, was inserted into the right flank of 'Group Vimy', between 16th Bavarian Infantry Division of 'Group Souchez' and 1st Bavarian Reserve Division. The troops had barely had time to orientate themselves than they were subjected to the biggest raid of the winter.

The Canadian Raid on 1 March
Hardly had the 79th Reserve Division settled into its new positions than the 4th Canadian Division stationed opposite attempted to launch strong forces forward in an ambitious attempt to inflict large scale casualties and to gauge the strength of the German defences. The Germans themselves felt subsequently that it was such a large operation that it had actually been intended as a surprise attempt to gain a lodgement on the ridge itself. The raid was directed against the northern section of the ridge which, with a depth of only 700 metres, was the sector where the Germans felt themselves to be most

Mortar Company RIR 262, commanded by Leutnant Matsch.

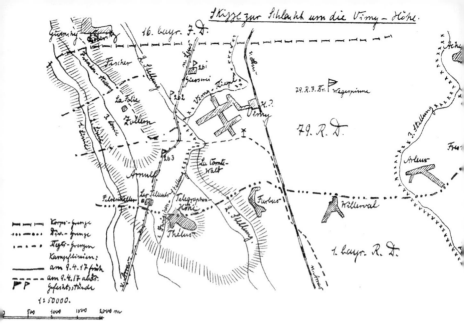

12. A German sketch map of the 79th Reserve Division Sector.

vulnerable to a breakthrough. A short, but extremely violent, concentration of artillery fire was intended to force the occupants of the front line trenches to keep their heads down and, at the same time, to neutralise the batteries in and around Vimy, which were swiftly shrouded in poisonous clouds of gas. The attackers' fire had a particularly severe effect in the area to the north of Vimy where, within a short time, three guns from a battery of Reserve Field Artillery Regiment 63 were destroyed [i.e. three out of four].

At 4.00 am, artificial smoke spread all along the battle trenches of the defenders. Simultaneously dense lines of Canadians lunged forward from their jumping-off points. One wave after another surged against the German positions. The clashes were particularly heavy against the trenches of Reserve Infantry Regiment 261 and these spilled over on the right against the sector of Bavarian Infantry Regiment 11 of the Bavarian 16th Infantry Division and left against Reserve Infantry Regiment 262. Flares shot up everywhere calling for artillery defensive fire. Every gun that was still operational fired as fast as it could, but artillery fire alone was insufficient to hold the attackers' assault. Fortunately for the defence, manning the trenches and shell holes were defenders with rifles and machine guns at the ready. As far as Reserve Infantry Regiment 261 was concerned, the main weight of the raid was held by 2nd, 4th, 9th and 11th Companies. Their combined fire mowed down the assaulting Canadians in dense masses and the attack petered out in front of the barbed wire obstacle. A renewal of the attack at 6.00 am suffered the same fate. Leutnant Hoppe and Vizefeldwebel Hentschel of 4th Company and Gefreiter Königstein and Signaller Soch of 2nd Company, in particular, distinguished themselves during the defeat of this raid.

Only to the right in Sector *Döberitz*, defended by Bavarian Infantry Regiment 11, did some Canadians succeed in breaking into the forward position, but a violent counter-stroke by elements of 1st Battalion Reserve Infantry Regiment 261 soon restored the situation. That was the final action of what had been a disastrous Canadian raid. Subsequent interrogation of two corporals and eight men of A and B Companies 72nd Battalion and two corporals and six men from B and C Companies 75th Battalion yielded a mass of detailed low-level intelligence, including the very significant point that although the attackers had been shown a model of the German trench system, there had been no rehearsals for this ambitious operation. Later raids and attacks were always preceded by careful practices – possibly as a result of this debacle. A very large number of dead Canadian soldiers lay out in No Man's Land, but the defenders also suffered some men killed and many wounded. During this battle, Leutnant Karl Lieser, 12th Company Reserve Infantry Regiment 261, became the first officer of the division to be killed on the Western Front. [Karl Lieser is buried in Block 9, Grave 533 of the German cemetery at Neuville St Vaast/Maison Blanche]. Fourteen other NCOs and men from RIR 261 were killed during the raid and fifty wounded, as were nine members of 6th and 7th Companies RIR 262.

The following day Oberstleutnant von Goerne, commander of Reserve Infantry Regiment 261, offered the Canadians a short ceasefire, so that they could recover their dead. Writing about the incident later, Goerne recalled:

Only the English [sic] *Major Lucas was hanging on the barbed wire obstacle; otherwise none of the enemy dead could be seen from the trenches* [the body of Major Frederick Lucas was recovered during the

Oberstleutnant von Goerne, commander of Reserve Infantry Regiment 261.

truce and is buried at Villers Station British cemetery in grave VI E 2]. *According to the statements of our men, the enemy must have suffered significant casualties. Because I wanted to convince myself of the existence of these allegedly enormous casualties, I went forward of the barbed wire under cover of the fog on the morning of 2nd March from the trenches of 9th Company. I was accompanied by Hauptmann von Koppelow, commander of the 12th Company. Here, hard up against the barbed wire, we came across the dead Canadians, who were indeed very numerous. In fact all the shell holes were filled with the dead. When we were approximately in the centre of No Man's Land, where we could just make out the outlines of the enemy trenches, a shot rang out from there. Hauptmann von Koppelow raised his stick and shouted towards the English [sic] trenches that they should cut out that stupid firing. I said, "Call out to them that the chap should come over here."*

I should here explain: Until he became a Fahnenjunker [Officer Cadet], *Hauptmann von Koppelow had grown up in England. His mother was English. Whenever he spoke German, his English accent was very marked. He also looked very much like an Englishman; to such an extent that, on several occasions, persons behind the front with nothing better to do, wanted to arrest him. Initially there was no response to Hauptmann von Koppelow's shouts. Finally a steel helmet and, gradually, a head appeared. Apparently the chap did not trust our peaceful intentions, but in the end he came forward. We asked him where his battalion or regimental commander might be and said that he was to tell him that he should come and meet us. It was still rather foggy, so that although they were only sixty metres away, we could barely make out the enemy trenches. Nobody fired, because Hauptmann von Koppelow had shouted out once more in his perfect English that nobody was to be so stupid as to shoot.*

After about ten minutes an English [sic] major arrived, accompanied by two runners armed with rifles. We saluted each other in silence. I opened the conversation, drawing attention to the many dead and pointing out that here and there amongst them there could well be wounded. If he was agreeable, we could negotiate a means of recovering the fallen. He agreed. In the meantime visibility had become clearer and curious faces were to be seen everywhere looking out from the trenches. We both called several men to us and gave instructions that the word was to be passed along the trenches that there was to be no firing. In addition both sides telephoned higher authority to request permission, which was granted. The artillery was also instructed not to open fire.

Meanwhile additional officers and runners had arrived from both sides. I had sent for Oberleutnant von Trotha, Oberleutnant Zickner, Rittmeister von Schwerin and several others. Oberleutnants von Trotha and Zickner [Zickner was later killed as a Hauptmann on 16 August 1917 at Langemark] in particular spoke good English. By now about ten Canadians and ten members of the 261st were standing next to one another. We agreed that a line, to which we would carry the dead, should be drawn in the middle. Here they would be received by the enemy. Assault ladders which had been intended for use during the assault and which were lying everywhere in profusion, were used to mark the line. Neither party was to cross this line and there was to be no fraternisation. Now the work began. Our men carried the dead on assault ladders to the centre and from there they were taken by the Canadians back to their own trenches. The whole of No Man's Land soon resembled an ant hill as, across the entire regimental front, men hurried to and fro with [these improvised] stretchers.

We officers stood together with the Canadians on one spot, all of us with pistols on our belts. There was no opportunity for either side to examine the opposing positions. A fleeting glance at the other positions was the most that could have been achieved. Eventually I offered the Canadian officers a cigarette. They all lit up, with the exception of the Canadian major, who put his cigarette away. I asked him why he was not smoking it and he explained that he wanted to keep it as a souvenir. I asked him if he would like another one to smoke and offered him one, which he lit. A conversation never really got going. There was really no point in asking anything, because nobody could have given an answer.

By 2.00 pm about 600-800 dead men had been carried over [This figure is somewhat inflated, though it is true that a great many bodies were recovered]. We then decided to call a halt for the day, so that it would be possible this same day to transport the dead further to the rear and agreed, having synchronised watches and decided on agreed signals, to resume work the following day at 8.00 am provided that our superiors were in

127

agreement. We further agreed that there would be no firing before 6.00 pm in order to facilitate the move to the rear of the fallen, but that after that the war would continue in the usual manner.

We went our separate ways at 2.00 pm and even shook hands. Shortly after we had parted, an English [sic] officer of the divisional staff appeared at our trench. He was there to pass on the particular thanks of the divisional commander and to state that the gesture would be reciprocated if a similar situation arose in future. I must state that the Canadians, by their upright military bearing and their behaviour made an outstanding impression on us. They could almost have been from the 261st!

Rittmeister von Schwerin had made use of the opportunity to verify the fields of fire of his machine guns and to adjust some of them. Unfortunately it was not possible to continue with the recovery operation the following day. Our superiors were in agreement, but our Bavarian neighbours, having initially agreed, withdrew their assent. All members of the 261st, who were present for this remarkable episode, the like of which never occurred on any other occasion during the war, will certainly often have pleasant memories of it.

On 5 March battle recommenced. As the weather cleared, it was possible from Vimy Ridge to observe a long way into the Canadian rear areas. The road from Arras to Souchez, which ran parallel to the front, the hill of Notre Dame de Lorette and the ruins of the villages of Souchez, Carency and Neuville-St. Vaast were all clearly visible. But the weather soon turned again. The mild spring days were followed by cold temperatures and sleet, or streaming rain, which filled both trenches and craters with water.

The Preparatory Artillery Bombardment
From the end of March the British massed their assault divisions opposite the German Sixth Army either side of Arras. With its main effort on the left flank, their aim was to break through between Souchez and Quéant via Vimy Ridge and along the banks of the Scarpe towards Cambrai. Simultaneously thousands of guns and mortars opened up destructive fire at the German front opposite, aided by numerous squadrons of aircraft. This fire soon put anything experienced on the Somme in the shade. A great deal more ammunition was fired - according to some estimates about twice as much ammunition was fired during the first week at Vimy as during

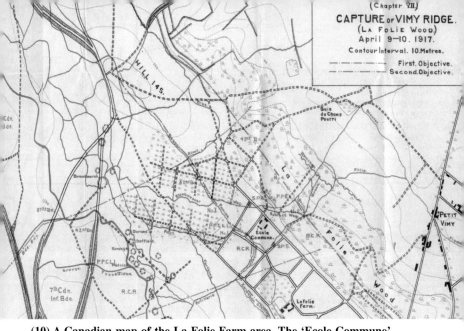

(10) A Canadian map of the La Folie Farm area. The 'Ecole Commune' was located alongside the Route Pietonnière, which runs through the modern Vimy Forest.

(30) Modern map of Visitor Centre and preserved trenches Vimy Memorial site [© VAC]. Note that maps 30-32 are slightly modified extracts from the map which accompanies the Self-Guided Tour pamphlet.

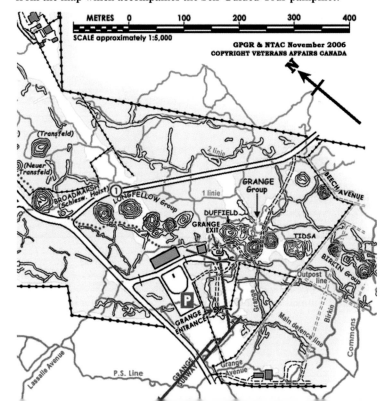

Diagram 3 Tunnels around the Grange Subway area. [© Durand Group]

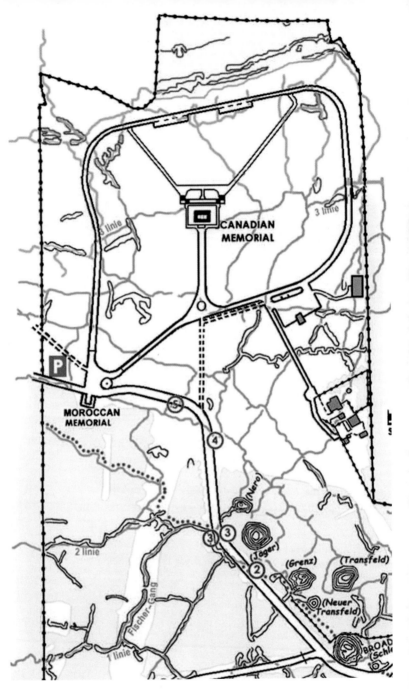

(32) Modern map Vimy Memorial site Broadmarsh Crater – Canadian
memorial Hill 145. [© VAC]

3

Above: German pump house beneath Vimy Ridge. [Photo: Durand Group]

Above right: Smashed trench mortar.

Right: Members of the Durand Group investigating the Goodman Subway.

Below: A waterproof bag containing ammonal.

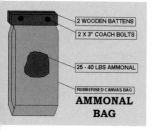

2 WOODEN BATTENS

2 X 3" COACH BOLTS

25 - 40 LBS AMMONAL

RUBBERISED CANVAS BAG

AMMONAL BAG

Head and names carved in Goodman Subway. [Durand Group]

Four leaf clover and the name and unit of AF Sutcliffe, Goodman Subway.
© Durand Group / VAC

A modern view towards Loos from Hanseatenweg on the eastern (reverse) slope of Hill 145.

A modern view of the Pimple and Givenchy Wood (in the distance on the right of the photograph) from Hill 145.

The Lorette Spur, viewed from Canadian Cemetery No 2.

3rd Canadian Division memorial.This is approximately on the site of La Folie Farm. Access is easy but parking is non-existent (just off the the Memorial-Lens Road) in Vimy National Forest. It is very poorly sign posted.

A Canadian Service of Remembrance at Canadian Cemetery No 2. The nearest Royal Canadian Mounted Policemen to the camera are standing almost directly above one of the exits from Tottenham Subway.

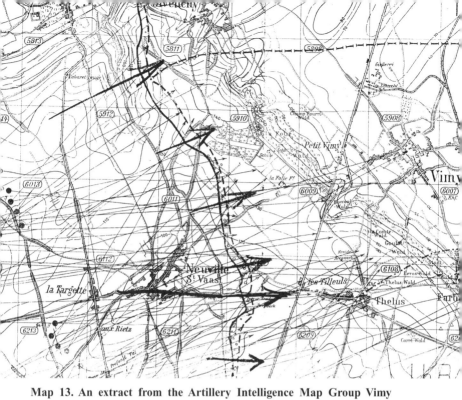

Map 13. An extract from the Artillery Intelligence Map Group Vimy showing battery positions which had definitely been located during the week 15 – 22 March.

A German 210 mm howitzer in action in Vimy April 1917.

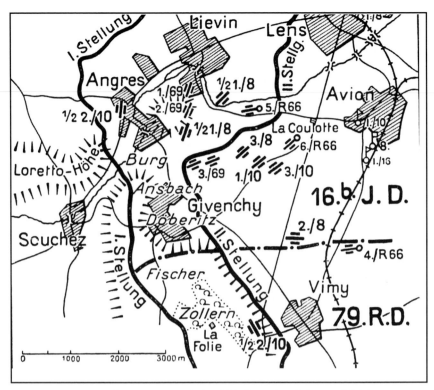

Map 14. A German map of the 16th Bavarian Infantry Division area, including battery locations.

the bombardment prior to the Battle of the Somme, whilst during the second week the figure was six times as much – and, furthermore, the length of front to be bombarded was considerably shorter. Soon all the positions north and south of the Scarpe were shattered and the German batteries were drenched repeatedly with gas.

The heaviest weight of fire was directed against the ridge between Givenchy and Farbus. Whilst it was possible during the first days of the artillery battle to establish the approximate weight of British artillery fire (most days 12,000 – 15,000 shells rained down on the positions of the 79th Reserve Division), later such was the intensity of the fighting that further attempts to count the quantities fired became impossible. Although initially the greatest weight of fire came down on Sector *Fischer*, later it switched, with even greater intensity, to Sector *Arnulf*. From the end of March built up areas and roads a long way behind the lines also suffered from British artillery fire. After several of the French inhabitants had been killed in this way, the local population was moved out of the endangered villages to the rear. The launch site of the observation balloon at Acheville was frequently a target for the British guns.

From the beginning of April it was no longer possible to make good the damage caused by the fire. Such was the effect of the heavy shells in conjunction with the overwhelmingly wet weather, that the positions were soon reduced to crater fields of glutinous mud, within which only a few of the dugouts survived the bombardment – and the majority of these were wrongly placed in the front line. Just to move a small load of ammunition trench stores or rations, took the whole energy of a man for a complete night. These conditions created gigantic problems as far as ammunition resupply was concerned – especially for the artillery. Wherever the wagons pulled by teams of eight horses were unable to go, manpower had to be substituted to haul forward the heavy loads. Despite all this, not only was it possible to move forward the division's daily requirements (on some days the divisional artillery fired up to 2,000 rounds), but also plentiful ammunition was stockpiled in the fire positions in anticipation of the need to counter the forthcoming major offensive. Although the constantly shot-up communications cables (even the cables buried two metres deep were broken again and again

Trenches on Vimy Ridge levelled by the bombardment, late March 1917.

131

Major Freiherr von Rotenhan, Commander RIR 262.

by direct hits), were supplemented by radio and light signalling stations, effective fire by the German artillery was constantly being disrupted, due to the destruction of observation posts and means of communications.

The numerical superiority of the British air squadrons made itself felt in a thoroughly unpleasant manner; this despite the fact that German airmen, above all the red aircraft of Rittmeister von Richthofen's (The Red Baron) squadron, flung themselves into battle, frequently driving them off with serious losses. Between 4 and 8 April 1917, for example, the RFC lost no fewer than seventy-five aircraft shot down and a further fifty six aircraft in accidents. At that time the German Albatross was more than a match for any of the British fighter types. Not for nothing was that month known as 'Bloody April'.

From the second half of March 1917 onwards there were raids and aggressive patrol actions every night. This inevitably led to prisoners being taken, which meant that as the day of the assault approached the defence was able to build up a more or less complete picture concerning Canadian intentions. Underground the battle swayed to and fro ceaselessly. Craters, which had been blown by German engineers, were immediately occupied by the German infantry. The German engineers decided, on the basis of reports from their listening teams during the first half of March, that the British sappers had worked their way round their tunnels and had begun to approach their lines closely in Sector *Zollern*. As a result, the engineer commander ordered the mine galleries in Mining Sector 1 to be charged and Galleries 35, 36, 37 and 38 to be blown. The war diary of the 2nd Battalion Reserve Infantry Regiment 262 records a statement by the miners that this was one of the largest explosions on the Western Front, if not the largest, up until that date. The plan was to blow the galleries using 700 Zentner [i.e. 700 x 50 kg = 35 tonnes] of explosive. The mines involved produced what the Allies later called the Longfellow Craters, which are located between Broadmarsh Crater and the Visitor Centre of the Canadian Memorial.

The explosion took place in the northern part of Sector *Zollern*

A gun of Reserve Field Artillery Regiment 63 moves forward through a contaminated area. Both men and horses are masked up.

which was the responsibility of Reserve Infantry Regiment 262. Their regimental history recorded the incident as follows:

During the night 22/23 March, charging of the four mine galleries was completed and the explosion took place at 4.10 am. Everything went according to plan. Our own lines were barely damaged and the rim of the easternmost crater, which was approximately four metres high, was occupied by us. The explosion took place in front of the 5th Company sector, which at the time was being commanded temporarily by Reserve Leutnant Mauer. The company was deployed on the right (northern flank) of the regiment (Zollern I.) Altogether four craters were produced. Unfortunately during this operation two of our comrades, Unteroffizier Gürtler and Grenadier Bartel, were shot through the head and killed by British [sic] snipers. With the death of Unteroffizier Gürtler, a secondary school teacher by profession, 5th Company lost a man who would never be forgotten because of his exemplary soldierly bearing and unshakeable calmness. The extent of the explosion, during which Engineer (Mining) Company 293 especially distinguished itself, was underlined by the fact that during the previous nights a relay

133

of 400 men of 1st Battalion Reserve Infantry Regiment 262
brought forward approximately 150 Zentner of explosives to the
front line.

Losses in men and equipment increased noticeably at the beginning of
April. Just before Easter it was possible to make a final check on the
fighting strength of those battalions of 79th Reserve Division who
were stationed forward. The general situation was as follows. There
were one to two companies forward in the first two lines of trenches.
One or two companies were stationed in the third trench, in support,
and the rest were under command of the battalion commanders in the
reserve role. The trench fighting strength of the companies varied
from fifty to ninety riflemen and this was reduced considerably further,

**15. A German map showing the main Allied thrusts and move of
reinforcements between Vimy Ridge and the Scarpe, 9 April.**

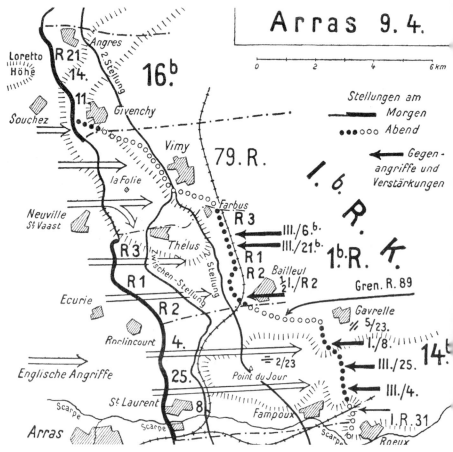

prior to the start of the major offensive. Because the battalion reserves were reduced to a few small groups, the Division directed the move forward of one company from each of the resting battalions into the battle zone in order to form, along with engineer companies, a small reserve at the disposal of the regiments. The machine guns, including the six belonging to Machine Gun Sharp Shooter Troop 20, which were only deployed at the end of March, were arranged in depth in amongst the craters where, in conjunction with the few remaining undamaged mortars, they formed the backbone of the positions, which by now were only thinly held.

The attackers' superiority in materiel was overwhelming. The Germans believed that for each kilometre of front north of the Scarpe, approximately 140 guns and 50 mortars were firing. As far as the 79th Reserve Division was concerned, this meant that the fire of over 400 guns and 150 mortars could be brought to bear. Against this, it could only deploy eighty-nine guns and a few mortars, of which many were destroyed during the preliminary bombardment. It is little wonder that the soldiers in the forward trenches were left with the impression that they were being sacrificed unprotected to the destructive fire. In the face of all the Allied preparatory fire, it became increasingly difficult to transport sufficient food forward to the front line. Frequently the soldiers were reduced to bread and water which, contaminated though it was with gas or other filth, they were reduced to collecting from the shell holes. Their psychological state was not improved either because they believed that there was a strong chance that Allied mining operations meant they were occupying locations which might be blown up at any moment. In the event the Canadian view was that the ground was already sufficiently difficult to traverse, without adding to the number of craters already in existence. Nevertheless all these pressures put together led to a noticeable decline in the strength and morale of the troops.

Throughout the bombardment extensive use was made of gas. On 4 April, for example, there was a concentrated gas attack on *Zollern* North. Because some men moving forward in a relief operation removed their gas masks too early through impatience or difficulty in seeing to move at night, there were numerous gas casualties. Reserve Leutnant Zeller of 7th Company RIR 262 reported the event as follows:

> *During the evening of 4 April my platoon was due to be relieved by another from 5th Company. The relief was to have started at midnight but suddenly, at 11.00 pm, the Tommies*

launched a gas attack. We were not totally surprised by the attack because we had heard the noise of the installation of cylinders over a period of several days. Being cautious, however, I ordered increased gas readiness as soon as the wind was favourable. In addition we were all outside in the trenches because the Canadians had attacked to our right a short while earlier. The Canadians released two gas clouds and it was possible for us to unmask in between the two waves. I remained unclear why the Canadians had released gas in this way without following it up by an attack. In the front line gas casualties were practically zero, but the relieving troops from 5th Company, who were underway, suffered worse. Some of them were gassed and had to turn about immediately and some men of the sections which completed the forward relief were affected the following day. As a result I, together with half my platoon, had to remain forward in the trenches for an extra day.

On 6 April, Headquarters Sixth Army received instructions from Army Group Crown Prince Rupprecht that they were to call forward formations designated to relieve the front line divisions, but the march forward of these divisions was so delayed that on 9 April they were still not in a position to carry out counter-strokes. After the battle, to this error was ascribed one of the principal causes of the loss of Vimy Ridge – Crown Prince Rupprecht was scathing in his condemnation, writing in his interim after action report on 21 April 1917:

Headquarters Sixth Army was directed to call for the move forward of the [reserve] divisions in good time. Army Headquarters demurred, stating that, 'it did not consider it to be appropriate to move the divisions at the moment. It would disrupt training and lead to over-concentration of forces in the forward area.' I was of the opposite opinion and sent an order by signal directing that the designated divisions, "were to be moved forward immediately into position behind your Group [sectors]". This order arrived at Sixth Army on 6 April.

Despite follow-up discussions on 7 April between the army group chief of staff and operations branch Sixth Army, during which assurances about the forward deployment were given, the moves did not take place and the price paid by the defence was high.

On 7 April the weight of artillery fire slackened noticeably, only to swell once more when the German batteries countered it fiercely. Then, on the afternoon of 8 April (Easter Sunday), it increased to violent drum fire which continued, sometimes at a lesser rate,

Thélus being bombarded, April 1917.

sometimes at a higher one, throughout the following night. It was the start of the final softening up process.

The Major Assault and Break in South of Thélus

When day dawned, wet and cold, at 5.30 am on 9 April, a storm of fire, unparalleled in anyone's experience, crashed down over the German positions. Its impacts were like the deafening roar and tossing of a sea lashed by a hurricane. Everywhere mighty fountains of earth rose in the air. The earth seemed to quake. Whilst the front line was engaged primarily with light guns and mortars, supported by massed machine guns, the support lines and battery positions came under fire from medium, heavy and super-heavy guns, as well as being drenched with gas. The fumes and smoke which hung over the German positions grew into dark masses of cloud, which glowed red. All the roads which the reserves, hurrying forward, would need to use were lashed by fire. Yellow flares rose all along the German lines, but before the defending batteries could begin to bring down defensive fire, the hail of fire lifted from the front lines, only to fall with increased violence on the depth positions. Even the curtains of machine gun fire, which had been raking the German front line parapets, permitting the sentries only to observe by the use of periscopes, lifted. In many places the earth itself opened as mines and subway entrances were blown.

Simultaneously, as an icy wind and squalls of sleet lashed the

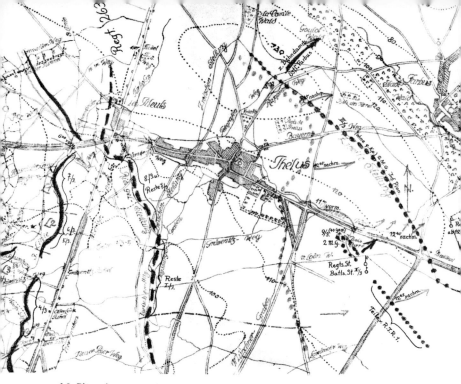

16. Situation map of Bavarian RIR 3-9 April, showing reverses in Thélus area.

muddy scene, from out of the trenches and craters rose the rested, well fed and supplied Canadian assault divisions who rushed towards the German trenches. In the lead were groups armed with hand grenades and pistols and behind them, in one dense mass after another came infantrymen, with their weapons slung and carrying large spades. In those places where the preparatory drum fire and exploding mines had extinguished all resistance, the German lines were soon overrun. But wherever German rifles and machine guns could bring fire to bear, the attackers were checked and their dead mounted up. Whenever bullets and grenades ran out, or where machine guns, clogged with mud failed, fighting continued with bayonets. Down to the south of Thélus, where groups of tanks crawled forward along the roads radiating from Arras, the German First and Second Positions were taken, whilst along the road Arras-Douai and in the valley of the Scarpe, the Third Position was also captured. Opposite Arras a gap twelve kilometres wide and temporarily practically devoid of defenders was created. This could only be closed gradually as reserves were rushed forward from neighbouring sectors unaffected by the attack, to meet the emergency but, due to poor positioning, the arrival of reserve divisions could not be expected before 10 April.

138

The Battle for Vimy Ridge

To the north of Thélus, where on Vimy Ridge the regiments of the 79th Reserve Division waited, nerves on edge, in mud-filled trenches and craters for the start of the offensive, the Canadian attack poured down on them with extreme violence. On the left flank, manning the forward trenches and with their machine guns all destroyed or out of action, were the men of Reserve Infantry Regiment 263, commanded by Oberstleutnant von Behr. Severely weakened by the intense bombardment, only a few of them were still fit to fight, but not until after they had mounted an obstinate defence with hand grenades were they finally overwhelmed. Along with many of his men, Leutnant Runge, commander of the 11th Company, was killed as he fought standing up above the parapet of his trench. Meanwhile resistance continued along the second line. The combined fire of the 12th Company and parts of the 10th Company brought the Canadian attack to a halt, whilst from the *Felsenkeller* [a mined dugout and command post of KTK South of Sector *Arnulf*] to the rear, the reserve platoon of the 10th Company under Vizefeldwebel Borcherding, stormed forward over the cratered landscape to boost the resistance of their comrades. Gradually, however, the deep break into the sector of 1st Bavarian Reserve Division by the 1st Canadian Division south of Les Tilleuls began to have an effect on Sector Arnulf. Constantly reinforced, masses of Canadian attackers advancing from the Arras-Lens road, forced their way against the flanks and rear of the 263rd, rolling them up from the south and surrounding them from the rear. The dead and wounded amongst the German ranks increased. Fighting back bravely at the head of the 4th and 10th Companies, Leutnants Patschek and Korb fell. The courageous Leutnant Zipp, who had rushed forward with his machine gun from the *Zwischenstellung* [Intermediate Position], was also mortally wounded and, nearby, Leutnant Hitzschke also met his death as he attempted to stem the Canadian break in with his machine gun.

It proved to be impossible to hold on to the First Position and, with it, went the Intermediate Position of the Regiment which ran from Thélus to Vimy. The mortars and grenade launcher weapons there fired on for a further twenty minutes, then fell silent. No member of their crews returned. At the very last minute, Major Meyer, (commander of the 1st Battalion) and his staff succeeded in breaking through to the railway embankment. In the meantime, led by the regimental commander, Oberstleutnant von Beyr, the 8th Company, which was in reserve, and remnants of the Engineer Company took up a blocking

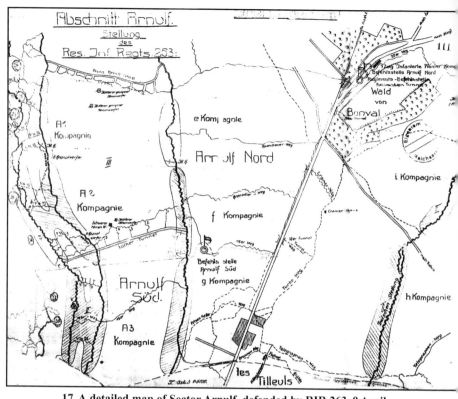

17. A detailed map of Sector Arnulf, defended by RIR 263, 9 April.

The railway underpass south of Vimy where the survivors of RIR 263 rallied on 9 April.

position south of Vimy. Here the attack was held up for hours. Leutnant von Rohrscheidt, commander of the 8th Company, and many other courageous defenders were killed. Finally, the very last of the defenders – five men under an Offizierstellvertreter – withdrew to link up with reinforcements which had arrived at the railway embankment to the south of the Vimy-Acheville underpass. At the Felsenkeller a desperate battle was waged by Hauptmann Geuinzius and Hauptmann Schmidt–Eberstein and the staffs of the 2nd and 3rd Battalions (because of a gas alarm and the onset of the final intense drum fire, the staff of the 2nd Battalion which had been relieved that morning had been unable to get away). They hoped constantly that a counter-attack would come to their rescue, but once one man after man was killed or rendered unfit to fight and machine gun after machine gun was wrecked, the last of the defenders were forced, in the face of overwhelming hand grenade attacks, back into the *Felsenkeller*, where a battle for possession of the final remaining usable exit raged. Two men armed with rifles and grenades kept watch there constantly. When one of the men guarding the entrance was killed or collapsed wounded, he was immediately replaced by one of his comrades, but the number of men fit to fight declined steadily. When on one occasion both men were knocked out simultaneously and were not immediately replaced, the attackers succeeded in forcing a way in. A vigorous intervention with hand grenades by Hauptmann Gueinzius and Hauptmann Schmidt-Eberstein themselves succeeded in driving out the attackers once more. The battle went on for hours, even though the many wounded in the mined dugout nearly suffocated as a result of the poisonous fumes of smoke grenades which the attackers dropped down a ventilation shaft. Not until around 11.30 am, when all the grenades had been thrown and there was no longer any prospect of timely relief, did the remainder of the garrison decide, reluctantly, to surrender. The final resistance in Sector *Arnulf* had been overcome.

Writing about the events of the day later, Major Meyer, commanding officer of 1st Battalion, whose command post in the *Schwabentunnel* in Sector *Arnulf* North was quickly rendered untenable by the outflanking manoeuvres to his south, reported:

> *At 5.30 am, 9 April enemy drum fire, supplemented by machine gun fire, began. It was impossible to observe the position and even flares were barely discernable through the dense smoke of the artillery shells. At 6.30 am the sound of very heavy small arms fire was heard and the message 'Heavy enemy attack' was sent to the rear by light signal. About half an hour*

later, Musketier Hagemann of 2nd Company, who had been wounded, passed the battalion command post with the news that the Canadians had broken through to the right of the battalion position and had already reached the third line. From later accounts of members of the 9th Company of the regiment, it appears that the Canadians overran the right flank of 1st Bavarian Reserve Division and then attacked our companies in overwhelming strength from the flanks and rear.

Musketier Hagemann's statements were unfortunately soon confirmed, because the battalion staff noticed that the Canadian infantry was already not too far off and was bringing a machine gun into action in a ruined house. Because no reserves were available to launch a counter-stroke, the officers and men of the battalion staff left their indefensible dugout and went to occupy the Intermediate Position, from which it would still be possible to organise the defence. On the way two officers and all the ORs, with the exception of two orderlies and three telephonists, were knocked out by heavy enemy fire. The regimental commander [Oberstleutnant von Behr] *was briefed in person by the battalion commander. Major Meyer then received orders, together with Oberleutnant Heinicke, to take 6th Company Reserve Infantry Regiment 261, ten machine guns of Reserve Infantry Regiment 263, three companies of 2nd Battalion Reserve Infantry Regiment 263 and approximately fifty men of 1st Battalion Reserve Infantry Regiment 263, who were back with the heavy baggage, and to defend the line of the railway embankment to the east of Vimy. The vulnerable point of this position was at Farbus Wood where the Canadians could close up to the embankment using covered routes. If they were to succeed in crossing the embankment the danger was that its entire length could be enfiladed by machine gun fire and therefore become untenable.*

Temporarily there was a similar danger for the right flank at Vimy Station, but this was removed through the deployment of 'Detachment von Block' (1st Battalion Infantry Regiment 118 and elements of Reserve Infantry Regiment 262), which subsequently succeeded in counter-attacking as far as the slopes of the so-called Telegraph Hill. During the afternoon of 9 April, large masses of Canadian soldiers were observed assembling in Farbus village, apparently in order to conduct an assault on the railway embankment. At that the battalion commander directed two machine guns into action at the southern underpass where

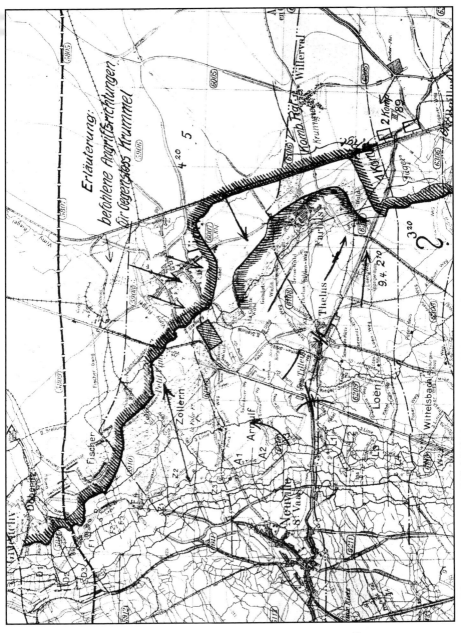

18. Situation map, afternoon 9 April 1917, showing planned counter-stroke Krummel.

143

they could bring enfilade fire down on Farbus Wood. In addition the deployment of 6th Company Reserve Infantry Regiment 261 and a platoon from 2nd Battalion Reserve Infantry Regiment 263, which had thus far been held back, meant that the left flank could be extended to a point to the south of Farbus Wood. The regimental commander was also requested to make forces available to reinforce and thus improve the security of the threatened left flank.

A little while later enemy cavalry was observed in the area of Willerval. At approximately the same time two companies (10th and 12th Companies Reserve Fusilier Regiment 34) arrived. One company was deployed to strengthen the left flank, whilst the other company remained concentrated behind the right flank in case the enemy succeeded in breaking through at Vimy. In the meantime the enemy kept the railway embankment and the two flanks in particular under fire by heavy shells and shrapnel. Towards evening Oberstleutnant von Behr arrived once more at the railway embankment in order to direct a counter-attack. This was to sweep round the flank of Detachment von Block, roughly in the area of Petit Vimy, and to be directed against Telegraph Hill. The troops which had been subordinated to Major Meyer were initially to support his attack by means of machine gun fire,

Canadian Cavalry patrol moving forward, 9 April.

then to undertake a frontal attack. This action was begun, but had to be halted when information arrived that the Bavarians had not succeeded in recapturing Farbus; that it was still in Canadian hands, which meant that the left flank of the attack would have been in acute danger.

During the night the companies were withdrawn to the railway embankment. They were reinforced by, amongst other units, elements of Reserve Infantry Regiment 224, which had been placed at the disposal of 1st Bavarian Reserve Division, but which had strayed rather too far to the right as they advanced and so had become mixed up with the battle line of Detachment Meyer. To the left 12th Company Reserve Fusilier Regiment 34 was now deployed, with its left flank resting on the road Willerval – Farbus Station. To its south there was a gap of 800 metres for which no troops were available to fill. Also that same night two machine guns were deployed in the area of the windmill at the southwestern exit of Vimy. Their role was to secure the left flank of Detachment von Block, which was located around the Vimy crossroads. During the morning of 10 April, Oberstleutnant *von Beyr, to whom Detachment von Block was also subordinated, withdrew on order of brigade to the cross roads about 1,200 metres further to the east. Two newly-arrived companies of Infantry Regiment 64 were deployed in the second line to the east of Farbus in order to improve the security of the railway embankment.*

A short time later 9th Company Reserve Fusilier Regiment 34 arrived at the railway embankment. Two of its platoons were used to occupy the southern edge of Vimy and so improve the security of the left flank of Detachment von Block and one platoon was deployed to the north of Vimy Station to secure up to the right. Towards the afternoon a weak enemy force attacked the left flank near to Farbus Wood, but was easily repulsed. During the evening Hauptmann Lüters, commander of 1st Battalion Infantry Regiment 118, who was in telephone contact with Major Meyer but not Hauptmann von Block, told the former that he had been attacked by strong forces and had been forced back into the Second Position. He had suffered about 30% casualties and required reinforcements, small arms ammunition and grenades. Because links to regiment were destroyed, Major Meyer allocated to Hauptmann Lüters 1st Battalion Reserve Infantry Regiment 262, 10th and 12th Companies Reserve

Fusilier Regiment 34 and 3rd Platoon 9th Company Reserve Fusilier Regiment 34. This information was passed immediately to brigade and later, when communications were restored, to the regiment. Patrols launched by 3rd Battalion Reserve Fusilier Regiment 34 established that the enemy was digging in along the wood edge to the south of Vimy. Weak sallies from this location were beaten off easily. The ground between the villages of Farbus and Vimy was free of enemy troops.

In Sector *Zollern*, which was defended by Reserve Infantry Regiment 262, the Canadian assault was preceded with massive mine explosions, which carried off much of the garrison of the front line. The few remaining defenders deployed in other positions were too few in number and could only put up temporary resistance. The attackers were not

Major Reschke, Commanding Officer Fusilier (3rd) Battalion RIR 262.

halted until just before the third line. As they then began to fall back in the face of the murderous fire laid down by the 262nd, masses more descended upon the flanks and rear of the defenders and forced them back in turn. Putting up a determined defence, Leutnant Niekutowski fell at the head of the 6th Company, along with many courageous grenadiers of the 2nd Battalion. Leutnant Wilke too was killed, together with many of his fusiliers. Isolated pockets of resistance were able to hold out temporarily, whilst other groups were able to break through to the rear, bearing reports of the imminent loss of the First Position.

The commanders of the engaged battalions – the Fusilier [3rd] and 2nd – deployed their weak reserves (the 10th and elements of the 7th Companies) in a counter-stroke. Major Reschke, commander of the Fusilier Battalion, soon found himself engaged, along with his staff and a few fusiliers, in hand to hand fighting. After a desperate struggle, he fell into the hands of the enemy, along with his few remaining men, almost all of whom were wounded. Command of the remainder of his battalion was assumed by Oberleutnant Freiherr von Richthofen. Further to the south the elements of the 7th and 10th Companies, which had launched a hasty attack, armed with hand grenades, succeeded in pushing the attackers back about 100 metres and in beating back repeated thrusts. Along with his adjutant, Leutnant Uhlhorn, Hauptmann Kröber, commander of the 2nd Battalion, was seriously wounded. He died a few days later in a field hospital. The reserves of the regimental commander, Major Freiherr von Rotenhan, which arrived about 8.00 am (9th Company and the machine gun reserves, which had rushed forward from Drocourt), were able in the course of a bloody struggle to hold on to the eastern edge of the ridge. Immediately to the soldiers' front the ruins of the chateau at La Folie could be seen being blown skywards.

The confusing experience of Grenadier Otto Schröder, a member of 12th Company RIR 262, must have been typical of many other defenders that day. Writing after the war, he recorded:

That night [8/9 April] we lay down, tired after night sentry duty, saying, 'Wouldn't it be nice to pull the blankets over our heads and go to sleep?' Suddenly heavy drum fire came down. The day sentries all bawled, 'Get out. Here come the British! [sic.]. We leapt up, all tiredness forgotten, then it was a life or death fight for the Fatherland. Every man was in his appointed place. As I was quickly passing up hand grenades, the entire trench was already full of firing. The British - they were Canadian troops - had broken through to our left, in the area of Bavarian Reserve Infantry Regiment 3 and, coming along the line of the road, were already rolling up our position. My section commander ordered me to go down into the dugout and fetch up the box of egg-shaped grenades. I immediately carried out his order, but once I was about half way up the thirty two steps of the dugout, my section commander suddenly shouted. "Come up at once. The Canadians have already pressed on beyond the trench on the left."

I quickly threw the egg-shaped grenades back down into the dugout and raced upwards into the trench. As I did so, I discovered that I was alone in the trench, accompanied only by a dead comrade, who lay there with his legs drawn up as though he was trying to launch himself up the wall of the trench. I knew only that he came from Hessen; I had quite forgotten his name. I risked climbing up onto the parapet and noticed that to the left, right and front there was nothing but

Hauptmann von Keiser, Commanding Officer 2nd Battalion RIR 262.

*enemy soldiers. In their 'straw hats' (steel helmets), they looked
as though they were hunting hares. As I later noted, they seemed
to have drunk a lot of schnaps. I had to do something, but what?
I dragged the dead comrade into a shell hole and lay down next
to him as though I was dead. In the meantime the waves of
attackers swept on past us. A long time went by.*

*Suddenly a very tall Canadian arrived and jabbed his fixed
bayonet into the dead comrade. It was for me the most terrifying
moment of my life. I moved and the Tommy shouted "Come
on!" At that I climbed up out of the shell hole (taking silent leave
of my comrade). He then pointed his bayonet at my chest and
asked me something. I did not understand him, so I just shrugged
my shoulders. As quickly as he had appeared, he disappeared
once more. Now I was once more all alone, so I raced off in the
direction of the Gießlerhöhe, where the Reserve Infantry
Regiment 261 positions were. As I was running past a parapet, a
Canadian soldier jumped out and shot at me, hitting me in the
upper arm. As I was running around wounded and confused, my
friend Cordes leapt up. He had been hidden away unwounded in
cover. The joy of meeting up with a good comrade whilst
surrounded by the enemy can only be imagined by someone who
has experienced the same thing.*

*We linked hands and raced aimlessly amongst the fallen who
had been mowed down here by machine gun fire. They included
both our comrades and Canadian soldiers. We arrived at a
dugout and settle down on the stairs to shelter from the heavy
fire that was falling on the Ridge. At that point the German
artillery brought the ridge under heavy calibre fire. Then we
tried to solve the mystery. Where were we: in our positions or
those of the Canadians. My mate thought that we were in the
enemy position, I that we were in our own. I said, 'Let's sit and
wait until our division launches a counter-attack, then we shall
be saved!'*

*Whilst we were discussing this, a door opened in a dug out
and a Canadian came out. We were amazed to discover that there
were six enemy soldiers sitting in this dugout. They were not
taking part in the assaults which were occurring up above, but
were leaving the war to its own devices and were happily playing
cards. Initially they did not notice us and continued to play cards
calmly. When their game was over a Canadian medical orderly
came over to me and said: "Hallo Fritz, how are you? Are you*

wounded?" I nodded; he examined me and said 'No gout' [sic]. He then bandaged me up and gave me something to eat and drink. A few more of our regimental comrades turned up. Once I felt stronger, the Canadian soldier took my hand and led me back to an advanced dressing station where I was examined by a doctor. Then a Tommy took me back to the nearest village. Here I saw the British reserves, some of whom were black. It was obvious to me that everything was going to be done to hold on to Vimy Ridge. Behind the front I arrived at a large prisoner collection point, where I met up with several comrades, including my former company commander Leutnant Schulz.

Leutnant Kopka, who with the 2nd Machine Gun Company of Reserve Infantry Regiment 261 was located in Vimy and who was put at the disposal of Reserve Infantry Regiment 262 to help meet the crisis, was killed in the front line by a shot to the head [Leutnant Peter Kopka is

buried in the Kameradengrab at Neuville St Vaast/Maison Blanche]. The left flank of the regiment, which hung in the air, was constantly threatened. However, thanks to the courageous defence put up by the 262nd, it was maintained, despite all assaults. On the right flank of the division, in Sector *Fischer*, the defence was the responsibility of RIR 261. Here the front line was held by 3rd Company (Balla), 1st Company (Wittkop), 11th Company (Wagner) and 9th Company (Neumann). Immediately to their front the great surging Canadian attack was halted forward in No Man's Land but, as has been noted, it had achieved greater success left and right in the adjacent sectors *Zollern* and *Döberitz*. In those sectors penetrations were made as far back as the third defensive line and preparations were made to roll up our first position from the rear. Hauptmann Zickner, who was in

Major Knobelsdorf, Commanding Officer Fusilier (3rd) Battalion RIR 261.

149

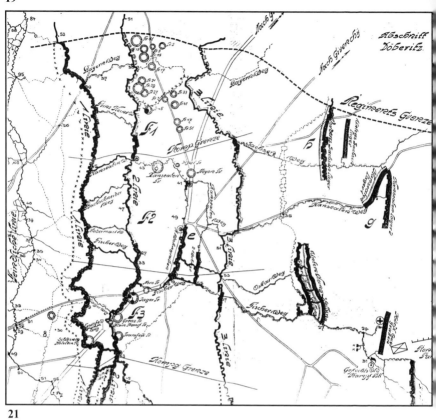

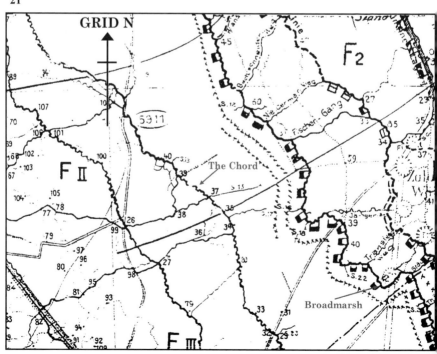

command of the so-called "Island Fischer" in the northern part of Sector *Fischer*, immediately launched a counter-attack by 2nd Company (Hoppe) and 4th Company (Ketzlick) from the Potsdamer Riegel [Postdam Stop Line]. The assault troops made almost immediate contact with the enemy in Potsdamer Graben [Potsdam Trench], capturing thirty men (including one officer) and a machine gun. They succeeded in pushing back the enemy lines as far as the crater field to the right of Prinz-Heinrich-Weg [Prince Henry's Way].

One platoon of 5th Company, commanded by the company commander, Reserve Leutnant Osthold, forced its way though to the 3rd Company which was locked in heavy fighting, whilst two and a half sections under Leutnant Degenhorst stayed back in Potsdamer Riegel to secure it. In the meantime the front line was sealed off by a party under Offizierstellvertreter Stracke, along the line of Hanseatenweg [Hanseatic Way]. Together with the last remaining section of 11th Company, commanded by Vizefeldwebel Rittershausen of 1st Company, they continued to beat off frontal attacks and, by means of a series of thrusts, succeeded in clearing the front line trench as far as 9th Company.

The situation remained essentially unchanged for hours. It was certainly extremely dangerous, though had sufficient reserves been on hand, certainly not hopeless. Up where Reserve Infantry Regiment 261 was still clinging on, the few machine gunners and riflemen who had escaped destruction brought down a hail of fire against the enemy. They fought like men possessed; some of them from a standing position, to bring fire to bear. The attack petered out bloodily in front of the regiment. But there was greater danger to the flanks. A flood of soldiers bore down from the south, from Sector Zollern, threatening to envelop the left flank of the Fusilier Battalion and to roll it up. Despatched forward by the battalion commander, Major von Knobelsdorff, in a powerful counter-stroke, the reserves (10th and elements of the 12th Company), succeeded at the cost of

20 Left above: Sector *Fischer*, April. Note the numerous minor stop lines dug in the attempt to overcome the inherent weakness of such a shallow position. Determined defence from these locations caused the Canadian 4th Division major problems and high casualties on 9 April.

21 Left below: Large scale map illustrating the German front line in Sector *Fischer*. The modern road between Broadmarsh Crater and Canadian Cemetery No 2 cuts straight through the meanderings of the front line. Note the faulty concentration of dugouts in the front line trench. [© GPG Robinson]

heavy losses in sealing off the enemy break in from the south.

Leutnant Koschmieder was mortally wounded as he brought a machine gun into action and by his side many brave infantrymen of the regiment also fell. Nevertheless the few remaining fit officers, NCOs and fusiliers held on grimly to the newly-won position. Captured Lewis guns reinforced their firepower. From the north too, the enemy, after blowing up large craters in the right hand neighbouring Sector Döberitz, broke in and swung south in large numbers to threaten encirclement. The right flank of the 1st Battalion was locked for hours in bitter hand to hand fighting against constantly reinforced groups. Here Leutnant Klabisch was killed amidst his faithful comrades, but one of the counter-attacks by the 2nd and 4th Companies, which the battalion commander Hauptmann Zickner launched, drove the Canadians attackers back in the course of a lengthy and bloody struggle. The success was dearly bought. Along with many grenadiers, Leutnant Ketzlick, the commander of 4th Company, and his platoon commander, Leutnant Lehmann, were killed.

In view of the vigorous resistance they had encountered, the Canadian 4th Division did not attempt further frontal assaults throughout the afternoon. However, when it went dark, a further massed attack was launched further to the north against Sector *Döberitz*, forcing back the line, weakened because of previous counter thrusts, withdrawing it from the craters. Leutnant Hoppe was wounded, Leutnants Ketzlich and Lehmann were killed and command devolved on Reserve Leutnant Fladt, who had suffered a head wound. His force conducted a fighting withdrawal towards the Potsdamer Riegel [Potsdam Stop Line] and the Intermediate Position (North). It was not possible for the battalion to respond to the urgent requests of Leutnant Balla for reinforcement, which had been brought through an area which was teeming with Canadian troops by the runners: Gefreiters Pilorz and Siefert.

Still the regiment clung on to the forward trenches in the centre with the remnants of the 3rd, 1st, 11th and 9th Companies, acting like a breakwater, but continuing attempts by the Canadians to break down this 261st wedge through the constant deployment of fresh forces, meant that the fighting power of the defence reduced more and more. When the crater belonging to Leutnant Balla, commander of the 3rd Company, was surrounded by a bombing party throwing grenades from a range of thirty to thirty five metres, the German grenadiers found that they were so exhausted that they could only throw theirs fifteen metres; it was as though their arms were paralysed. At one point the

Canadians were kept at bay by the fire of a single rifleman who, lying behind a firing shield, maintained his fire for hours, reporting after every shot, Yet another! During this battle, the courageous Vizefeldwebel Stracke was killed close by Leutnant Balla. During the morning a British aircraft appeared with the intention of attempting to deal with the craters that were still holding out by dropping bombs on them. By a lucky chance the Germans fired white flares at it, whereupon it flew away without dropping bombs. White flares were the recognition signal for friendly forces that day.

During the afternoon reinforcements arrived at last. Oberstleutnant von Goerne despatched two platoons from his final reserve, the 5th Company, to the Fusilier Battalion and, with their help, it was possible to secure the link to Reserve Infantry Regiment 262. One platoon under Leutnant Osthold, which was sent to the 1st Battalion, pushed forward to Leutnant Balla and was able to join in the life and death struggle there. A short pause in the battle meant that many lightly wounded could be sent to the rear and the severely wounded moved into the mined dugouts. But the question on everyone's mind was, would a counter-stroke in strength be launched?

Deployment of the Reserves

As the drum fire of a violence never before experienced worked its way back towards its command post during the early hours of 9 April, 79th Reserve Brigade alerted the battalions which were resting. Immediately after that the Division ordered an increased state of alert for the entire area. During the early fighting, until 7.00 am and in some cases until 8.30 am, the divisional artillery, despite heavy losses, maintained its defensive and destructive fire. However, because the situation in the infantry front line was unclear, it had to continue to fire on its previous defensive fire zones. The batteries which were deployed in Sector Arnulf, at least those whose positions were west of the railway embankment, were drawn into the close quarter battle and for a long period had to beat off infantry attacks, firing over open sights or using rifles and hand grenades. 3rd and 8th Batteries, Reserve Field Artillery Regiment 63, succeeded in pulling their guns out of action in the midst of small arms fire and taking up new positions to the east of the railway embankment. The 1st and 6th Batteries, against whom the enemy had succeeded in closing right up to the barbed wire obstacle to their front, had to blow up their guns after they had fired their final rounds. Two heavy field howitzer batteries – 10th and 11th Foot Artillery Regiment 10 – which were located in Sector *Zollern*, were assaulted by infantry, but with friendly infantry support were able to maintain their fire positions, despite fighting at close quarters.

Once the alert state had been increased, the divisional reserves, comprising 2nd Battalion Reserve Infantry Regiment 261 (5th Company regimental reserve in the Lower Slope Position), 1st Battalion Reserve Infantry Regiment 262 (2nd Company regimental reserve in and around Vimy) and 2nd Battalion Reserve Infantry Regiment 263, which had just been relieved in the forward position (8th Company regimental reserve in Vimy; Staff and 5th Company not yet returned from the First Position), were ordered to move closer to the battle zone. Whilst they were on the march, news arrived that the enemy had succeeded in penetrating the area of 1st Bavarian Reserve Division to the south and that they had taken the First Position. Soon information came in that the enemy had also succeeded in breaking in on the left flank of the 79th Reserve Division and was rolling up the position from south to north. It was also reported that there had been a further break in north of the Division. The Brigade then gave orders to the forces at its disposal (2nd Bn RIR 261 under Hauptmann von Goerne and 2nd Bn RIR 263 led by Oberleutnant Heinicke), to head in the direction of the railway embankment south of Vimy and to send their machine gun companies ahead at the double. 2nd Bn

Hauptmann **von Goerne**
Commanding Officer
2nd Battalion RIR 261.

RIR 262 under Hauptmann von Block was despatched to the cross tracks at La Gueule d'Ours, east of Vimy, as divisional reserve.

The first of the reserves who were hurrying forward to arrive was a Machine Gun Company of RIR 261, which was greeted joyfully at the railway embankment and deployed to reinforce the weak forces from RIR 263 who were already there. They were followed by 2nd Bn RIR 263 which was completely exhausted, 6th Company RIR 261 and later by a company from RIR 262. The other elements of the Brigade Reserve, namely 7th and 8th Companies RIR 261, together with the 2nd Machine Gun Company RIR 263, were despatched by Brigade to RIR 261, with orders to hold the Second Position at all costs and make contact with RIR 262. (According to radio and light messages, which had so far been received, it had to be assumed that the enemy had already outflanked and encircled RIR 262 and that it was effectively unable to exercise command and control of the battle.) The 2nd

Machine Gun Company, which had been located in Vimy had, as has already been mentioned, placed itself on its own initiative at the disposal of RIR 262. Altogether this meant that at least the most urgently required support had been secured for the troops who were being most heavily pressed. Unfortunately the reserves available were insufficient and too weak to carry out an immediate counter-stroke to restore the situation. Sergeant Dorrmann, of 6th Company, Reserve Infantry Regiment 261, later provided a vivid description of the day from the perspective of one of the reserve sub-units.

'During the early hours of Easter Monday a dull rumbling from the front woke us. Soon we received the order, 'Get your assault order on. Everything else must stay here!' Each man was to take a piece of bread with him. The most senior of the NCOs were placed in charge of sections of soldiers and then the company set off, leading the battalion. The field artillery was going into positions to the left and right, with British shells landing in amongst us. Nevertheless we reached the railway embankment near Vimy unscathed. The 210 mm howitzers of a Saxon foot artillery regiment were in position here. My group took up position near some of these monsters. With each shot I thought that my eardrums would burst. In addition shell fragments and pieces of ballast from the embankment were flying everywhere and hitting our helmets. Later the Tommies lifted their fire more to the rear areas, where I could observe the approach of our ammunition columns. A

A medical aid post in Vimy, April 1917.

gunner standing jacketless by one of the guns stopped a wagon and swiftly unloaded it. Then, just like a baker placing loaves of bread in the oven, he loaded one shell after the other into his gun, which was readjusted right and left after each shell. If I had been allowed to leave my post, I would have run over to this comrade to express my appreciation.'

As things became a little calmer, we left sentries up on the embankment and took cover in the dugouts of the artillery. Towards 9.00 pm, we were ordered forward. I went with Leutnant Rahlfs at the head of our platoon. The artillery fire of both sides hindered our movement. Wearing our gasmasks, we leapt from one crater to another, dodging the falling gas and phosphorous shells. In the meantime the sky had darkened so much that it was impossible to see the next man, even if was possible to touch him. There was then a shower of hail which, even though it was thoroughly unpleasant, saved us. We were not far off from the howitzer position which had once been German, when we came under fire from there. Because our flanks were hanging in the air, we were later ordered back to our jumping off point. Unfortunately two men were missing and we never heard anything of them again. Towards 4.00 am we were meant to be launching another assault, but this was cancelled later.

Gradually we began to feel hungry, because we had each only brought a piece of bread forward with us. The gunners and our sister regiment 263, to whom we had been allocated, gave us something to eat; the number of casualties meant that not all the rations had been consumed. During the morning [presumably 10 April], heavy fire continued to fall on the rear areas and during the afternoon on our position too. A shell wounded the sentry in front of our dugout and we took him to the medical dugout at the railway underpass. I then went and checked on the sentries, noticing that Grenadier W., who was always very fearful when he had not had a drink, was flinching whenever a shell landed. I moved him ten metres to the left and said, 'Keep your chin up, they're not shooting at the place where you are standing now.' The sentry who had been relieved and I continued on, when suddenly a shell exploded, we flew through the air like dolls and found ourselves lying on our stomachs with wounds to the shoulder and arm. We moved to the medical dugout, where we were bandaged and had the well-known labels attached to us. I reported to the company commander and requested to be

156

allowed to stay with the company, but he said, 'My dear Dorrmann, you are the father of a family and wounded. Even though your wound may not be very severe go where you are sent. Nobody knows what is going to happen here, or even if anyone will come out of it alive!' We parted with a powerful handshake and, with his good wishes ringing in my ears, I made my way to the medical company.

Towards midday, orders arrived at Division from GHQ that the lost Third Line was to be recaptured. At the same time information was received that two fresh battalions – 1st Bn IR 118 (56th Division) and 3rd Bn RFR 34 (80th Res Division) were on their way. General von Bacmeister, who in the meantime had been able to obtain a more-or-less clear picture of the overall situation, now decided to fill the wide gap which had opened up between RIR 262 and I Bavarian Corps and to recapture Telegraph Hill [Hill 135, north of Thélus] by means of a counter-attack, code named Krummel. For this purpose, he allocated 1st Bn IR 118 and one company of Machine Gun Sharpshooter Detachment 20 to the Brigade.

From 1.40 pm the Brigade Staff had been located at La Gueule d'Ours, the cross tracks to the east of Vimy. It issued an order which placed Oberstleutnant von Beyr in charge of the attack and allocated the following forces to Hauptmann von Block: 1st Bn IR 118, 1st Bn RIR 262 (less two companies) and one company of Machine Gun Sharpshooter Detachment 20. Von Block was ordered to launch the attack against Telegraph Hill from the area of the foundry (north of Vimy) along the line of the road Lens-Arras and to link up with RIR 262 on the right. Oberleutnant Heinicke, with the forces from RIR 263 which were located at the railway embankment, was to attack Telegraph Hill frontally from the south of Vimy, conforming to von Block's assault and linking up with the assaulting troops of 1st Bavarian Reserve Division. Whilst the artillery was firing a preliminary bombardment against the heights north of Thélus in support of the counter-attack, the battalions which had been allocated to the division began to arrive at the ridge to the east of Vimy. Because of the increasing quantity of artillery fire which was coming down there, they were forced to cross this in widely dispersed formations. Not until about 6.00 pm could Hauptmann von Block's attacking force traverse Vimy.

A combination of darkness and snow squalls hindered a swift conduct of the attack, which having cleared the Canadians out of the ruined village, could not cross the Second Position, its right flank linked up with the left flank of RIR 262 and its left anchored on La Compte Wood [the northwest extension of Goulot Wood], until late evening. Because the assault force from 1st Bavarian Reserve Division advancing to the south was well to the rear, the counter-attack of the left assault group, advancing from the railway embankment, also made only slow progress and finally stalled along the track Vimy-Farbus due to heavy artillery fire. Completely out of contact in the constant flurries of snow, the regimental commander withdrew them to the embankment once more. At a result, during the night, the Brigade allocated Oberstleutnant von Beyr 3rd Bn RFR 34 (less two companies) and some machine guns, so that he was able to occupy the southern edge of Vimy and establish contact with von Block's group. Despite great difficulties, as well as the fact that Vimy was under heavy fire with both conventional and gas shells, these courageous troops succeeded in achieving this by morning. There was still a wide gap to the left hand neighbouring division, which could not be closed during the hours of darkness. As a result, the Brigade allocated the reserves which had arrived, namely one company RIR 34 and two engineer mining companies, to RIR 263 in order to strengthen its left flank.

The End of the First Day of the Battle
As it went dark up on Vimy Ridge, fresh Canadian troops renewed their violent assault on the narrow salient of RIR 261which stuck out well forward. It had proved to be out of the question for further runners (commanded by Unteroffizier Kremer, 1st Company) to break through to Leutnant Balla and his command, which had been almost wiped out by mortar fire, with instructions; nevertheless they succeeded in bringing in some Canadian prisoners. Pressed in by overwhelming forces, the garrison had to surrender the position, which it had succeeded in holding until evening. Leutnants Balla, Wittkop and Osthold (severely wounded) were captured, along with the remnants of the 1st and 3rd Companies, which had been involved in constant close quarter grenade and bayonet fighting. *Offizierstellvertreter* Stracke (1st Company), Leutnant Klabisch (3rd Company), Leutnants Lehman and Ketzlich (4th Company) had been killed, together with a large number of the most courageous NCOs and men. Three machine guns, which were no longer capable of being fired, were destroyed with hand grenades. The light mortars of the regiment, which had fired off all their ammunition, were buried and the crews continued the fight with rifles.

Once the last of the grenades had been thrown and the final bullets fired, the commanders decided to give orders for a withdrawal to the next position to the rear, but no sooner had the last of the fighters leapt out of the craters in order to race towards their objective, than they were caught by a sudden concentration of fire from the British guns, which scattered them. Some of them became prisoners of war of the British. The fate of one of these men provides a dramatic impression of the scene at the end of the day. Leutnant Balla, having with a heavy heart given the order to withdraw from the positions which had been held with such sacrificial courage, lost his footing in the darkness and fell into a huge shell hole which was full of water. In order to avoid sinking, he hauled himself with his last reserves of strength up the side of the crater, where he lay, unable to move or even without outside assistance, to free himself from the mud. There he lay totally exhausted until he was found and rescued by some Canadian soldiers. Only a very few defenders made their way back and were able to bring news about the final stages of the day's fighting.

The deployment of the last of the troops of RIR 261 meant that the Intermediate Position on the eastern edge of the ridge could be held. That night the first relief came with the arrival of 3rd Company Engineer Battalion 18, which was sent forward by Brigade. The bitter fighting continued during the night on the front of RIR 262. An energetic thrust led by Oberleutnant von Richthofen succeeded in winning some terrain back from the Canadian 3rd Division. Fighting was particularly heavy on the left flank of the regiment until the advance of Hauptmann von Block removed the risk of encirclement. The following morning brought further relief when a company of RIR 34 arrived. All along the battlefront there was a shortage of small-arms ammunition, hand grenades, flares and barbed wire, but resupply took place that night. The northern sector was supplied from the ammunition depot in Bétricourt via the narrow gauge railway which led to the railway embankment; the southern by trucks which were unloaded under heavy fire.

The divisional batteries suffered heavy casualties in exactly the same way as the infantry, which fought with their very last reserves of strength. By the evening of 9th April, out of twelve field batteries [i.e. forty eight guns], only seventeen guns were battleworthy. In order best to meet the demands of the battle, they were organised into two groups; Group North under Major von Pressentin and Group South under Hauptmann Döring. Three of the batteries of Reserve Field Artillery Regiment 63, which had been withdrawn from the battle zone west of the railway embankment, took up positions by Brigade Headquarters at

La Gueule d'Ours. They were joined by 3rd Battery Field Artillery Regiment 25, which had been allocated by Division. Major von Pressentin moved his headquarters to the area of 2nd Battery Reserve Field Artillery Regiment 63 by the railway embankment, where he was followed during the morning of 10th April by the staffs of RIR 261 and RIR 262. Hauptmann Döring moved to the cross tracks, near to which the staff of RIR 263 and the Heavy Artillery were also located. This made it possible for the Brigade to conduct the infantry battle in close coordination with the artillery groups. By order of 79th Reserve Division, the British battery positions around Neuville St Vaast were engaged with gas shells and the villages of Les Tilleuls, Thélus and Farbus, along with the roads leading to the German battle positions, were kept under heavy fire.

Hauptmann **von Block Commanding Officer 1st Battalion RIR 261.**

In the meantime, thanks to the resistance put up by the forward defenders, the Germans felt that the immediate crisis of the battle had been overcome. Already during the late evening two battalions of 111th Infantry Division, which was moving up, had arrived at Acheville and Arleux to occupy the third line. They were followed on 10 April by the remaining units of the division, which were at the disposal of GHQ and went into bivouac in the built up areas behind the Third Position. During the early morning, 2nd Bn IR 73 and 3rd Bn Infantry Regiment 164 were subordinated to 79th Reserve Division, which immediately allocated them to the Brigade. They arrived at La Gueule d'Ours at 10.00 am, where their arrival had been eagerly anticipated. Two companies and some machine guns were immediately despatched forward to each of the exhausted fighting regiments. The Brigade retained half of 3rd Battalion IR 164 as a reserve which, together with eight machine guns, was readied to protect the left flank of the division.

The Battle for the New Defensive Front

The front in the area where the break in had occurred now ran as follows: western edge of the village of Givenchy – eastern edge of Vimy Ridge – south of Vimy to the railway embankment – from there south of Bailleul eastwards, bending backwards along the western edges of the villages of Gavrelle, Monchy and Wancourt. The deployment of new and complete divisions either side of the Scarpe removed the most immediate danger and the occupation of the rearward positions by fresh battalions and batteries strengthened the defence further. As a result, subsequent attempts by the Canadians to push forward on 10 April were not believed to represent a serious threat. A British attack supported by tanks via Bailleul – Farbus during the afternoon and directed at the rear of 79th Reserve Division, was halted by concentrated counter fire, including that of the left flank of 79th Reserve Division. Much the same happened to an attempt to break through south of the Scarpe.

Towards evening heavy fighting broke out on Vimy Ridge once more, during which its eastern edge, which despite an heroic defence had been temporarily lost, was retaken by an immediate counter-stroke. Everywhere the performance of the German troops, including those from outside the division, was notably effective. Alongside many brave NCOs and men of RIR 261, Leutnants Florenz and Schnioffsky were killed. Leutnant Wiese, who was severely wounded, was captured by the Canadians. He died of his wounds on 17 May. Within a short time, the situation of 1st Battalion RIR 261 was extremely critical, as constantly reinforced masses pressed in on it from the flanks.

Nevertheless it could not bring itself to withdraw from the ridge and drop down to the Second Position. It remained manning Potsdamer Graben [Potsdam Trench] and the Intermediate Position (North), as the Canadians dug in to its front. Its hopes of reinforcement were met to a limited extent. Between 2.00 and 3.00 am 3rd Company Pionier Regiment 18 arrived, as did 6th Company IR 73, under Leutnant Gipkens, the following morning. Heavy fighting for the Intermediate Position, which was now the front line, took place. Suffering under heavy enemy and also [misdirected] German, artillery fire, the decimated garrison, unable to find cover, pulled back to the Sachsenlager in the face of a massed Canadian attack. *Unteroffizier* Piesker, who had already distinguished himself through his outstanding courage, covered the withdrawal with the last remaining serviceable machine gun. *Vizefeldwebel* Petersen (4th Company) guarded the left flank, whilst the remainder, which had closed in around the battalion staff, barricaded themselves into Sachsenweg [Saxon Way], preventing the enemy from advancing further.

It was already evening when it became increasingly obvious that the battalion was completely outflanked, that the remainder of the slopes of Vimy Ridge were controlled by the Canadians and that there was no prospect of the arrival of reserves. Finally the battalion decided that there was nothing more they could do in order to save the Ridge so, in order to avoid further useless casualties, the decision was taken to exercise the discretion given it the previous evening and to pull back to the Second Position. Leaving behind deception forces, the remnants of the 1st Battalion and 1st Company Pionier Battalion 18 moved back across ground swept by heavy shrapnel fire and gas, to the Second Position, taking with them all the wounded, the telephones and the reserve rations. There were pitifully few of them, because the companies had already left behind on the ridge, or evacuated to the rear, large numbers of wounded men.

The Phased Withdrawal of 79th Reserve Division from the Battle
The infantrymen of 79th Reserve Division had spent many days and nights in action, enduring snow, cold and mud, with insufficient food and sleep. Their battleworthiness had been stretched to the limit and would soon have been fully exhausted. General Headquarters decided, therefore, to give up the eastern edge of Vimy Ridge which up until then had been held, to withdraw the remnants of the battalions of the 79th Reserve Division during the night 10/11 April and to replace them in the Vimy Position with troops of 111th Infantry Division. Once 2nd Battalion IR 76 along with its regimental staff and 2nd Bn IR 164 had arrived, the relief of the 79th Reserve Division commenced, being controlled by Brigade. Despite the greatest difficulties, before dawn on 11th April the sectors had been reorganised and the relieved battalions withdrawn. Only in Sector *Zollern,* on the eastern edge of Vimy Ridge, which was lightly covered with fresh snow, there remained a weak force of RIR 262, which it had not been possible to withdraw before dawn. On 11 April, too, they held on devotedly to their forward position, despite being pressed on all sides. Finally the last of the fighters was withdrawn on the night of 11/12 April from their positions along the heights, for which, in accordance with their orders, they had fought for so hard.

The battle line of the 79th Reserve Division now ran along the line of the Second Position, bending back from the south western corner of

Vimy to the railway embankment. The divisional, brigade and sector commanders maintained command of their sectors and the troops of 111th Infantry Division, even after their own infantry had been relieved. During the night 10/11 April, when Vimy Ridge was evacuated, the final batteries which were still deployed west of the railway embankment were withdrawn. Some took up new fire positions near La Gueule d'Ours; others behind the Third Position. A British attack against Vimy on 11 April was shot to a standstill by the

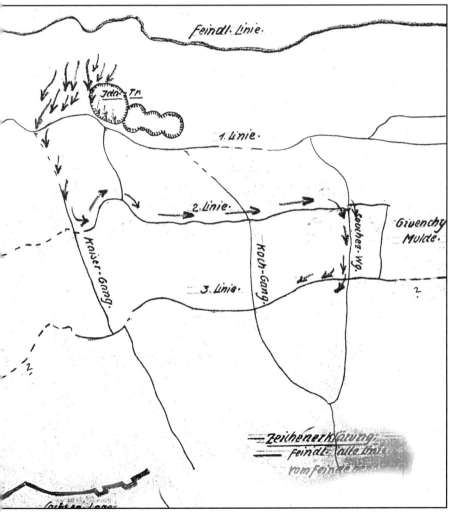

21. Allied penetrations, Sector Döberitz, 9 April.

163

defensive fire of the German artillery batteries, whose other preoccupation was to observe the Canadians up on the ridge and to harass the approach routes. After repair, the number of available guns increased. By the evening of 11 April, 22 field- and 12 heavy guns were operating in front of the Third Position.

During these days, the main British assaults were along the line of the road Arras-Cambrai. Thanks to overwhelming firepower and the use of tanks, they were able in this way to take Monchy. The overall situation had developed in such a way that in order to produce a more bearable situation, the Army Group decided to pull clear of the enemy and to withdraw to the Third Position along the line Lens-Avion-Méricourt-Acheville-Arleux-Oppy-Gavrelle. The bulk of the artillery had to take up fire positions behind this line during the night 11/12 April. Nevertheless, 79th Reserve Division left the Infantry Brigade two field batteries east of Vimy, in order that they could continue the close quarter battle. When day dawned on 13 April, the German Positions from Liévin via Vimy to Gavrelle had been evacuated. Only weak rearguards remained, to yield only when enemy pressure built up. Command of the former sector of 79th Reserve Division then passed to 111th Infantry Division and on 14 April the batteries of Reserve Field Artillery Regiment 63 were also withdrawn from the battle.

The main battle for Vimy Ridge was over, but there had been a sharp fight for the Pimple on 12 April. Bavarian Infantry Regiments 11 and 14 of the 16th Bavarian Infantry Division had suffered particularly heavily during the bombardment and the initial actions, so the decision was taken to move forward fresh troops from 4th Guards Division to reinforce, then relieve, the hard-pressed Bavarians. This meant that on 12 April, the Fusilier [3rd] Battalion Grenadier Guard Regiment 5 and 1st Battalion RIR 93 defended this important feature. Arriving tired, unfed and thirsty in the area of Bavarian Infantry Regiment 14 at 2.00 am on 11 April, it took until 6.00 am for companies of Grenadier Guard Regiment 5 to deploy into position. 9th, 12th and 10th Companies occupied the front line, with the 11th behind them. In reserve was 2nd Battalion Bavarian Infantry Regiment 14. Battalion HQ was established back down at *Angres-Kreuz*.

The situation of Grenadier Guard Regiment 5 was anything but promising. The trenches were levelled and full of mud and icy water; the artillery fire rained down on the largely defenceless fusiliers. Worst of all, lack of numbers meant that the front line contained several gaps, between 100 and 300 metres wide, which represented a disaster waiting to happen. No more troops could be made available, so the

22. The wrecked trench system Sector Ansbach. The gaps in the solid black lines in A1 and A2 indicate where the position was now longer tenable. This is where the main breakthroughs occurred on 12 April.

165

companies had to make the best of the situation. Communications were bad. There were no working telephone lines and light signalling was not possible. Runners maintained with great difficulty the link between battalion and companies whilst, to the rear, messenger dogs and carrier pigeons were employed.

At midnight 11/12 April, artillery fire crashed down all over the positions, pounding the men, who had not been fed a hot meal for two days. Crouched in wet, muddy shell holes, worn out, soaking wet and freezing, the fusiliers could only sit and wait as casualties mounted. About 4.00 am the first of the assaults began. This was largely beaten back with small arms fire and grenades but, at 4.50 am, shielded by a snowstorm which cut the visibility to nothing and artillery fire, which hammered the depth positions, a Canadian attack in considerable force came in behind a rolling barrage. Some of the Canadians were alleged to be wearing German steel helmets, rather than their own flat plate-shaped helmets as a deception measure. [It is impossible to judge the truth of this statement. It is possible but, equally, a man wearing a German helmet in poor visibility ran the risk of being shot by his own side.] Every third or fourth man of the leading wave was said to have been carrying a machine gun.

German defensive fire, when it eventually arrived, was late and too light to cause the Canadians serious problems and they broke into the German positions with relative ease, exploiting the wide gaps. Isolated groups of German soldiers fought on with rifle and hand grenade until they were overrun. The remnants of 9th Company, commanded by Vizefeldwebel Bröker, for example, held out for some time until, reduced to four men still on their feet, Bröker ordered them to break out to the rear. Staying behind himself to cover the others, Bröker was killed. Of the whole company only Fusiliers Heinrichs, Koog and Palubitski made it back. That story was mirrored all over the Giesslerhöhe and Givenchy Wood, where small groups fought their way back via the various sand and gravel pits and the web of trenches, until eventually the survivors were forced back into Givenchy.

On a day of serious casualties, the battalion commander, Major Roosen, was killed later when his temporary command post was destroyed by a direct hit, killing also his dog handler and one of the two messenger dogs, which had maintained the links to regimental headquarters throughout the fighting. The company commanders of the 9th, 10th and 11th Companies (Leutnants Kurt Bronsch, Erich Riemke and Kurt Hühnerbein) were also killed, as was Leutnant Paul Schmidt, Roosen's orderly officer. None of them has a known grave.

Reserve Leutnant Ueckert, commander 2nd Company RIR 93, which was deployed to the south of Grenadier Guard Regiment 5, survived the battle and later produced a detailed account of the time he spent on the rear slopes of the Pimple to the south of the Givenchy Mulde:

It was immediately obvious when we arrived at the appointed position that it had been the scene of heavy fighting. Those companies of the Bavarians which had not been completely wiped out were down to a strength of about ten men and they were completely intermingled along the main defensive line. The relief was extremely difficult to carry out because the front line trace varied throughout its length. Dawn was already appearing on the eastern horizon by the time the companies of the 1st Battalion had occupied their designated sector. The Givenchy salient was very like Thiepval. On the right flank (Souchez-Gang = Souchez Way), the Third Line was occupied by 1st Company, whilst the left flank was held by the 3rd Company, with sentry positions distributed from Kaisergang = Emperor's Way down to the lower Sachsenlager = Saxon Dugouts.

Forward at the most prominent part of the salient there was a large gap between the companies. This was because this point was already occupied by the enemy. To the 2nd Company fell the task of closing the gap. I made use of part of the existing Koch-Gang = Cook's Way, and caused a new line to be extended right through the crater field to the right flank of the 3rd Company. Fortunately this re-grouping went very well and was completed swiftly. As a result, by the time it was fully daylight the company was dug in all along the new line. Despite the extremely difficult situation in which we found ourselves, everyone was alert and ready for the coming operations. Most of 11 April was taken up with the exchange of considerable quantities of artillery fire on both the forward positions and routes to the rear.

My main concern was the left flank of the company and the battalion, which was hanging in the air, because I expected an outflanking enemy attack from the south from La Folie Wood. [In 1917 the remains of this wood extended all the way into Sector Fischer]. *In the event completely the opposite happened. It went dark early, because the skies were full of threatening snow clouds and an icy wind blew across the battlefield. Reinforced night sentries went on duty. The need for reliefs meant that there was little opportunity for rest in the dugouts. Those off duty had to lie there with their equipment on, helmets pushed back on their heads, rifles to hand; ready at any moment to be torn out of their slumbers by the shouts of alarm of the sentries in the trenches.*

In the enemy trenches all was quiet. There was no sign that any operation was to be undertaken that night. Suddenly, in the early hours of 12 April, the sentries raised the alarm. Within a minute the company was out of the dugouts and stood-to along the parapet. Squally snow showers blotted out the dawn and it was impossible to see more than five metres. Insanely violent drum fire came down on our trenches and the village of Givenchy. Under the protection of the driving snow, the enemy had attacked and had gained a lodgement in the sector of the Grenadier Guards. Suddenly the enemy appeared in Koch-Gang as well and began to roll up the company position, taking some prisoners. Everyone was taken by surprise by this sudden appearance of the Tommies in the trench. Nobody could explain it. Had the 1st Company been surprised?

I immediately launched a counter-stroke. The Canadians left the trench rapidly, pulling back to the Souchez-Graben. In an instant the entire trench garrison of the Koch-Graben launched forward charging after the enemy. Within a few moments, Vizefeldwebel Beutel and his platoon had caught up with them, capturing two officers and nine men. The remainder of the enemy were scattered and the prisoners they had taken were freed. Other remnants of the enemy were captured by 1st Company. Meanwhile 2nd Company had returned to Koch-Gang. The snow squalls eased off and the drum fire died away gradually. The whole business had only lasted a few minutes. The entire company was elated. One thing was clear: the Tommies had been given a bloody nose by 2nd Company.

The same fate had befallen the enemy in front of 1st Company which, under the command of Leutnant Roland Müller, had energetically beaten them off. The 3rd Company was not involved in this attack. At the end of it the 1st Battalion was in complete control of the sector which it had taken over on 10 April. The situation was a good deal worse in the area of our right hand neighbours, the Grenadier Guards. Despite a vigorous defence the enemy had broken into the trench system and were working their way forward along Souchez-Graben. The enemy break-in had occurred to the north of Fünf-Wege-Kreuz [Five Way Junction]. We realised that the prisoners were very drunk. Later there was unanimous agreement the enemy assault troops were completely drunk. [This accusation occurs repeatedly in German personal accounts of the battles of the Great War. Certainly large tots of high proof rum were given before battle, so men would have had the smell of it on their breath, but drunkenness in the trenches was severely frowned on and the veracity of these reports is at least questionable.]

The situation became serious for us once more. Enemy parties had worked their way forward about 300 metres along the Souchez-Graben. I ordered the company to occupy the whole of Koch-Gang and to block off Souchez-Gang, to avoid the risk of being cut off from Givenchy. This meant that the company was occupying a narrow wedge-shaped position, which meant that gradually it was having to defend two fronts. To our front there was the eerily silent, but ever present, threat from the salient to our front. Luckily the enemy did not seem to appreciate exactly where our positions lay and we were left alone from that direction. The entire attention of the company was directed towards the Souchez-Gang and the hollow to its rear. We could watch large scale enemy movements there and the sentries engaged them. Enemy patrols were constantly pushing forward in order to determine the size and shape of our positions.

For the most part, these patrols were shot up by our grenadiers. This provided an important lesson to the infantryman, who in this way learnt once more to appreciate the value of their own weapons. Trench warfare had meant that the

A German artist's impression of the battle for Givenchy, early evening 12 April.

hand grenade had become the principal weapon, with the rifle playing only a subordinate role, but rifle fire could have a devastating effect on the enemy – even at short range. The whip-like crack of the shots, coupled with their sharp sound through the air had a much greater demoralising effect on the enemy than the dull thuds of the hand grenades and so it was near Givenchy. Our well aimed rifle fire held the Tommies completely in check, forcing them to bring forward fresh troops in order to be able to continue the advance.

By now the sky had cleared and the afternoon brought spring-like warmth from the sun. Our situation became ever more threatening, as the arrival of enemy reinforcements increased the pressure on us. Towards 5.00 pm strong enemy columns were seen forming up, front facing southeast, behind the wire and level with Fünf-Wege-Kreuz. Similar enemy detachments could be seen massing in the salient to our front and further to the south. In view of this perilous situation I immediately discussed fresh defensive measures with Leutnant Roland Müller. Then, at 5.30 pm, we were surprised to receive an order from the battalion, ordering a withdrawal by 1st and 3rd Companies to Givenchy then on to Avion. 2nd Company was to remain in position as rearguard.

It would be no easy task to hold the position until 3.00 am, because a major enemy attack from north and south could be launched against Givenchy at any moment. The grenadiers, who had been absolutely staunch up until this point, began to get somewhat uneasy in view of the changed situation, but were nevertheless all prepared to defend themselves and their position to the utmost. Shortly before 7.00 pm, 1st and 3rd Companies withdrew from their positions and pulled back to Givenchy, where they occupied positions in the Souchez-Gang left and right of Battalion Headquarters. [There must be something wrong with the timings at this stage of the report, but the course of events is nevertheless clear.] *My grenadiers suddenly felt an oppressive feeling of being isolated. I had to take immediate measures because the enemy, who had spotted the withdrawal of 1st Company, immediately began to tighten the noose around us by occupying the abandoned trenches south of Souchez-Gang.*

2nd Company, every man of which was stood-to, brought the groups of enemy under fire. I had stops erected in the trenches to block off the trench to the north and south. In Souchez-Gang things remained lively, with the grenadiers bringing down rapid rifle fire whenever they detected the flat helmets of the Tommies. It was absolutely vital that our blocks were not overrun, otherwise the line of our withdrawal to the village would have been cut. The enemy columns were assembled like gathering thunder clouds on the heights to the east of Fünf-Wege-Kreuz, ready to launch an attack on Givenchy. The masses increased in size before our eyes and we waited tensely for the moment when they would launch forward. Then, about 6.30 pm, a runner arrived from the battalion bearing the following order: '2nd Company is to pull back to Command Post Augsburg. Only the rearguard will remain in Koch-Graben. (Enemy about to launch an attack).' Everybody heaved a sigh of relief as I directed the company to prepare to move out. Leaving one platoon behind as a rearguard in Koch-Graben, the other two pulled back to Givenchy. The withdrawal was spotted by the enemy, but although we came under heavy fire we had no casualties. It now fell to the 1st Battalion to hold the village of Givenchy until 9.00 pm.

Shortly after 7.00 pm the enemy columns attacked with the evening sun behind them from their positions east of Fünf-Wege-Kreuz. At that the final rearguard pulled back from Koch-Gang. Firing from a small heap of rubbish near the command post, four machine guns from the 1st Machine Gun Company under Leutnant Jeibmann, supported by some rifle sections from 1st and 2nd Companies, brought down a torrent of rapid fire on the unsuspecting enemy. There was complete confusion. The attackers all went to ground and stretcherbearers came forward to carry back the wounded. The attack was beaten off without the aid of a single German gun, but the British artillery lost no time in bringing down revenge fire.

Heavy shells crashed down around the firing positions and they had to be abandoned. It was now 9.00 pm and high time to depart if the battalion was not to be surrounded; the enemy was already in Givenchy and in rear of the 93rd. Finally the companies began to fall back. First to go was 3rd Company, followed at fifteen minute intervals by the 2nd, 1st and 4th. Enemy artillery fire increased minute by minute to drum fire. The enemy seemed to be preparing or another attack. At the double we pulled back along Souchez-Gang to the Kronprinzen-Lager [Crown Prince Dugouts], *straight through a hail of British shells.*

171

An intense box barrage sealed off the rear of the village. Near the church, everything was in flames. We were witnessing the funeral pyre of Leutnant Jaap of 4th Company, who met his end at that time.

He had intended to blow up his dugout and, to facilitate that, had carried sacks of powder and mortar bombs into it. When it was time to go he ordered everyone out, placed several packets of flares on the charge and lit the fuse. As he raced up the stairs, he saw that the entrance was blocked by his men who were unwilling to brave the move into the open and the hell of the British drum fire. A heavy shell suddenly crashed down into the entrance of the dugout collapsing the timber framework of the entrance and hurling several of the men at the top of the stairs (including Leutnant Jaap) back down. Simultaneously the charge went off with a dreadful crash. Flames, metres long, roared up, engulfing both the men and their commander. All attempts at rescue were in vain. [Given the reported circumstances of his death, it is hard to credit that Leutnant Jaap is believed to be buried in the *Kamaradengrab* of the German cemetery at Neuville St Vaast/Maison Blanche. Nevertheless, his is an unusual name and the German *Volksbund* is satisfied that he lies there. The name Jaap appears on the bronze panels.]

With the skilfully conducted evacuation of Givenchy, the final scenes of the battle for Vimy Ridge were played out. 1st Battalion RIR 93 was fortunate, emerging with casualties of only nine killed, sixty-eight wounded and twelve missing, seven of whom were accounted for when six men died with Leutnant Jaap in the dugout. RIR 93 was lucky not to be the main focus of the fighting, but its companies had been forced effectively out of their trenches. Out-manoeuvred and ultimately out-fought, the German defenders who had borne the brunt of the fighting for Vimy Ridge were withdrawn to rest, recuperate and count their losses, which were high. The survivors of 79th Reserve Division were proud ever after to be counted as *Vimykämpfer*. They felt that they had given a good account of themselves against the odds and the name Vimy appeared in the place of honour on their regimental banners after the war. Paying a final tribute to their comrades, whom they had had to leave amongst the fallen on the ridge, RIR 262 turned to poetry:

> *Sie ruhen und schlafen aus von der Not*
> *Vom Leid und der Mühsal im Kriege*
> *Und küßt ihre Gräber das Morgenrot*
> *Dann träumen sie lächelnd vom Siege*

Regimental Banner RIR 261 at the unveiling of the regimental war memorial in Berlin, 17 August 1922. Note the name 'Vimy' in pride of place. The motto translates as 'Always stand fast; never stand still'.

(Strötgen)

They rest and sleep free from danger
From the pain and the trials of war's history
When the red of the dawn comes and kisses their graves
Then they dream with a smile of the victory

(Strötgen)

In truth of course there was no German victory to celebrate at Vimy. They had fought hard and well, but this was a Canadian triumph, which no amount of public bluster or weasel wording could disguise. Writing in his diary, the army group commander, Crown Prince Rupprecht of Bavaria, noted pessimistically, 'It is questionable if we can hold on the face of artillery fire of this increasing intensity. This prompts the further question: In these circumstances, is there any point in continuing to prosecute the war?' Generalfeldmarschall von Hindenburg, writing in his memoirs, admitted that 9 April cast a dark shadow across the birthday of Ludendorff, which fell on that day:

> *On 9 April the evening briefing painted a dismal picture. There was much shadow and little light. Nevertheless it is essential to look for light in cases like that. There was one ray of sunshine, even though its outlines were a little unclear. The British did not seem to understand how to exploit their success to the full. On this occasion that was lucky for us as it had been on occasion before. After the briefing was over I shook my First Quartermaster General [Ludendorff] by the hand and said, "Well we have lived through worse situations than today together." Today, on his birthday! My trust remained unshaken. I knew that we had fresh troops marching on to the battlefield and that trains were rolling in its direction as well. The crisis would be overcome. As far as I was concerned, it was already over. The battle would continue.*

At one level Hindenburg was justified in his confidence. Swiftly the German defenders withdrew five to six kilometres to their Third Position which had already been prepared in anticipation of such an eventuality. There they were sufficiently far to the east to neutralise the advantage that possession of Vimy Ridge gave the Allies and there the front stuck for weeks and months to come, whilst the German chain of command analysed this shock reverse and devised the tactics they would later use at Ypres when the Passchendaele campaign opened three and a half months later.

War memorial RIR 261.

War memorial RIR 262.

Chapter 6

A TOUR OF THE VIMY AREA

It should be noted that in the companion Battleground Europe volume,
Vimy Ridge, *there is a very detailed tour of the Allied side of the line
about which visitors might like to be aware. Its contents are almost
entirely different from this tour, which concentrates to a large extent on
the German side of the line. There is often also a fuller description of
many of the cemeteries and memorials than will be found here.*

<u>Summary</u>
Notre Dame de Lorette – Angres – Givenchy - Vimy – La Gueule
d'Ours – Beehive Cemetery - Willerval – Orchard Dump Cemetery –
Bailleul – St Laurent Blangy (German) and Bailleul Road East
Cemeteries – Roclincourt – Thélus – Farbus – Thélus - Nine Elms and
Arras Road Cemeteries – Neuville St Vaast – La Targette - Maison
Blanche – Zouave Valley and Souchez.

23. Car Tour.

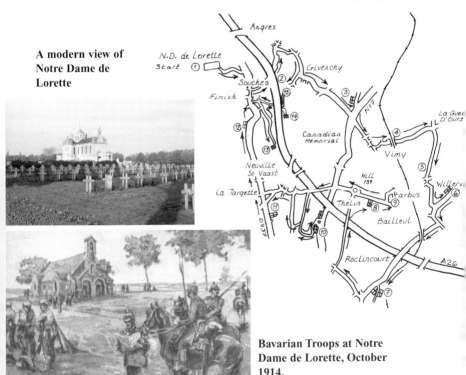

A modern view of
Notre Dame de
Lorette

Bavarian Troops at Notre
Dame de Lorette, October
1914.

This is a comprehensive and long circuit of the Vimy Ridge area, which is laid out in this manner for ease of description. It is not the intention of the authors to suggest that it be followed all at once. The route can easily be sub-divided for your personal convenience. The walking tour of the Canadian Memorial site can be undertaken at any time during the tour and there are suggestions for supplementary visits and walks to provide variety, during what should probably be a two-day visit to this fascinating sector of the Western Front. The tour is designed for cars and minibuses. Anybody who is contemplating following some, or all, of the route by coach, should ensure that this is preceded by a detailed route reconnaissance, in order to avoid places where, for example, it is impossible to turn a large vehicle or park it. It is recommended that visitors obtain a copy of IGN map 2406E (1:25,000) Arras. This map provides far more information than this description can hope to achieve.

The tour begins at Notre Dame de Lorette, (1) which is accessed from the D 937 Arras – Béthune road to the north of Souchez. Now the site of a massive French cemetery, memorial basilica, ossuary and tower, it was first occupied on the morning of 5 October 1914 by men of Bavarian Reserve Infantry Regiment 10 and Bavarian Reserve Cavalry Regiment 5. Thereafter it was the scene of intense fighting with heavy casualties on both sides until spring 1915, when the French army succeeded in recapturing it from the German army, which had been occupying this dominating point for eight months. From this high ground there are extremely extensive views, best seen from above the

The main road through Souchez prior to the battle.

German front line positions Angres South, with Fosse 6 Angres to be seen top left.

A modern view of the Kuhlsenke Givenchy.

German defensive positions in Sector *Burg*, east of the Pimple on the *Giessler Höhe*.

building which houses the headquarters of the association responsible for the site, or from a specially constructed viewing point a few metres away. This is complete with bronze orientation table, which presents the events of 1915. From here Givenchy Wood, the Pimple and the entire length of Vimy Ridge and its great memorial can be seen clearly. This is, in fact, one of the best points from which to appreciate the importance of the Pimple. Modern tree growth restricts views of that area from many angles.

There are also excellent sightlines to the south, though some detail is obscured by the ridge between Ablain St Nazaire and Carency, which is where the German line ran prior to the 1915 battles. In the far distance Mont St Eloi, the centre of the Canadian pre-battle build up, is also easily distinguished. Having seen the view, this is a suitable opportunity to visit the French cemetery and ossuary and the museum, which is open daily from to 9.00 am to 8.00 pm and is well worth seeing. Refreshments are available here, as is a diorama, filled with a very large number of three dimensional (when viewed through the machines) photographs taken during the war and an area of reconstructed trenches and shelters to the rear of the museum. As you head back down from the ridge, there are good views in the direction of the Loos battlefield to your half left and as far north as the high ground south of Ypres and Vimy Ridge, especially the Givenchy end, opens up dramatically in front of you. It is clear at a glance why the possession of these heights was an essential prerequisite for the assault on Vimy Ridge.

At the foot of the hill rejoin the D 937, heading towards Arras. At the traffic lights in the centre of Souchez, **turn left along the D 58 E2 towards Angres and Liévin (Rue Jean Jaurès)**. Proceed beneath the A26 autoroute until you reach Angres. At this point the autoroute follows the Allied front line. On the far side you enter the German Sector *Burg*, which was defended by Bavarian Reserve Infantry Regiment 21 of 16th Bavarian Infantry Division on 9 April 1917. An important communication trench, *Patrouillenweg* [Patrol Way], ran parallel to the road you are currently driving along. As you enter Angres, you will pass a supermarket, which sells petrol and diesel at competitive prices. **Take the first exit (D51) at a roundabout signposted Givenchy and Vimy**. On the way out of Angres there is a general store which is open seven days a week. **Carry straight on at a further set of traffic lights.** The route is now signposted Mémorial Canadien. On entering Givenchy the road ascends in a slight left hand curve. You then **take a right turn signposted Neuville St Vaast, Givenchy and Mémorial Canadien (Rue Artur Lamendin)** and continue through the built up area until you arrive at the **Rue Victor Hugo. Turn right and right again** to follow a narrow road, which soon becomes a track. This area, known as Sector *Ansbach* and the responsibility of Bavarian Infantry Regiment 14, was of considerable significance during the battles of 12 April 1917. **(2)**

French memorial stone
Givenchy Wood.

Optional Walk
Park your car off the track and follow the path down to an obvious wicket gate. You are now standing in sub-sector *Burg* North. To your left was an area of low ground known as the *Kuhlsenke* [Kuhl = German surname; Senke = Hollow] and a track ran southwest uphill from here past a series of gravel pits to *Fünfwegekreuz* [Five-Way Junction] near the Pimple. There is a prescribed circuit in the wood, which has been cleared of unexploded ordnance and you should stick to it in order to avoid contravening local by-laws. The wood provides an extremely atmospheric experience. Responsibility for it was divided between Sectors *Burg* and *Ansbach* and all three lines of the German First Position, together with numerous communications trenches were located within its boundaries. As a result there are trench lines and

Vimy church in ruins.

innumerable shell holes throughout the wood.

If you choose to follow the circuit clockwise, after a few hundred metres you will come across a private memorial to Louis Pique and Maurice Cabrielle of the French 413th Infantry Regiment, who were killed on 9 May 1915 during an attack on the Pimple. This memorial is located more or less on the German Second Line of the First Position. Soldiers of the 44th and 50th Battalions (chiefly the latter) fought here against 3rd Battalion Grenadier Guard Regiment 5 on 12 April 1917. A little beyond it, where the circuit turns to the right (northwest), it is possible to follow a rough path forward which cuts the German front line and emerges out of the wood on a track which leads left up to the Pimple, but you approach the Pimple this way at your own risk. It is probably best to delay a visit to it until the end of the tour, because it is easily accessible from Givenchy en Gohelle cemetery. Continue on around the circuit and return to your car.

Retrace your steps to the **Rue Marcel Sembat**, head back to the main road and **turn right at the halt sign** in the direction of Vimy (D51). As you exit Givenchy, there are excellent views of Vimy Ridge on your right. Follow the road until you reach a roundabout, **where you take the last exit in the direction of Lens**. N.B. The layout of this roundabout and surrounding area is likely to alter when the new Thélus bypass is completed. A short distance later, **fork to the left** towards La Chaudière CWGC. This busy junction is signposted Avion and ZAL

Fosse 7. Stop at the cemetery. A blockhouse or large pillbox in this area, whose exact position is not known, was the regimental command post for Reserve Infantry Regiment 261 during the period its battalions were deployed forward on Vimy Ridge. From here Oberst von Goerne directed the battle for the northern end of the ridge from 9 – 12 April 1917. **(3)**

The cemetery contains numerous Canadian soldiers who were killed during the fight for the ridge. The cemetery also contains the grave of **Private John George Pattison, 50th Battalion Canadian Infantry (Alberta Regiment), who was killed on 3 June 1917; he won his VC on Hill 145 during the battle**. Back in Canada, Mount Pattison in Jasper National Park is named after him. In row 8E is buried a group of men from the 75th and 54th Battalions, killed 1 March 1917. It must be assumed that they were wounded and captured during the major raid that day, or recovered by the Germans prior to the truce. From the rear of the cemetery there are good views of the reverse slopes behind the Vimy Memorial. The ground is absolutely flat, bare and open, so it cannot have been an easy task to have been employed as a runner back to the regimental command post when the battle was going on. One man who did the journey on foot on 9 April 1917 took three and a half hours to get here from the front line. There is also a pair of graves belonging to Captain George Barclay

Private John George Pattison VC.

Lockhart and Lieutenant Alexander Philip Wilson of the Royal Flying Corps at VI D 17 and 18. Lockhart and Wilson were shot down on 14 April 1917. April 1917, known as 'Bloody April', was a month of very heavy losses for the RFC.

Retrace your steps back to the Lens - Arras road (N 17) and turn right in the direction of Arras. At the roundabout **take the D 51 in the direction of Vimy.** There are various shops in Vimy. Carry straight on at a set of traffic lights, the road bears round slightly to the left and continues towards the church. **Take the next left turn, signposted Méricourt.** This is the D 46E2 (Rue Voltaire). Follow the road to the railway embankment. Go through the underpass and **stop. (4)** This place was the site of a casualty clearing point. From here it was possible to continue evacuation by motor vehicle and a narrow gauge railway, which ran through the underpass and continued in an easterly direction back to Rouvroy, could also be used for this purpose. This location gives a good impression of the railway embankment, behind which the men of 79th Reserve Division rallied during the afternoon of 9 April 1917 as they waited for reinforcements to get forward. Note that it had always been planned to exploit the defensive value of this major embankment. Located between the German Second and Third Positions, its defensive potential was continued to the north by the *Vimy Riegel* [Vimy Stop Line], which ran north from this point, passing to the west of Avion in the direction of Lens.

If you turn left after the underpass (north) and follow the road round to near the site of an old *Briqueterie* [Brickworks], there are very good views back towards Vimy Ridge. After the underpass continue to the east towards the Gueule d'Ours [The Bear's Mouth] and the junction with the D 50E. To your right there are views across the rising ground to the prominent Beehive Cemetery, which is marked by four field maples. In the close proximity to this complex road and track junction

were the dugouts containing the command post of Generalleutnant Dieterich's 79 Reserve Brigade and that of the artillery commander of 79th Reserve Division.

There is a French helmeted demarcation stone at the road junction and there is plenty of space to park and examine the stone. However it is almost certain that the Germans were stopped here in 1918 by the British army. According to an inscription the marker, which is a good example of a dwindling number of such markers, was the gift of the people of Quebec. Driving down towards Willerval there are excellent views all along the rear of Vimy Ridge, Farbus church and Farbus Wood [Bois de Berthonval on the modern map]. Note, too, the embankment of the Arras – Lens railway, which in this area too played an extremely important role on 9 April 1917 as a fall back position for the defence.

Demarcation stone at La Gueule d'Ours.

Turn right on the D 50E, signposted Willerval. As you drive towards Willerval, not only are the views of the wooded section of Vimy Ridge excellent, but the significance of its extension to the southeast becomes very clear. As you clear the obvious crest along this road, the importance of the area around Beehive cemetery becomes obvious. It occupies a position on the reverse slope of the line which played a prominent part in the battles of later spring 1917, when the German army had pulled back to the Third Position. The views of Arleux en Gohelle in one direction are excellent, as are those of Farbus and Farbus church to the west.

As you approach Willerval look out for signs to Beehive cemetery on the right. (5) The sign is obscured until you are very close to it, so approach it slowly. The turn off to the right up a farm road is about 120 metres before the roundabout in Willerval. Find a suitable place to park and put on your Wellington boots if you have them with you. The route up to this cemetery gets very muddy at times. The cemetery contains about fifty burials, all but a handful of these are Canadians who died from May 1917 onwards, indicating the length of time they spent in the area. There are only two unknown burials and the burials are well spaced out, so this is not a battlefield clearance cemetery. It would appear that it was established near an aid post of some description. This location offers exceedingly good views over the Douai plain in the direction of Lens and Loos and the full length of Vimy Ridge as seen from the German perspective, so it is well worth visiting. To the right of the Vimy Memorial, it is possible to see the hill of Notre Dame de Lorette (direction indicated by a large antenna with a flashing light). The basilica and ossuary are also visible with the aid of binoculars. Return to your car and head towards Willerval.

During the afternoon of 9 April 1917 Canadian cavalry patrols attempted to exploit eastwards out of Farbus. According to the after action report of Bavarian Reserve Infantry Regiment 3, of the twelve man patrol which attempted to head towards Willerval at 3.30 pm [4.30

Railway underpass east of Vimy looking west. The aid post was on the verge to the right of the opening.

Beehive Cemetery.

The view of Vimy Ridge from Beehive Cemetery.

Vimy   Vimy Memorial   Givenchy

pm German time], six were brought down by small arms fire, two were captured in Willerval itself and the rest escaped. A similar patrol, which attempted to advance along the railway line in the direction of Bailleul, was shot down with the exception of two men. The fate of these patrols should be born in mind whenever criticism is made about the failure to attempt to exploit to the east using mounted troops on 9 April 1917.

At the roundabout in Willerval continue straight on towards Bailleul (D 50E1). As you drive south out of the village, there continue to be good views of the southern end of Vimy Ridge. At a T junction with the D919 **turn left (signposted Arleux and Rouvroy)**. Orchard Dump cemetery, the object of this short deviation, is also clearly marked. **(6)** Although there is space to park at Orchard Dump, this is a busy road, so exercise caution. Orchard Dump, a beautifully maintained cemetery, is unusual in that the land upon which it stands was donated by Madame Wartelle in memory of her husband Capitaine Wartelle of the French 72nd Regiment of Infantry, who fell on 22 August 1914. Orchard Dump cemetery is only about 750

Orchard Dump Cemetery.

metres short of the German Third Position, which in this area ran north – south just to the west of Arleux. Clifford Wells, whose letters are quoted in the text, is buried here in IX J1

Return to your car and turn round. Head in the direction of Bailleul, passing the turn off to Thélus and continue to follow the D 919, which skirts the main part of the village. A prominent right turn is signed to Roclincourt and St Laurent Blangy. As you exit Bailleul there is a signpost to Albuhera Cemetery, which you may wish to visit. You are now in the rear area of Sector *Eberhard*, the right hand sector of 14th Bavarian Infantry Division, which was defended on 9 April 1917 by Bavarian Infantry Regiment 4. Continue under the railway line. There used to be a much more complex network of field tracks in this area and the place where a track leads off to the left about 600 metres beyond the railway used to be a significant crossroads. The German Second Position ran roughly north-south along two of tracks and the command post of Major Hoderlein, commander of Bavarian

Infantry Regiment 4, was located here on 9 April 1917. Continue on across the A26, from which elevated point it is possible to see a prominent British cemetery (Bailleul Road East), where you will be taking the left fork, which is signposted to the German military cemetery of St Laurent Blangy. **(7)**

Deutscher Soldatenfriedhof 1914-18
ST LAURENT BLANGY
Cimetière Militaire Allemand

Find a parking place and enter the cemetery, which is located on the line of the German *Zwischenstellung* [Intermediate Position] in Sector *Schwaben*, which at the time of the battle was the responsibility of Bavarian Infantry Regiment 25, commanded by Oberstleutnant Seemüller. This cemetery is an expansion of a German battlefield cemetery, originally established in 1915. At first glance this place appears to be of modest size; in fact it is enormous. With almost 32,000 burials, it is one of the largest German cemeteries in the world. The mass *Kamaradengrab* contains the grotesquely large number of 24,870 men (more than two Tyne

Lieutenant Clifford Wells, photographed in the summer of 1916.

Cots!), of whom 11,587 are unknown. When it first came into use in 1921, it appears to have been treated by the French military authorities less as an honoured last resting place for the fallen than a convenient

The mass grave St Laurent Blangy.

landfill site to dump unwanted bodies. Some dignity was restored at an early date when the German *Volksbund* built a stone wall round the *Kamaradengrab* in the 1920s. In 1956 the German cemetery at Comines in Belgium was closed and a further 4,238 burials were concentrated at this site, which assumed its current form in 1972 when the metal crosses were installed.

If the cemetery directory is missing, note that the block number appears on each of the crosses. Block One is to the left as you go through the gate and Block Three to the right. Remarkably few of the German casualties of the 1917 battles in the Vimy area appear to have known graves, but this cemetery contains a few individuals who were killed during the period of extensive raiding leading up to the main battle and whose graves are worthy of your attention.

Reserve Oberleutnant Anton Breher Bavarian Infantry Regiment 11 killed 13 Feb 17 (B1 G323)

Reserve Leutnant Friedrich Reuter Bavarian Infantry Regiment 11 killed 13 Feb 17 (B1 G329)

Breher and Reuter, together with an unknown additional number of men of their regiment, were killed as a result of a large scale raid, launched by the 44th, 46th, 47th and 50th Battalions 10 Brigade, 4th Canadian Division and commanded by Lieutenant Colonel Davies of 44th Battalion. Each battalion provided one officer and eighty men and the raid was rehearsed the previous day at Bouvigny. At 4.00/5.00 am on 13 February 1917 a heavy bombardment by artillery and mortars came down the full length of Vimy Ridge and at 4.15/5.15 am a heavy Canadian raid in three waves was launched against the two right hand companies in Sector *Döberitz*. The front line was breached in several places and a prolonged period of close quarter battle ensued until the raiders withdrew thirty minutes later. The raid did not achieve its objective of pushing through to the third line of the First Position, because the response by the German artillery was swift and deadly and the trench garrison fought back hard, causing the attackers numerous casualties. Five Canadians were captured. Four of them were seriously wounded and the fifth, a sergeant from 44th Infantry Battalion, was later interrogated at length.

Grenadier Michael Burg 3rd Company Reserve Infantry Regiment 262 14 Mar 17   (B3 G1081)

Grenadier Emil Nilly 6th Company Reserve Infantry Regiment 262 1 Mar 17 (B3 G1089)

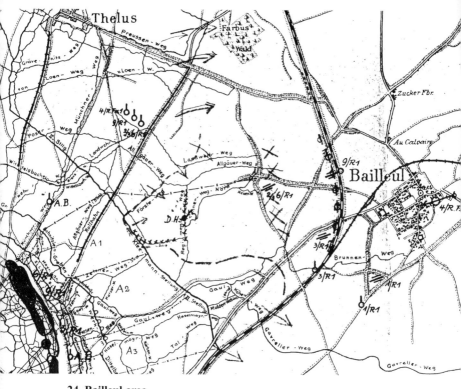

24. Bailleul area.

Reservist Hermann Mönch 6th Company Reserve Infantry Regiment 262 1 Mar 17   (B3 G1091)

Burg and Nilly were killed during the disastrous raid by 4th Canadian Division on 1 March 1917, which is described in Chapters 2 and 5.

Reserve Leutnant Johann Niebauer Bavarian Infantry Regiment 11 2 Apr 17 (*Kamaradengrab*).

At the rear of the cemetery, the Lens – Arras railway runs in a cutting. The command posts of the *Bereitschaftstruppenkommandeur* [BTK = Commander of the Supporting Troops] of Bavarian Infantry Regiments 4 and 25 were located in dugouts in this cutting. That of Infantry Regiment 25 was located more or less level with the southern tip of the cemetery and that of Infantry Regiment 4, 250 metres to the north. **Return to your car.**

As you exit the cemetery note that the command post of the *Kampftruppenkommandeur* [KTK = Commander of the Forward Troops] of Bavarian Infantry Regiment 25 was located on the right of the track about 500 metres further along. Leave your car where it is and walk back to Bailleul Road East Cemetery. On your left as you approach the cemetery was the site of a major German dump for mortar ammunition, whilst the site of the cemetery itself was used to store engineering equipment and materials by a German concrete troop, responsible for the construction of pillboxes in the area. The most famous burial in this cemetery is that of the noted war poet Isaac Rosenberg. The Special Memorial at V C 12 notes that Rosenberg, a private soldier of the King's Own Regiment, is known to be buried near this spot. Although not physically robust Rosenberg, who was born in 1890 and who was living in South Africa in 1914 for the sake of his health, returned to England, volunteered his services and spent three years in the ranks, until his untimely death on 1 April 1918. His poem, *Break of Day in the Trenches*, in which he has an imaginary conversation with a rat, warning him that he risks being shot for consorting equally with both British and German soldiers, is widely regarded as being one of the very best of the poems to come out of the Great War.

Special memorial of the war poet Isaac Rosenberg.

What do you see in our eyes
At the shrieking iron and flame
Hurled through still heavens?
What quaver – what heart aghast?

What indeed? With that thought return to your car, retrace your route to the junction and **turn left** onto the D 919.

Arras is visible in the distance, as are the blue and white buildings of Roclincourt aerodrome, as you approach the right turn for Roclincourt. Since leaving the cemeteries, you have been driving through the forward area of Sectors *Eberhard* and *Schwaben*, defended with notable lack of success on 9 April 1917, by the already worn down 14th Bavarian Infantry Division. **Turn right onto the D60 signposted**

189

Roclincourt and Aérodrome. From this point, which (confusingly) was also known in 1917 as Maison Blanche, you are traversing the battlefield of the 34th Division and the 51st (Highland) Division. A few metres after the junction you cross the German front line, No Man's Land (which was barely one hundred metres wide at this point) and the British front line. As can be seen on the area map, mining operations were continued right down to this area in 1916.

As you proceed down the hill into Roclincourt slow down and look for a minor turn to the right at a barely recognisable roundabout. To your front is a café and there is small white sign (not a normal road sign) indicating the turn to Thélus. Immediately after the turn you should pass the Mairie and a war memorial. There are signs to two British cemeteries up to the right as you exit Roclincourt. Just before the fork that leads right up to a cemetery, you crossed back into the German lines in Sector Rupprecht, which was defended by Bavarian Reserve Infantry Regiment 2 of 1st Bavarian Reserve Division and commanded in April 1917 by Oberstleutnant Ritter von Brunner, who was captured in controversial circumstances (but later cleared by a military Court of Honour of any personal failure), on 9 April 1917. 750 metres along the track which runs past the cemetery was *Münchener Haus* [Munich House], the command post of the right hand KTK of Bavarian Infantry Regiment 2. As you proceed towards Thélus you also cut through Sectors *Wittelsbach* and *Loën*, the responsibility of Bavarian Reserve Infantry Regiments 1 and 3 and commanded by Oberstleutnant Ritter von Füger and Major Anton Meier respectively.

Memorial to Lieutenant Henry Labesse near Roclincourt.

On your left, shortly after you pass the turn to the cemeteries, a small yew hedge encloses a private memorial to Henry Labesse, a decorated lieutenant of the French 2nd Infantry Regiment, who died aged 24 on 16 June1915. Beneath is a plaque in French which states: 'Near to this spot ran the trenches of the Allied front line in front of Roclincourt for a period of thirty one months. Those who came to do battle here included troops of France, (Savoy, Brittany, Gascony and Limousin), Algeria, Senegal, Great Britain, Canada, South Africa and New Zealand.

As you cross the A26 there are good views to the left across the ground traversed by the 1st Canadian

Division on 9 April 1917 and also across to Farbus and Bois Carré to your half right. On the southern side of Bois Carré was the regimental command post of Bavarian Reserve Infantry Regiment 3, known as *Leipziger Hütte* [Leipzig Cottage] and from which Major Meier directed operations during the battle for Vimy Ridge. At a halt sign opposite the church in Thélus, where there is a CWGC sign to the Bois Carré British Cemetery Thélus, **turn right** onto the D 49. **(8)** Parking outside the cemetery at Bois Carré is awkward. There is room to drive a car or minibus onto the kerb, but this would not be possible for a larger vehicle. In Bois Carré Cemetery, in the plot furthest from the gate and just in front of the Cross of Sacrifice, there are large numbers of burials from 9 April 1917, mostly from the 3rd and 4th Canadian Divisions. A great many of these men were concentrated from the battlefield cemetery C-D 27 (Neuville St Vaast) about two kilometres west of Petit Vimy, which contained the bodies of

Bois Carré cemetery.

forty eight soldiers who fell on 9 April 1917. Almost all belonged to the 54th and 102nd battalions, though there are two officers from the PPCLI here as well.

Return to your car and continue in the direction of Farbus. On your

25. Maison Blanche area.

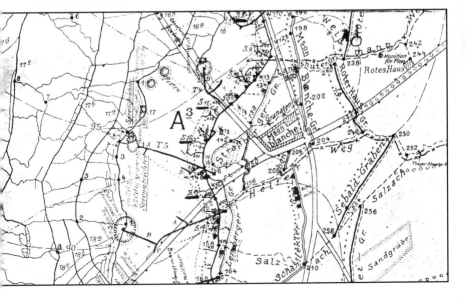

right, about 300 metres along the road, is the memorial to the 1st
Canadian Division. There is just about enough room for one vehicle to
stop, provided that it is pulled well in to the side. At the junction of the
D49 and the D50 a single story building to the east of the junction
stands on the site of the Commandant's House (known to the Germans
as *Gries Haus*), which is a little short of the Canadian Brown Line and
only a hundred or two metres north of the boundary with the 51st
(Highland) Division. Turn left and follow the road along a right hand
bend down into the dip which contains the Bois de Berthonval. The
Germans referred to this as *Farbuswald* =Farbus Wood. **(9)** It is in dead
ground to anyone approaching the Brown Line from the west and was
used to house artillery batteries.
Optional Walk

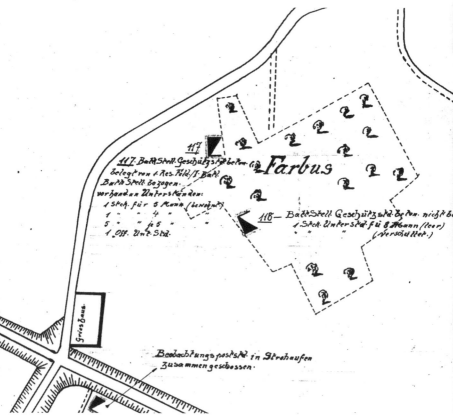

**26. German Battery positions 117 and 118, Farbus Wood [Bois de
Berthonval].**

192

Farbus Wood, April 1917.

The approach to Farbus Wood. Note the use of old railway lines and screw-in barbed wire pickets to support the modern fence.

A destroyed German gun in Battery Position 117…

and the remains of the concreted gun pit today.

Continue past the track that leads into the wood and stop at an obvious parking space. There would be space for a coach here. Park your car and walk back along the roughly tarmaced track marked *Rue des Queuettes* to the wood. This wood is extremely atmospheric, as is Givenchy Wood and, fortunately, a track leads right through it. To the

left of the entrance track there are numerous sections of narrow-gauge railway line and screw-in barbed wire pickets in use as fence posts. The wood is full of warnings including *Zone Piégé* (traps in use). Therefore it is important not to stray off the tracks, but it is worth traversing the entire wood, because the German Second Position ran northwest – southeast along its western edge. This wood has been heavily shelled. It contains pill boxes and several well-constructed concreted gun pits, which are the remains of the German Battery Position 117. At the time of the battle, in addition to the concrete shelters, the position featured six five man dugouts, one four man dugout and one officers' dugout which served as a command post. The nearest gun pit and shelter to the track has

Original battle scarred tree stump Farbus wood.

two feet of overhead cover, which has been hit by shells. Adjacent to it is a one man observation post, almost certainly used to watch for flares calling for fire. It is clear that no significant clearance or restoration work took place in this wood after the war. It contains considerable quantities of dud ammunition, which on no account should be disturbed. There are indications here and there that the shell holes were linked to create defensive positions associated with the Second Position. There is also good evidence of communication trenches, particularly in the area heading up to the shelters, where a very obvious trench leads away to the east.

Return to your car. You may wish at this point to drive down the

Memorial stone outside Farbus church.

hill into Farbus itself. Outside the church there is a memorial erected in 1988. It may be assumed that it is made from a stone which survived the battle, because it is heavily scarred. It is dedicated to the memory of all the soldiers who fell at Farbus. The church is interesting. A lot of money and effort obviously went into its renovation after the war. From Farbus retrace your steps in the direction of Thélus. At the top of the first hill out of Farbus a good track runs away to the northwest, parallel to the wood on your right. It soon deteriorates, but is passable with a 4x4 vehicle. For those who wish to experience the atmosphere of another heavily shelled wood, it can be followed easily on foot for about 1,000 metres to a track junction and a track leading down into the wood (Bois du Goulot), through which the German Second Position ran. At this point the track is marked *Sentier de la Couture Comblet*, and it is possible to follow it to the east, down to Farbus and a railway underpass through the embankment northeast of Thélus which played a prominent role in the April battle. If you turn left at the track junction, the feature you are climbing is Telegraphen-Höhe [Telegraph Hill = Hill 139 on the modern map]. There was a chalk mine on the eastern flank of the hill, which was used as a troop shelter, known as the *Felsenkeller* [Rock Cellar]. Telegraph Hill was the objective of the failed German counter-attack during the late afternoon of 9 April 1917.

Continue back to the Commandant's House and **turn right on the D 49** (sign posted Thélus). Carry straight on through Thélus towards Neuville St Vaast. The *Zwischenstellung* ran roughly north-south through the village along the line of a minor road about 250 metres beyond the church. Go straight across the N17 Lens-Arras road. On your right by the traffic lights there is a memorial to the Canadian artillery. At this point the road runs westwards, just inside Sector *Arnulf*, which was the responsibility of Reserve Infantry Regiment 263 of 79th Reserve Division. Cross the A 26 and look down to your left to see Zivy Crater Cemetery, then continue until you see a sign on the left for Arras Road and Nine Elms Cemeteries. This road has been specially improved to facilitate access to these two cemeteries. It runs to the south, more or less along the Canadian front line (within a few metres it goes over Zivy Cave), then cuts back through the three lines of the First Position of Sector *Wittelsbach*, defended in April 1917 by Bavarian Reserve Infantry Regiment 1 of 1st Bavarian Reserve Division. The road then swings north to Nine Elms Cemetery. (10)

There is ample parking here, large enough for a coach. Enter the cemetery, which was originally a 14th Canadian Battalion battlefield cemetery, then move to the western wall. To your front is an obvious crest line, which is where the German front line trench was located. The overwhelming majority of burials in this cemetery relate to the Battle for Vimy Ridge, but there are also numerous French graves dating back to the fighting in 1915. A large number of graves of men from the 1st Canadian Mounted Rifles all bear the date of death as 7 – 10 April 1917, which suggests that there must have been a problem at the time with their records. Row 1A is obviously a trench burial dating back to the time of the battle for Vimy Ridge. Most headstones in this row commemorate two men. There are also numerous concentrations of men of 5th, 15th and 16th Canadian Battalions. In grave IV E 11 lies Private Charles Barnabus Searle, 16th Canadian Battalion, who was killed, aged 20, on 9 April 1917. It is quite possible that this is the 'C.B.S.' who carved his initials on the wall of the church at Ecoivres three days earlier. Look out for this poignant reminder of a young life lost when you get to Ecoivres later in the tour.

1st Canadian Division memorial near Thélus.

...and its accompanying tablet. It is unfortunate that funds appear to be lacking to provide this important monument with a sign post worthy of it.

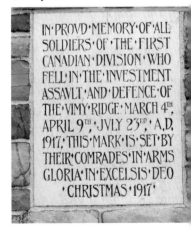

Also buried in this cemetery in Grave IV E 1 is Corporal Alfred Henry (Hal) Clubbe, who is typical of many thousands of tough, clean-limbed young Canadians who flocked to the colours during the course of the Great War and made the Canadian Corps one of the outstanding formations in the British army. Born on 28 December 1890 into a large

CPL. A. H. CLUBBE MISSING.

Corporal A. H. Clubbe, who enlisted at Winnipeg in March, 1916, in a Highland battalion, has been missing since April 9, according to word received by his mother at Rosseau, Ont., Pte. Clubbe went overseas in August last, and had been in the trenches only a few months.

Corp A. H.Clubbe

Newspaper report that Corporal Clubbe was missing in action. His date and place of enlistment are stated wrongly.

Corporal Clubbe's original grave marker in the 1920s...

...and his modern headstone, bearing the epitaph chosen by his family from St. John 15: 13
'Greater love hath no man than this; that he lay down his life for his friends.'

family in Rosseau, Ontario, he had moved west to Saskatchewan before the war to become a farmer, taking advantage of the very favourable terms on offer at the time from the Canadian government. At the time of his enlistment in April 1916 he was living and working in Landis, but went to Saskatoon (which, coincidentally, had a large German immigrant population in those days), together with a fairly large group of other farmers, to join up. Initially he became a member of the 96th (Overseas) Battalion, but later transferred to the 21st Battalion Canadian Infantry, which was based on his native Ontario. Hal, who had been promoted to corporal whilst in France, was killed during the assault on 9 April 1917 by 4 Brigade 2nd Canadian Division on the Thélus area.

Continue on north towards Arras Road Cemetery, which takes you into the centre of Sector Loën, defended in April 1917 by Bavarian Reserve Infantry Regiment 3 of 1st Bavarian Reserve Division. Dugouts are known to have existed under the northeast corner of this cemetery, whilst a larger dugout under the southwest boundary was the command post of the KTK of Bavarian Reserve Infantry Regiment 3, known as *Neuburger Haus* (Neuburg House). This dugout is described in detail in the account of the 13th Battalion's part in the attack; it was used as their Battalion HQ. The cemetery contains a large number of graves of men of the 7th Battalion Canadian Infantry, in many cases

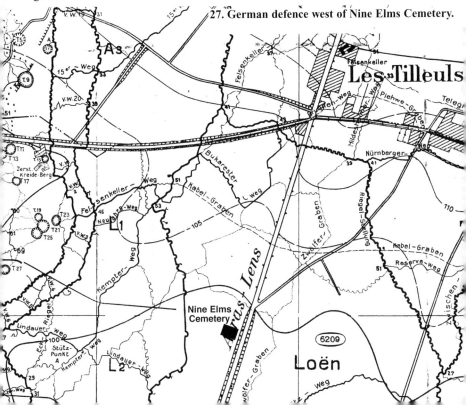

27. German defence west of Nine Elms Cemetery.

with uncertain dates of death. Some are identified as being 9 April 1917, but most carry the formula 8-10 April 1917. Row 2A has a whole group of soldiers from the Highland Light Infantry who died between 14 and 19 December 1914. These men were all casualties of the fighting south of Ypres. From the western side of the cemetery there are excellent views from the German perspective of Ecurie, Maroeuil Wood, the German cemetery of Neuville St Vaast, then around to the north to Notre Dame de Lorette. In all the view encompasses much of the frontage of the 2nd, 3rd and 4th Canadian Divisions, whilst to the south Arras and Monchy le Preux are both visible.

Retrace your route until you are once more heading north along the Allied front line and keep an eye open for a slightly rough, but perfectly drivable, track leading off to the left. Follow this track for about 900 metres until it intersects the D 49E. Known as the Labyrinth, this area was strongly disputed during the 1915 battles. **Turn right** and make for Neuville St Vaast. 750 metres up the road on the crest of the hill is a private memorial to the French *aspirant* Augustin Leuregans, who was killed aged nineteen, whilst serving with the 236th Infantry Regiment; it is on the site of a pre war mill. At the T junction to the east of Neuville St Vaast, **turn left** on the D49 and proceed through the village, **taking a left fork** down the D55 (signposted Arras and La Targette). At the next crossroads turn left along the D937 (signposted Arras). Directly opposite at this junction is the Relais St Vaast, which is a good choice for a lunch stop, but be aware that opening hours are quite restricted. On the opposite side of the road is an entrance to a deep cave, used amongst other things as an advanced divisional HQ by the Canadians.

Drive south for 800 metres and pull into the parking space by the German Cemetery of Neuville St Vaast (Maison Blanche). **(11)** With no fewer than 44,833 burials, this is the largest of the German Great War cemeteries in France. It was originally created between 1919 and 1923 by the French military authorities, who concentrated German war graves from 110 communes here. The memorial to the men of the Hanoverian Infantry Regiment 164 was moved here during this work from one of the cleared cemeteries in Boiry-Ste.-Rictude. Men from more than 100 different infantry divisions are buried here, together with gunners, engineers, airmen and men from a multitude of support services, who fell in battle throughout Artois, at Notre Dame de Lorette, Vimy Ridge and even as far away as the Somme.

Because the cemetery was established where there had been intense fighting, initially the crosses stood out starkly from disturbed white chalk, but over the years there were repeated attempts to improve matters. An intention to invest millions of Reichsmarks for improvements at the end of the 1930s came to an end with the outbreak of the Second World War and it was not until the 1950s that serious work began. The communal *Kamaradengrab* was walled and the metal crosses installed over a four year period from 1974. Fixed to the wall outside is a replica of a Cross of Peace presented by the Commune of Neuville St Vaast at the conclusion of one of the first international Youth Camps, which worked to renovate the German war cemeteries after the Second World War. It bears the inscription 'Peace to men of good will' and the original was carried in procession by members of the youth camp on 28 June 1959 and erected on the spot where the great steel cross stands today.

It has proved to be remarkably difficult, even with reference to some detailed regimental records, to pinpoint the graves of men who fell during the battles for Vimy Ridge between 9 and 12 April 1917, but the cemetery does contains some clusters of burials relevant to your visit, which are probably indicative of larger numbers killed in roughly the same areas. Your attention is drawn, in particular, to the men of Reserve Infantry Regiment 262, buried between Graves 255 and 279 of Block 2, which is located through the main entrance and to the right. Also worthy of note is the grave in Block 9 of Leutnant Karl Lieser of Reserve Infantry Regiment 261, who fell during the major raid of 1 March 1917. Lieser was the first officer of his regiment to be killed following its return from the Eastern Front. If you also visit the mass *Kameradengrab*, which contains the bodies of 8,040 men, only 842 of whom are identified, then your walk will have taken you on a route which truly reveals the appallingly large dimensions of this place. The name Jaap is quite unusual, so the German *Volksbund*, the charity which cares for German war graves outside the Federal Republic, is fairly certain that Leutnant Alfred Jaap lies buried in the *Kameradengrab*.

Grenadier Max Lukaschek 6th Company RIR 262 2 Apr 17 B1 G229
Grenadier Fritz Griphan 4th Company RIR 262 6 Apr 17 B1 G245

The memorial to the fallen of Infantry Regiment 164. The inscription translates as; 'The 4th Hanoverian Regiment No 164. To the comrades who fell here for the Fatherland.'

Unteroffizier Otto Weiß 3rd Company RIR 262 1 Apr 17
B1 G248
Reserve Leutnant Ignatz Reisacher RIR 261 1 Apr 17
B2 G172
Gefreiter Jakob Nowak 1st Company RIR 262 5 Apr 17
B2 G255
Grenadier Johannes Bernges 4th Company RIR 262 6 Apr 17 B 2
G262
Grenadier Karl Schoppe 1st Company RIR 262 5 Apr 17
B2 G263
Ersatz Reservist Karl Schäfer 3rd Company RIR 262 1 Apr 17B 2
G264
Grenadier Hermann Hinkebeen 7th Company RIR 262 2 Apr 17
B2 G267
Grenadier Wilhelm Wieland 1st Company RIR 262 4 Apr 17 B 2
G269
Gefreiter Wilhelm Kespohl 1st Company RIR 262 10 Apr 17 B 2
G279
Füsilier Max Männig 10th Company RIR 262 21 Mar 17
B5 G178
Füsilier Heinrich Finke 10th Company RIR 262 9 Apr 17
B6 G558
Grenadier Willy Dettmann 2nd Company RIR 262 14 Mar 17 B8 G
84
Grenadier Ernst Kömpf 6th Company RIR 262 3 Mar 17
B9 G373
Lt Karl Lieser   RIR 261 1 Mar 17
B9 G533
Grenadier Robert Padberg 1st Company RIR 262 19 Mar 17
B11 G823
Gefreiter Albertus Spanjer 3rd Company RIR 262 7 Apr 17
B13 G903
Grenadier Alfred Straube 1st Company RIR 262 11 Apr 17
B13 G996
Grenadier (Wrongly described as Musketier) Heinrich Büscher
2nd Company RIR 262 DOW 11 Apr 17
B13 G1006
Gefreiter Kurt Schulze 4th Company RIR 262 7 Apr 17
B14 G788
Grenadier August Wenzel 3rd Company RIR 262 10 Apr 17
B27 G1416

Lt Peter Kapka RIR 261 9 Apr 17 Kamaradengrab
Kam.Grab
Lt Alfred Jaap 4th Company RIR 93 12 Apr 17
Believed to be buried in the Kamaradengrab (surname only)
Kam. Grab

Return to your car and retrace your route north along the D937 to La Targette.

Optional Additional Loop: The Canadian Rear Areas
For this extra tour, it would be useful to have the IGN map 2406 O (1:25,000) Avesnes le Comte. At the D55 turning for Neuville St Vaast, along which you have already come, **turn to the left**, the D55's continuation to Maroeuil. Almost immediately on your right you will see a small British cemetery, completely dwarfed by a huge French cemetery adjacent to it. **(A)** The crosses nearest to you date from the Second World War. Beyond are those of the Great War; along with Notre Dame de Lorette, these are a stark reminder of the cost to the French of their offensives in the Artois, particularly in 1915.

At the junction with the main road, the D341, t**urn right**. Stay on this road for about two kilometres, noting the great bulk of Moreuil

28. Car Tour Extra Loop.

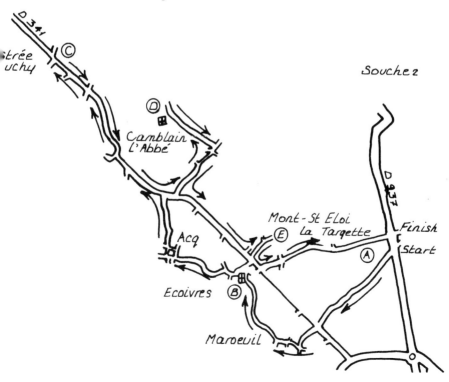

Wood on your left, behind which concealed much of the Canadian logistics efforts, including a large light railway terminus near the small village of Bray. Soon after cresting a hill, with the ruined towers of Mont St Eloi abbey visible to the right of the road, you will come to a crossroads, clearly indicated by an isolated house. **Take the turn to the left, the D49, marked Ecoivres** and with a CWGC sign for Ecoivres Military Cemetery. Ignore the turning to the left (on the Mont St Eloi side of which were two camps, Superior and Ontario) to the CWGC cemetery, as parking and turning places are both limited on what can be a surprisingly busy road, but instead park in the large space available, shortly beyond that turning, on the left. Walk into the civil cemetery and a fairly easy hop over a low hedge will bring you into Ecoivres Military Cemetery, one of the most beautifully situated ones in this area. **(B)** There are numerous French graves from fighting earlier in the war; the British headstones often follow a fairly consistent chronological order. Casualties from the Vimy fighting are towards the top end of the cemetery, and several of them are mentioned in the text.

Return to your car and continue into Ecoivres. After a couple of sharp bends in the road you will see the village church on your left; there is a minor road going off to the left just before the church, and ample parking and turning space is available off this. Go to the left side of the church and look along the walls towards the far end. Amongst more modern and less artistic graffiti will be found some from soldiers

of the CEF. A little further down this minor road was Erie Camp, whilst the 1st Division had its HQ in the building behind the high walls adjacent to it; doubtless soldiers whiling away idle moments decided to leave their mark in the soft stone.

Graffiti on the walls of the church at Ecoivres. 'CBS' may be Private Charles Barnabus Searle 16th Canadian Battalion, who is probably buried in Nine Elms Cemetery.

Return to the D49 and proceed through Ecoivres; after about half a kilometre or so there is a significant bend to the right, with a road going down to the railway line on the left. Near here was another camp, Huron, adding to those named after the Great Lakes: only Michigan seems to have been left out. Continue on into Acq and **take the second major turning on the right, the D58**, situated by the village church. After about two kilometres this will bring you out on the D341, a major road that eventually goes to Bruay. **Turn left** and stay on this for about eight kilometres. It will take you through Camblain l'Abbé, the location of the Canadian Corps HQ, past Quatre Vents and on to Estrée Cauchy, almost inevitably known to the troops as Extra Cushy. Between Quatre Vents, (exceptional only for a CWGC cemetery off to the right on the D75), where the D75 crosses the road and Estrée Cauchy, was the ground over which much of the training for the battle took place and to which constant references are made in regimental histories. When you reach Estrée Cauchy **(C)** turn around and retrace your route.

On leaving Camblain l'Abbé and the large wood off to the left beyond it (in which was situated Artillery Camp), and after the D58 turning to Acq on the right, about 300 metres further on there is a turning on the left, **the D58 to Villers au Bois**. After a few hundred metres you will see a large house on the left: this was the 2nd Division's HQ. Continue well into the village, **driving slowly, as the D65 turning to the left, signposted Servins and with a CWGC sign for Villers Station Cemetery, can be quite easily missed** in the excitement of being on the alert for cars exercising their entitlement to priority from the right. Near this turning, in the village, was the 3rd Division's HQ. Villers Station cemetery is in open country on the left, about two kilometres from the turning, and up a drivable track, part of an old railway line – indeed the old station house is still there (D). Many of the casualties from the abortive raid of 1st March are there, including the two commanding officers who were killed. As at Ecoivres, many of the burials are in chronological order; bodies were brought back from the front using the various railway lines that ran up to the support lines in Zouave Valley.

Return to the junction with the D65. To the left, several hundred yards along the road, and off to the right, is the Chateau de la Haie, used as the 4th Division's HQ. Stop a while to consider the view. Opposite you is the bulk of the Bois de la Haie; in the vicinity of the chateau, to the north and to the east, were camps with names such as Canada, Beaver, Niagara, Vancouver and Lawrence, as well as the more mundane and self evident Chateau de la Haie. This area would have been a teeming hive of activity in the days immediately preceding the attack, as literally thousands of troops moved off to the front from here, often collecting their final battle stores from dumps located in the area.

Return to Villers au Bois and then back along the D58 to the D341, where you should turn left. Almost immediately after you do this, just to the right side of the road, was another terminus for the railway system that ran into Bray. About three hundred metres after the road commences an incline to the right there is a minor road on the right heading into Acq. This junction is known as Le Pendu; in the

Heavy traffic and an inadequate road network led to problems during the logistic build up.

open ground to the left as you proceed were a number of camps, situated on the edge of the woods, the further east being Bois les Alleux. The camps nearest to the road were Pendu, Assinboine and Bois des Alleux; towards the far side of the wood, on the north eastern edge, were Woodman, Dumbbell, Pioneer and La Motte. Proceed carefully into Mont St Eloi; **ignore the first turning on the left, but take the second,** only fifty or so metres further on; there is a signpost indicating a memorial to a French Dragoon regiment. Drive up to the abbey ruins (the ruining commenced at the time of the French Revolution; the war then added its contribution to the proceedings); there is car parking opposite. Then walk back down the road on the left hand (east) side and walk up the path to the Communal cemetery, which is set well back from the road. There are a few British graves from the Second World War, from the 1940 fighting when Frank Force was doing not a bad job in holding up the advancing Germans. Proceed straight ahead and slightly to the left to the hedge line so that you can get the best view possible over much of Vimy Ridge and Arras.

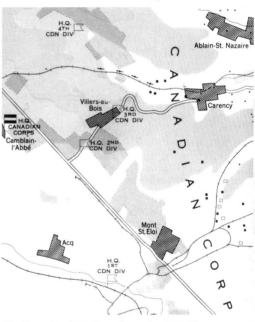

Return to your car and retrace your route to the D341, where you turn left (with great attention!). As you climb up the hill out of the village you are on the road upon which the transport would pile up in the evening with supplies for the front line, waiting for the light to fade so that it could make its dash in relative safety over the crest

29. Canadian HQ Locations, April 1917

ahead to feed the military machine at the front. At the house where you turned left to go to Ecoivres, **turn left and follow the D49 towards Neuville St Vaast.** For some of the distance along here there was a light railway; whilst also alongside the road the Royal Naval Air Service had an airfield, established in May 1917. This route should also enable you to consider the horrific racket that characterised the

207

Canadian troops resting in a village in the rear area prior to the battle.

time before the battle, for scattered all around, using all the folds and natural security that could be found, were batteries of guns, wheel to wheel.

After about fifteen hundred metres the road bends to the right; look into the fields on your half left and you will see Berthonval Farm, surrounded by trees, where Byng had his advanced HQ for the battle. Beyond it is the mass of Bois l'Abbé, or Bois Berthonval. It was from the rear (western) edge of this wood that much of the Moroccan Division assembled before its notable advance up to Hill 145 in May 1915; alas, it was an advance that could not be consolidated because of the failure of flanking troops. Continue into La Targette; at the junction with the D937 there is a surprisingly large military museum on the left, owned by the same proprietor as that at Notre Dame de Lorette. There are numerous mannequins dressed in uniforms from both the First and Second World Wars as well as plenty of interesting artefacts. It seems to be open every day of the week and the opening hours are generous; we have never found it shut. **Turn left on to the D937 and continue the tour.**

Continue straight on through La Targette in the direction of Souchez. As you climb out of La Targette you pass on your right a Polish memorial and almost opposite, on your left, a Czech cemetery. The burials are almost all from the Second World War. There are good views in the direction of Bois l'Abbé on your left and the Vimy Memorial on your right. It is also possible to see Canadian Cemetery No. 2 beyond the autoroute. Away in the distance the slag heaps of the Loos battlefield can be seen as you approach Cabaret Rouge cemetery which, with 7,091 burials, is the one of the largest British cemeteries on the Western Front **(12)**. This is a busy road, with a solid white line in the centre, so the only safe and legal way to visit this cemetery is to drive past it until there is somewhere safe to turn in Souchez and return to the car park by the entrance. The body of the unknown Canadian Soldier, now entombed at the National War Memorial in Ottawa, was taken from here in May 2000. A headstone marks the site of the original tomb, VIII E7.

As the road bears sharply to the left to enter Souchez, the area of the Pimple stands out clearly on the far side of the autoroute. As you approach the centre of Souchez look out for CWGC sign posts to Zouave Valley and Givenchy en Gohelle Cemeteries. **Turn sharp right** here, passing the church on your left. After a few hundred metres **bear right** following the cemetery signs, then take the right fork to Zouave Valley cemetery **(13)**. The slopes up to the Pimple and the remains of a zig zag communications trench, named Uhlan Alley, are very obvious on your left. Stop outside Zouave Valley cemetery, which dates back to

Canadian light railway operating in the rear area April 1917.

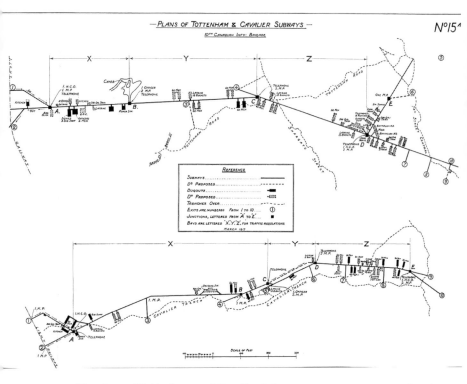

The plans of Tottenham and Cavalier Subways. [Courtesy of the Durand Group]

1916 when the British army took over the Vimy Sector from the French. Most of the casualties of this lengthy period of trench warfare were taken back by narrow gauge railway to cemeteries much further to the rear, so it is not completely clear why this cemetery was originally placed here. Be that as it may, it contains a substantial number of Canadian burials associated with the truce which followed the failed 4th Canadian Division raid of 1 March 1917.

Six of the subways built to facilitate the assault on 9 April 1917 were dug from dead ground in Zouave Valley. The entrance to Tottenham Subway was in a field 250 metres west of the southwest corner of Zouave cemetery. Its two exits emerged right in the middle of what is now Canadian Cemetery No. 2, directly in front of the Cross of Sacrifice. If you walk along the rough track leading south up the rise from the cemetery, the entrance to Cavalier Subway, which emerged in the area just southeast of Givenchy Road Cemetery, within the grounds of the Vimy Memorial, was located only a few metres from the track junction where the track begins to follow the line of the autoroute. As you head back down the valley, proceed slowly. The road bends right, then left and a rough track or distinct field division runs off to the left. Opposite the track on the right of the road is a small wood. Vincent Subway began on the left of the road about ten metres beyond the rough track.

Continue down the hill a further 250 metres to a point level with the northwest tip of the next small wood to the right of the road. The twin entrances of Blue Bull Subway were located a few metres up the bank near this corner of the wood, which is fenced off and in which various spoil heaps can be seen. From the same point an area of scrubby bushes and trees can be seen about three hundred metres away to the northeast. This copse screened the entrance to Gobron Subway. Had the German Operation Munich been launched during the period leading up to 9 April, at least four of the most northerly subways would probably have been affected in some way. Speculation about the potential consequences for the assault on Vimy Ridge is pointless; Operation Munich was postponed and then cancelled.

Continue down the road to **a sharp turn to the right**, sign posted to Givenchy en Gohelle Canadian Cemetery. The road bears round to the right and then to the left where it crosses Uhlan Alley. It then passes under the A26, which at this point runs along almost the precise line of the Canadian front line. The German interdivisional boundary between Sectors Döberitz and Fischer was a few metres to the south. These sectors were defended by Bavarian Infantry Regiment 11 and Reserve Infantry Regiment 261 respectively on 9 April 1917. **Park here.** It is difficult to turn even a short vehicle near Givenchy en Gohelle Cemetery **(14)**.

Optional Walk

If you head to the left here, you can follow a road for about 1,000 metres to a point where there is easy access to the Pimple **(15)**. As you go up the hill at the beginning of this road, over almost immediately on your right was the site of Montreal Crater. It is, in fact, feasible to drive this first section. Apart from the excellent views, a visit to the Pimple is less rewarding than it used to be. The last vestiges of the memorial to the Canadian 44th Battalion have all been cleared away, whilst the numerous craters which were dotted about everywhere were refilled and the land reclaimed when the autoroute was constructed. Nevertheless Sector *Döberitz*, in particular this area and the ground dipping away back to Givenchy, were fought over hard later in the

The view looking north up Zouave Valley from the CWGC cemetery. The wooded slopes on the right concealed the entrances to several subways.

battle, so it is a good idea to have studied the ground in person; it makes the battle descriptions easier to follow.

Return to where your car is parked and **walk to Givenchy en Gohelle** Cemetery, which is located just inside Sector Fischer. Somewhere in the dense scrub just forward of the A26 underpass was where Gobron Subway emerged. From a point just short of the cemetery, look to your right (west). Ersatz Crater was located precisely on the line of the autoroute. This cemetery can also be accessed by means of a one kilometre walk from the Canadian Memorial on the ridge. **Return to your car and retrace your route down to Souchez.** As you descend, notice the views of Cabaret Rouge Cemetery and Notre Dame de Lorette. The tour ends in Souchez.

Chapter Seven

A WALKING TOUR OF THE VIMY MEMORIAL SITE AND NEIGHBOURING AREA

Most people who come to the Vimy Memorial site spend relatively little time here; a quick walk around the Observation or Outpost Lines, possibly a tour of the Grange Subway if there are places and there are forty five minutes or so spare, and a trip up to the Monument. Even this abbreviated tour can take anything up to two hours. For a first time visitor this can be quite enough; the cratered and shell damaged ground, trenches, the subway and the silent eloquence of the eleven thousand names on the Memorial provides a tremendous amount of food for thought. Yet a quirk of history has provided the modern visitor or pilgrim with one of the most extensive battlefield sites, changed as little as practicable, on the Western Front. Canada was eventually ceded some 250 acres by France and the major national memorial (one of eight) was constructed here, a tortuous business that took years of labour before it was finally 'unveiled' in 1936. The benefit to today's visitor is not only the memorial but the extensive grounds that go with it. Thus the site now acts as a memorial to the Battle of Arras as well, just as Beaumont Hamel does for the Somme.

Viewing the battlefield here is complicated by trees and by the fact that most of it is off limits to the visitor. The reason for the trees is that it was part of a massive reforestation programme by the French state after the war – and we have to be grateful that we have the adjacent Vimy National Forest as a consequence of this. The mass planting of trees was part of a project to deal with land which was considered to have been so devastated by war that it could not easily (if ever) be returned to its former use. The best known example of this in France is the Verdun Forest. The reasons that people are excluded from wandering around the site are various. In the early days uncleared munitions were a major concern; and these still exist. Nasty caltrops lurk just beneath the surface and there is always a risk of ground subsidence into underground workings, something that becomes more likely rather than less with the passing of the years. More recently, health and safety concerns and the risks of litigation mean that every care has to be taken to ensure visitor safety.

The site is a victim of its own success too. Tens of thousands of battlefield visitors come every year, seemingly in ever increasing numbers. Other visitors include joggers and those who use the site for recreational purposes, who are mainly completely indifferent to the fact that this is a memorial site – what matters is that it is green, there is plenty of fresh air and good views and exercise can be pleasantly taken here. If they were allowed to go all over the site, the damage to the remaining earthworks would be considerable. It is quite notable even now how the craters in front of the preserved Observation Lines have recovered so well from the days before 2000 when all asundry could walk or run in and out of them. Until 2008 or 2009 the access from the Lens road is likely to remain closed whilst the new Thélus by-pass is built. It is assumed that most people will come in to the site from Neuville St Vaast, though a slightly tortuous route (well sign posted) is also available from the Givenchy (eastern) side.

Park your car at the car park near the new Interpretive Centre, the preserved trenches and the entrance to the Grange Subway. It is recommended that your visit begins with a visit to the Centre (Open every day except Christmas and New Year's Day: summer months, 10am – 6pm; winter months 9am – 5pm). There is a new display about the work undertaken on – or rather under - the site by the Durand Group, as well as a brief explanation about military mining. The rest of the centre gives some account of the Canadian Corps, there is an audio visual commentary on the battle of Vimy and there are a number of photographs and artefacts. There is a small book and postcard shop administered by the Friends of Vimy. You may also get a Self Guided Tour of the site. Honesty requires that we declare that it was co-authored by Nigel Cave, but it is a very useful means of obtaining more from your visit. The map alone is well worth it. The charge is currently one euro; should you wish to return it in a good condition after you have used it, your money will be returned. Inquire from one of the Canadian Student Guides at the desk to see if a tour of Grange Subway is available. These are conducted in French or English, so it is useful to know when might be the next one in a language suitable for you. Bear in mind that tours are often pre-booked and Health and Safety conditions strictly limit the number who can be below the surface at any one time. Young children may not go underground. It is often easier to get a tour at short notice in the school holiday period.

Leave the Centre and pause to look towards Walter Allward's architectural masterpiece, the Vimy National Memorial, in the distance. He always intended that there should be glimpses of the memorial through the trees that threaten to hide it from almost all directions except from the north. Much closer to you, almost within

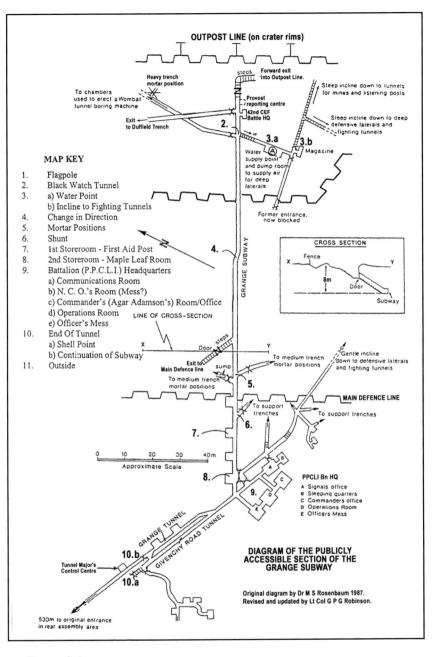

OUTPOST LINE (on crater rims)

Heavy trench mortar position

To chambers used to erect a Wombat tunnel boring machine

Exit to Duffield Trench

steps

Forward exit into Outpost Line.

Provost reporting centre

42nd CEF Battle HQ

Steep incline down to tunnels for mines and listening posts

Steep incline down to deep defensive laterals and fighting tunnels

2.

3.a

3.b Magazine

Water supply point and pump room to supply air for deep laterals

Ⓐ

Former entrance, now blocked

MAP KEY

1. Flagpole
2. Black Watch Tunnel
3. a) Water Point
   b) Incline to Fighting Tunnels
4. Change in Direction
5. Mortar Positions
6. Shunt
7. 1st Storeroom - First Aid Post
8. 2nd Storeroom - Maple Leaf Room
9. Battalion (P.P.C.L.I.) Headquarters
   a) Communications Room
   b) N. C. O.'s Room (Mess?)
   c) Commander's (Agar Adamson's) Room/Office
   d) Operations Room
   e) Officer's Mess
10. End Of Tunnel
    a) Shell Point
    b) Continuation of Subway
11. Outside

4.

GRANGE SUBWAY

CROSS SECTION

Fence

X

Y

8m

Door

Subway

LINE OF CROSS-SECTION

X

Door steps

Y

Exit to Main Defence line

To medium trench mortar positions

sump

To medium trench mortar positions

Gentle incline down to defensive laterals and fighting tunnels

5.

MAIN DEFENCE LINE

To support trenches

To support trenches

6.

7.

0   10   20   30   40m
Approximate Scale

8.

9.

B

A

C

D

E

PPCLI Bn HQ

A Signals office
B Sleeping quarters
C Commanders office
D Operations Room
E Officers Mess

GRANGE TUNNEL

GIVENCHY ROAD TUNNEL

10.b

Tunnel Major's Control Centre

10.a

530m to original entrance in rear assembly area

DIAGRAM OF THE PUBLICLY ACCESSIBLE SECTION OF THE GRANGE SUBWAY

Original diagram by Dr M S Rosenbaum 1987.
Revised and updated by Lt Col G P G Robinson.

Grange Subway.

throwing distance, are the lips of the Longfellow Crater. It is quite clear how considerable was the change in No Man's Land that these four mines made when they were blown by the German *Pionier* [Engineer] Company 293 on 23 March 1917. Walk towards the Outpost (or Observation) Line. Go past the old Guide Kiosk and go slightly to the left of a fenced off area where you will see a plaque mounted on a low plinth. This is a tribute to Lieutenant Colonel Mike Watkins, one of the founders of the Durand Group, who was killed in 1997 in the nearby forestry area whilst conducting further subsurface investigations. He had already played a major part in ensuring the rendering safe of mines near this area, most notably, perhaps, the disarming of the Durand Mine, which is located a few metres from this spot.

Walk past the flagpole and up to the preserved trench line. Note one of the entrances to the Grange Subway on the left; another one is to be found a couple of hundred metres down the gravel path to the right; this latter emerged into the main front line trench. Follow the path over the bridge (which crosses the continuation of the Grange Communication Trench) and stop at a convenient point at the Canadian

Aerial view, 1917, craters near Grange Subway to La Folie.

Outpost Line. You can walk along this. Note there are frequent short saps. This system should not be confused with a front line trench proper. Because of the sheer extent of the underground war here, there were tens, if not hundreds, of craters along the front in this sector. Both sides rushed to occupy their side of the crater and established sentry posts, which were later expanded, more often than not, into a continuous line, with numerous small saps pushed forward to guard against sudden attack and to provide vantage points (note the metal plates) for both observers and snipers. Most regimental histories refer to this line as the Observation or Crater Line.

Continue into No Man's Land. There are descriptions in the book of raids conducted by various battalions in the line here; given the short

Communications room Grange Subway.

Longfellow Crater, present day.

distance between the lines some of them seem almost unbelievable. To your left is the Grange Group of craters, and over to your right is the Tidsa Group; the second crater on your right is probably Patricia; a full description of its firing and what happened subsequently is in the main text. Looking to the right, along the line of craters, you look into the Forestry Area of the site, closed to public access. Approximately from the car park to the limit of easy viewing you have walked along the front of the 42nd Battalion on the left, the PPCLI where you are now and the RCR on the right on 9 April. Further over, where the forest becomes dense, was the area of 8 Brigade, the other part of the 3rd Division that took part in the initial attack.

Cross to the German line, which was part of Sector *Zollern*, held by RIR 262 between 1 March and 9 April 1917. The small bunker was designed as a shelter for an observer – note that he would have had a good view over No Man's Land to his left. You will also find a blocked off concrete entrance to a German mine shaft in one of the trenches. As you leave the German Observation Line, keeping to the path, you will find a bay that was probably used as a mortar position. You will soon cross the German first line system, with its associated communication

218

trenches. The path will bring you out to a road that was constructed after the war that leads eventually to the Lens road. Turn right and after a matter of ten metres or so you will come to a gate. Look over it down into the forestry area; you will see an avenue of magnificent beech trees planted after the war, but for what purpose is not certainly known. There was considerable fighting to the left and right of the avenue in late 1915 and early 1916, as the Germans sought to push the French further away from the summit of the ridge.

Cross the road and turn left. If you look to the right you will see, well to this side of the fence that separates the site from the Vimy National Forest, the remnants of the German second line (of the front line position). After a while there is a clearing, fenced off. It is worthwhile going to the top right of this and locating the still quite deep German second line that disappears off into the trees. Return to the road and you will see a wooden marker post that has the number (1) on it. This refers to the Self Guided Tour. From here you get an excellent view of the German side of the Longfellow Crater. Continue along the path; on the right, where the wooded area once more takes the place of the clearing, you can make out traces of the German front line trench.

Shortly before you come to the road junction you will cross the boundary between the 3rd and 4th Canadian Divisions, between 7 and 11 Brigade, on 9 April 1917. As the path bends around to the right, the considerable cavity of the Broadmarsh (*Schleswig Holstein*) crater becomes fully evident. You are now in Sector *Fischer*, which was defended very effectively on 9 April 1917 by RIR 261. Approximately under the road junction the British laid a mine charged with some twenty thousand pounds of ammonal, to be fired in conjunction with the attack on 9 April. In fact it was not used, probably because the German firing of the Longfellow mines made crossing No Man's Land difficult enough without providing a new obstacle. The Durand Group had their origins in the essential need to know whether the mine had been defused: twenty thousand pounds of explosive going off under such a well used road junction could have had disastrous consequences: and mines had been known to go off years after the war. The result of the investigation showed that it had been defused and most of the explosive had been removed. The film account of the investigation, *One of Our Mines is Missing*, is available on DVD.

The German line ran around the forward edge of the Broadmarsh Crater. It was from here that snipers were able to interfere with the efforts of the 42nd Battalion to consolidate its side of the Longfellow

Broadmarsh Crater Summer 1916.

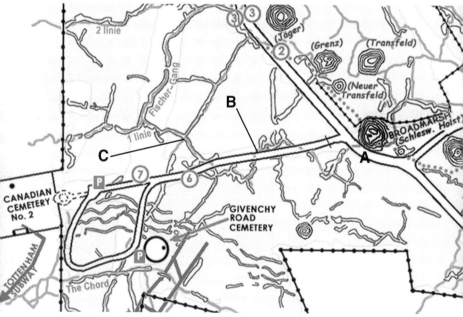

31. Modern map Vimy Memorial site Broadmarsh Crater – Canadian Cemetery No 2.

Pionier Frese exits Broadmarsh Crater January 1917. Location: Map 31
Point A.

Leutnant Olaf Grieben, a young engineer officer makes his way along the front line January 1917. Location: Map 31 Point B.

Crater. Broadmarsh also marks the southernmost point of the highly successful limited German attack of May 1916 against the British. Possession of the crater left them with good views along the new front both to the south west and north east. The crater also marks the approximate western limit of the disastrous Canadian brigade sized raid on the night of 28 February – 1st March. Cross the road and note from the map how the German line also shifts across to this side. Take the road leading down to the two cemeteries, and notice how the German line moves to and fro across it. At this point the Canadian line was just inside the tree line on the left.

Continue along the road, always bearing in mind that it was along

Pionier Dohl moving along from one tunnel to another near Fischerweg January. 1917. Location: Map 31 Point C.

BROADMARSH.
CRATER.
36ᶜ S ·21ᵈ·9·9·

Broadmarsh Crater from the air March 1917.

here that such fierce fighting took place during the raid. At Marker 6
look into the woods slightly to the left of the circular Givenchy Road
Cemetery. There were exits from the Cavalier Subway in this area. At
Marker 7 look up towards the Memorial. The ground between here and
the road at the top was heavily fought over on 9 April and Feldwebel
Paul Radschun, an Offizierstellvertreter [Officer Deputy] with 3rd
Company RIR 261 left a graphic, if somewhat vainglorious, account of
the fighting for the slopes below Hill 145:

> *Foggy, grey and dull, Easter Monday dawned to an icy wind
> and squalls of snow. Relief was due to take place that night.
> Suddenly in the early dawn, thousands of British guns opened up
> as one, pouring their thunderous hail of iron on our positions.
> For the regiment a bombardment of such violence was totally
> unprecedented. In all directions an endless dense series of
> fountains of clay shot upwards. Rocks were reduced to dark dust
> and tiles into red dust clouds. There was a constant terrible
> banging and crashing and, now and again enormous
> thunderclaps, which could be heard above everything else, as
> ammunition dumps blew up. Passively, but tense, von Goerne's
> regiment stuck it out in its trenches, completely surrounded by
> dreadful circles of roaring, blood-red fire, but with hands*

clutching the butts of the weapons tightly, determined to defend every last foot of ground to the last, in accordance with Prussian tradition. Then the Canadians came. As the fire which had been coming down intensely for hours lifted to the rear, the sentries of RIR 261, peering through the dark blanket of mist and mud, caught sight of dense columns trudging forward through the clinging clay of No Man's Land with their rifles slung around them.

At long last! Now there was going to be a battle with the same weapons, on even terms, shot for shot, throw for throw. As the enemy came up to the barbed wire, there was a sudden burst of fire as Goerne's Grenadiers opened up on them, strengthened by their tough, firm and knightly soldierly spirit. The machine guns and rifles of the grenadiers crashed constantly. The dense Canadian columns were broken up and scattered by this determined defensive front. Heaps of khaki-clad bodies began to pile up in front in front of the trenches. Unfortunately, on the left flank the heavy enemy fire had destroyed almost all the machine guns. Only here did the enemy have it easy. Favoured by the

Canadian Memorial undergoing restoration work in 2006, viewed from the German front line. The important communication trenches Fischerweg, Bachschneiderweg and Hanseatenweg ran away up the slope across this torn ground and in the wood blocks left and right of it.

Givenchy Road cemetery.

bumps and dips of the craters, they succeeded in breaking
through along the boundary with our neighbouring unit and
were able to threaten our left flank and rear.

Hand grenades fell in dreadful numbers among the brown-
clad enemy. Finding themselves embroiled in the toughest of
defensive battles, the flanking companies began to bleed to
death. Only a few men succeeded in breaking out and some
survivors fell into the hands of the enemy. But the Canadians
also succeeded in breaking through on the right boundary. Once
again there was bitterly hard fighting everywhere. The cracks of
the infantry small arms were mixed with the drum beats of the
hand grenades and roaring above it all was the thunder of the
guns. The grenadiers fought on, doggedly enraged. Heroism and
faithful duty escalated to titanic heights. Heavily outnumbered,
the German grenadiers fought on. The weather conditions,
namely the damp and the cold, caused stoppages in the feed
mechanisms of the machine guns. Sometimes it was possible to
clear them quickly but, at other times, no amount of blows,

shaking or rattling would free the damp belts of these precious weapons and they remained silent, to be replaced by the use of grenades and the bayonet.

In the meantime the enemy losses rose steeply, but again new brown masses surged forward, threatening to encircle the regiment, which fought on in a superhuman way. Everywhere the battle had broken down into a dreadful close-quarter battle, man against man. Without being able to help, my company commander, Leutnant Balla had to look on, whilst his company was reduced to a tiny handful of men. Smoke, noise, wild shouts gradually died away in the evil, muddy battlefield. It was all over! Honour these heroes, who hoped to cheat death! - Through the iron curtain, the fusiliers of the regiment, together with elements of 5th Company and the Infantry Engineer Company continued to fight on and before this fresh defensive wall, which was inspired by the same spirit as the remainder, the last waves of the Canadians burnt out and the dreadful storm of steel ebbed away.

A circling infantry cooperation pilot was able to make out the message of the signalling panels: 'We are holding the line'. During the morning of the following day came the moment of relief. The regiment lost 20 officers and 860 NCOs and men during this tough battle. It had not yielded. It had defended its appointed place to the last drop of blood; worthy of its fathers; worthy of its parent formation the Prussian Guard; worthy of the heroic spirit of its beloved commander, who had always taught it to stand firm against the odds in all circumstances.

Turn around and look past the circular cemetery and you will see the ruined towers of Mont St Eloi Abbey dominating the skyline. Also visible is Bois l'Abbé/Berthonval Wood, behind which is Berthonval Farm, Byng's Forward HQ. Follow the road round to the left towards Givenchy Road Cemetery, a battlefield cemetery created immediately after the battle and filled almost entirely with those who were killed in the assault. The closely set headstones indicate that these were trench burials, possibly making use of at least some existing earthworks. The disturbed ground to left and right as you approach the cemetery is a mixture of trenches from the time when the British front line was much closer to the Memorial, an outpost line for the main Canadian front line trench and possibly saps and assembly trenches for the assault. A recent (filled in) ground subsidence to the south of the cemetery, probably an incline into a dugout under the cemetery itself, illustrates

German prisoners being marched away.

the continuing problems of sudden earth movement as a consequence of the underground war.

Continue, following the road around to the right (east). To your left the relatively deep trench was the Canadian front line in this area. Depending on the crops, as you approach the bend in the road, the top of Cabaret Rouge cemetery may be seen in the distance, as well as the various features of the French cemetery at Notre Dame de Lorette.

Go into Canadian Cemetery Number 2, a concentration cemetery with bodies brought here from all over the Western Front, some from as far as the North Sea coast. Originally all the cemeteries had a register number; this cemetery has the last register number for CWGC cemeteries in France, indicating that it was probably the last to be completed (although, of course, other bodies were added to cemeteries in Belgium and France as they were [and are] discovered). Roughly in the mid point of the cemetery and in front of the Cross of Sacrifice there were exits from the Tottenham Subway. Go to the back of the cemetery, where there are excellent views of Notre Dame de Lorette, and note the red and white mast in the middle distance. It was at approximately this point that the German line angled to the north, towards the Pimple. The German line here ran about fifty metres north of the cemetery wall (Cross of Sacrifice side) and angled its way towards the mast. The raid on 1st March was relatively speaking a little more successful at this western end of the attack. Retrace your steps back to the road through the Memorial. You might opt now to collect your car and move it to the car park near the Memorial site.

A German machine gun cupola prior to the bombardment.

Assuming you carry on the walk, at the junction turn left towards the Memorial. Marker 2 indicates the crater line; at this point you are just behind the old British/French front line. Further on Marker 3 (one on either side of the road) indicates the approximate point at which the old front line crossed the present road; note that in this immediate vicinity the Germans transformed it into their second line. Marker 4 is placed to encourage a pause to consider the damage inflicted by the barrage on 9 April; obviously there would have been a large number of shell holes before, but this cleared area gives a graphic impression, even now, of the destruction wrought by shell fire. In the text a quote relates how some of the wounded who fell into the water filled shell holes were drowned. It is difficult to relate this pastoral scene, with sheep often working away at keeping the grass under control, with the sheer horror of what happened on the battlefield. Cross the road and stop at Marker 5. Look down towards the cemetery road; you are looking over the advance (mainly) of 11 Brigade and, to the right and into the wooded area, of 12 Brigade. The attack here stalled, it would seem mainly because of a flawed decision not to shell a portion of the German line, but there is no doubt that the Germans put up a ferocious defence in this area.

Continue to the Moroccan Memorial, which commemorates the

considerable achievement of advancing several kilometres to this point during the First Battle of Artois, in May 1915. In the near vicinity is the place where Major MacDowell captured over seventy Germans almost single-handedly. It is also near a part of the German defences where there were considerable deep dugouts with a capacity to hold anything up to 250 men. It is also a point where you can begin to appreciate the nature of the Germans' defensive problem on the ridge in general and here in particular: there was very little space in which to conduct a defence in depth. Cross the road and follow the road around to the left of the Vimy Memorial. You will get (on a clear day) excellent views across the Douai Plain as you head gradually down the slope on the east side of the Ridge. To the half left you can see the two distinctive slag heaps that effectively mark the southern limit of the Battle of Loos, September-October 1915; whilst on a good day the hills near Ypres may also be seen – about forty or more kilometres away as the crow flies. As you proceed down the hill you pass another German defensive line, indicated by the ruined bunker on the left.

On the left, as the road begins to bend away to the right to go around the Memorial, there is a footpath to Givenchy. Go a little way down here and look to your left rear: from here one can begin to appreciate why the Pimple was a problem for the attackers. Until this point its tactical position and value has been disguised by the wood that has grown up around the Crosbie Craters (amongst others) and Givenchy en Gohelle Canadian Cemetery. Return to the road and look to the left, to the area below the 'parade ground' on the far side of the road. This was a major German defensive line, known as the *Hangstellung* [Slope Position]. The Canadians were not the only ones to have subways, and the Germans it is almost certain (though none have been accessed) had similar, if less complex, systems, as well as deep shelters for large numbers of men. You can now either continue walking the circular road (there is an entrance to the Vimy National Forest (or La Folie Wood) more or less in line with the side of the Memorial on the far side) or you can return and access the Memorial from the car park site. The real enthusiast could walk through the National Forest and thereby cover almost the whole of the 3rd Division's front; but the wood is so dense that, although evocative, with numerous remnants of earthworks and shell holes, it does not really help understanding of the battle.

The Memorial has undergone a major restoration over the last couple of years. There was a design flaw with it; the technology available when it was originally constructed could not deal either with some slightly inadequate stone nor the ravages of wind and, in

230

Church Parade in the caves beneath Arras Easter Sunday 1917.

particular, water. The statues that adorn the structure, however, have stood up remarkably well to the passage of time, as have the iconic pylons, symbolic of France and Canada. The re-engraving of the names of the Canadian Missing in France (ie with no known grave – those in Belgium are commemorated on the 'Imperial' memorial, the Menin Gate in Ypres) has been an extraordinarily time consuming and technically difficult task. If you decide not to do the entire walk, it is possible to drive back down to Broadmarsh crater, take the left turn there and follow the road for just over a kilometre to the sign for the Third Division monument, which was placed on the site of La Folie Farm. There is room to park opposite and no traffic to speak of, all the time that work on the Thélus bypass makes this a cul de sac. When access is possible from both directions once more, extra care will have to be taken at this point. You are now in a position to resume the main tour or head for a nearby café to refresh yourself after a healthy walk – and to give yourself time to contemplate what you have been seeing – for this is a thoroughly evocative battlefield; one which grips the emotions of the visitor.

GERMAN – BRITISH COMPARISON OF RANKS

German	British
Generalfeldmarschall	Field Marshal
General der Infanterie	General of Infantry}
General der Kavallerie	General of Cavalry} General
General der Artillerie	General of Artillery } N.B. The holder of any of these last three ranks was at least a corps commander and might have been an army commander.
Generaloberst	Colonel General
Generalleutnant	Lieutenant General N.B. The holder of this rank could be the commander of a formation ranging in size from a brigade to a corps. From 1732 onwards Prussian officers of the rank of Generalleutnant or higher, who had sufficient seniority, were referred to as 'Exzellenz' [Excellency].
Generalmajor	Major General
Oberst	Colonel
Oberstleutnant	Lieutenant Colonel
Major	Major
Hauptmann	Captain
Rittmeister	Captain (mounted unit such as cavalry, horse artillery or transport. This rank was also retained by officers if they joined the Flying Corps)
Oberleutnant	Lieutenant
Leutnant	Second Lieutenant
Feldwebelleutnant	Sergeant Major Lieutenant
Offizierstellvertreter	Officer Deputy N.B. This was an appointment, rather than a substantive rank.
Fähnrich	Officer Cadet
Feldwebel	Sergeant Major
Vizefeldwebel	Staff Sergeant
Sergeant	Sergeant
Unteroffizier	Corporal
Gefreiter	Lance Corporal
Musketier	}
Grenadier	}
Füsilier	} These equate to private soldier
Schütze	}
Infanterist	}

CASUALTY ANALYSIS: RESERVE INFANTRY REGIMENT 261

Just as this guide was going to press the detailed Roll of Honour for Reserve Infantry Regiment 261 became available for study. Because that regiment played a prominent role in the defence of Vimy Ridge this section, which is devoted to the outcome of that work, has been added in. According to the regimental history of Reserve Infantry Regiment 261, the last of the regiments to be withdrawn from Battle for Vimy Ridge, the defence had cost it fatal casualties of nine officers, nineteen NCOs and eighty six junior ranks. Five officers, thirty six NCOs and 199 junior ranks were wounded, whilst the list of missing amounted to six officers, sixty nine NCOs and 451 junior ranks. The overall totals: twenty officers, 124 NCOs and 736 junior ranks were high, reflecting the intensity of the fighting and the stubborn defence the regiment mounted. Closer examination of the regimental Roll of Honour yields a number of interesting facts.

In addition to the 114 definitely killed on Vimy Ridge on or after 9 April 1917, a further 94 were listed as missing (presumed killed) during the same period. This suggests, in turn, that a total of about 430 of the missing were in fact captured. The 208 fatal losses did not fall on the companies equally. The hardest hit were 1st (31), 9th (29), 10th (33) and 11th (24). At the other end of the scale were 6th (3), 7th (2) and 8th (1). In part this was a reflection of their different roles. The front line was manned from south to north by the 9th, 11th, 1st and 3rd Companies. The 9th and 11th fought on, until surrounded at around 3.30 pm on 9 April 1917. Very few men from these companies fought their way back through to the positions in rear; the majority of the survivors, wounded or not, must have been captured, thus boosting the numbers of missing after the battle. The 10th Company mounted a series of local counter-attacks throughout the morning and early afternoon: hence their heavy losses. Any of its wounded must also have been captured.

The companies of the 1st Battalion fought on for the longest period, with the 1st and 3rd holding the front and 2nd and 4th Companies involved in a series of counter-attacks. When this battalion was ultimately withdrawn, it was greatly reduced in strength, but there were relatively few prisoners from this source. A total of eight officers, thirty eight NCOs and 280 junior ranks had already been killed or evacuated wounded. The 2nd Battalion was in Brigade reserve and, with few exceptions, spent most of the battle manning the Second

Position, suffering far fewer casualties in the process, although 5th Company, which was involved in defending the Intermediate Position, suffered seventeen fatal casualties.

Of the 208 killed, or missing believed killed, during the battle and a further sixty nine who fell during the previous six weeks, only forty eight have known graves. Forty five are listed below and three others in the car tour section. Of these, only eight were killed on or after 9 April 1917. In other words a mere three point eight per cent of the total fatal casualties during the main battle were buried and recorded in the correct manner and the body of one of these (Fusilier Wilhelm Pohl) was not discovered until after the war when, for some reason, he was taken all the way to Sissonne (near Laon) for burial. Of the sixty nine other members of the regiment who were killed between the end of February 1917 and 8 April, forty (fifty eight per cent) repose in known graves. If those who were killed during the final bombardment are excluded the proportion properly accounted for rises sharply. It is a stark illustration of the care the German defenders took to recover their dead whenever possible, compared with the unmarked burial in shell holes or abandoned trenches of the German fallen by the Allies after the battle. One strange fact is that, according to the German Volksbund, Füsilier Wladislaus Dronczkowski appears to have two graves in the cemetery at Neuville St Vaast/Maison Blanche.

Just as there is a cluster of men from Reserve Infantry Regiment 262 in Block 2 at Neuville St Vaast, the same applies in Block 9 for the men of Reserve Infantry Regiment 261. Try to make time to visit their last resting place as you tour the area.

Grenadier Johann Stachon 5th Company 6 Apr 17 Neuville St Vaast (NSV) B1 G218
Landsturmman Heinrich Kriege 5th Company 2 Apr 17 NSV B1 G234
Grenadier Karl Randau 2nd Company 1 Apr 17 NSV B2 G157
Gefreiter Fritz Königstein 2nd Company 1 Apr 17 NSV B2 G167
Grenadier Wilhelm Püthe 6th Company 1 Apr 17 NSV B2 G180
Gefreiter Richard Kittler 1st Company 9 Apr 17 NSV B2 G861
Füsilier Heinrich Mewes 11th Company 9 Apr 17 NSV B2 G863
Musketier/Füsilier Wilhelm Hoppe 10th Company 9 Apr 17 NSV B6 G310
Schütze Wilhelm Schneider Machine Gun Company 20 Mar 17 NSV B8 G83
Landsturmmann Max Fohl 8th Company 31 Mar 17 NSV B9 G169
Füsilier Wladislaus Dronczkowski 12th Company 26 Feb 17 NSV B9 G 173/368
Grenadier Franz Michnik 8th Company 31 Mar 17 NSV B9 G184
Schütze Wilhelm Laaf Machine Gun Company 27 Mar 17 NSV B9 G293

Füsilier Karl Börner 12th Company 16 Mar 17 NSV B9 G296
Gefreiter Otto Fechner 7th Company 26 Mar 17 NSV B9 G299
Grenadier Gustav Dürr 7th Company 16 Mar 17 NSV B9 G303
Gefreiter Josef Bokel 1st Company 20 Mar 17 NSV B9 G 304
Gefreiter Karl Sebering 8th Company 31 Mar 17 NSV B9 G321
Füsilier Johann Galonska 12th Company 27 Mar 17 NSV B9 G323
Grenadier Valentin Buchwald 8th Company 31 Mar 17 NSV 9 G329
Grenadier Johann Spitzenberg 1st Company 1 Mar 17 NSV B9 G364
Grenadier Erwin Suhl 3rd Company 1 Mar 17 NSV B9 G372
Grenadier Otto Kirstein 2nd Company 1 Mar 17 NSV B9 G489
Grenadier Andreas Zieße 1st Company 1 Mar 17 NSV B9 G491
Grenadier Gustav Reetze 4th Company 27 Feb 17 NSV B9 G496
Landsturmmann Bruno Sauermann 8th Company 31 Mar 17 NSV B9 G504
Grenadier Herrman Hoff 8th Company 28 Mar 17 NSV B9 G507
Gefreiter Heinrich Bachmann 9th Company 1 Mar 17 NSV B9 G511
Grenadier August Simon 4th Company 1 Mar 17 NSV B9 G518
Gefreiter Felix Hellwig 4th Company 1 Mar 17 NSV B9 G524
Gefreiter Robert Wietfeld Machine Gun Company 1 Mar 17 NSV B9 G527
Grenadier Georg Pfau 4th Company 27 Feb 17 NSV B9 G535
Gefreiter Oskar Pietzschke 12th Company 1 Mar 17 NSV B9 G537
Vizefeldwebel Heinrich Becker 12th Company 1 Mar 17 NSV B9 G550
Grenadier Robert Schumann 3rd Company 9 Apr 17 NSV B11 G644
Musketier/Füsilier Gerhard Thomas 9th Company 9 Apr 17 NSV B21 G1222
Grenadier /Musketier Johannes Orlob 1st Company 9 Apr 17 NSV B21 G1223
Reservist Hermann Göppert 1st Company 9 Apr 17 NSV B26 G1473
Grenadier Gustav Olldag 3rd Company (DOW) Barlin BG G5
Krankenträger Paul Trumpf 4th Company 11 Apr 17 Billy-Montigny B1 G195
Gefreiter Walter Schaer 2nd Company 17 Mar 17 Billy-Montigny B2 G157
Füsilier Richard Schmidt 11th Company 7 Mar 17 Billy-Montigny B3 G209
Gefreiter Gustav Holtkamp 10th Company 10 Mar 17 Billy-Montigny B4 G510
Unteroffizier August Hilke 2nd Company 4 Mar 17 Billy-Montigny B5 G 276
Füsilier Wilhelm Pohl 12th Company 10 Apr 17 Sissonne B3 G615 (Near Laon)

INDEX